ETHNIC AMERICANS for the HEALTH PROFESSIONAL

Norma Jean Downes, R.D.

KENDALL/HUNT PUBLISHING COMPANY
4050 Westmark Drive   Dubuque, Iowa 52002

Copyright © 1994 by Kendall/Hunt Publishing Company

ISBN 0-8403-9752-6

All rights reserved. No part of this publication may be reproduced, stored in a retrieval system, or transmitted, in any form or by any means, electronic, mechanical, photocopying, recording, or otherwise, without the prior written permission of the copyright owner.

Printed in the United States of America
10 9 8 7 6 5 4 3 2 1

Contents

INTRODUCTION 1
   Stereotyping 1
   Terminology 2
      African American or Black 2
      Asian American 2
      Latino 2
      Native American and American Indian 2
      Pilipino 2
      White 3
   Objectives 3
   References Cited 3

PART 1
OVERVIEW OF CULTURE IN THE UNITED STATES

Chapter 1 CULTURE 7

Definitions 8
   Acculturation 8
   Assimilation 8
   Culture 8
   Cultural pluralism 8
   Cultural shock 8
   Discriminate 8
   Egalitarian 8
   Entitlement 8
   Ethnic 8
   Ethnocentrism 9
   Matriarchy 9
   Matrilineal 9
   Prejudice 9
   Race 9
   Racism 9
   Stereotyping 9
   Traditional health care 9
   Xenophobia 9
American Culture 9
   World view 9
   Interactional styles 10
   Time and space 10
   Values 10
Minorities 11
Tradition 11
Poverty 11
Conclusions 12
References Cited 12

Chapter 2 DEMOGRAPHICS 13

Socioeconomic Status 14
Health Status 15
Conclusions 17
References Cited 18

Chapter 3 MULTICULTURAL COMMUNICATION 19

    Beliefs and Values 19
    World View 20
    Social Organization 20
    Rules of Communication 20
    Context 21
    Verbal Communication 21
        Language 21
        Interpreters 21
    Non-Verbal Communication 21
        Space 22
        Time 22
        Eye contact 22
        Expressiveness 22
        Body language and gestures 22
        Posture and gender 22
        Other non-verbal behaviors 22
    Implications for Health Care 23
    References Cited 24

Chapter 4 HEALTH BELIEFS AND PRACTICES 25

    Etiology of Illness 25
    Treatment of Illness 26
    Medical Practices in the United States 27
        Allopathic medicine 27
        Homeopathic medicine 27
        Osteopathic medicine 27
        Chiropractic medicine 27
    Western Medicine in Other Countries 28
    Traditional Medicine 29
    Medical Pluralism 30
    Implications for Health Care 30
    References Cited 31

Chapter 5 FOOD, CULTURE, AND RELIGION 33

    Food Patterns in the United States 33
    The American Diet 33
    Food and Health 34
    Acculturation 34
    Religion 35
        Jewish food customs 35
        Muslims 35
        Christians 35
    Ethnicity 36
    References Cited 36

Chapter 6 UNITED STATES IMMIGRATION POLICY 37

    References Cited 40

Chapter 7 **GENDER   41**

    Child Care   41
    Sex and Gender Role   41
    Communication   42
    Sexism   43
        Employment and income   43
        Medical care   44
    Implications for Health Care   44
    References Cited   45

PART 2
INDIGENOUS GROUPS, IMMIGRANTS, AND REFUGEES

Chapter 8 **NATIVE AMERICANS   49**

    World View   51
    Family Structure and Interactional Styles   52
        Children   52
        Gender roles   53
    Communication   53
    Health Beliefs and Practices   54
        Harmony with nature   54
        Causes of illness   54
        Healers   54
        Treatment   55
    Health Status   55
    Food and Nutrition   57
    Implications for Health Care   58
    References Cited   59

Chapter 9 **LATINOS   63**

    World View   65
    Family Structure and Interactional Styles   65
    Communication   67
    Health Beliefs and Practices   67
        Causes of illness   67
        Mental illness   68
        Treatment   68
    Health Status in the United States   70
    Food and Nutrition   72
    Implications for Health Care   73
    References Cited   74

Chapter 10 **AFRICAN AMERICANS   77**

    World View/Life Experiences in the United States   78
    Family Structure and Interactional Styles   79
    Communication   81
    Health Beliefs and Practices   82
        Causes of illness   82
        Traditional treatment practices   83
        Caribbean immigrants   84
    Health Status in the United States   84
    Food and Nutrition in the United States   87
    Implications for Health Care   88
    References Cited   89

Chapter 11 CHINESE AMERICANS 93

World View 95
    Philosophical principles 95
    Social rules 95
Family Structure and Interactional Styles 96
Communication 97
Health Beliefs and Practices 97
    Treatment methods 99
    Mental illness 99
Health Status in the United States 99
Food and Nutrition in the United States 100
Implications for Health Care 101
References Cited 101

Chapter 12 JAPANESE AMERICANS 103

World View 104
Family Structure and Interactional Styles 105
Communication 106
Health Beliefs and Practices 106
    Shinto religion 106
    Chinese medicine 106
    Western medicine 106
Health Status in the United States 106
Food and Nutrition in the United States 107
Implications for Health Care 107
References Cited 108

Chapter 13 KOREAN AMERICANS 109

World View 110
Family Structure and Interactional Styles 111
Communication 112
Health Beliefs and Practices 112
Food and Nutrition in the United States 112
Implications for Health Care of Chinese, Japanese, and Korean Americans 112
References Cited 113

Chapter 14 SOUTHEAST ASIANS 115

World View 116
Family Structure and Interactional Styles 116
Communication 118
Health Beliefs and Practices 118
    Health beliefs 118
    Health practices 118
Health Status in the United States 119
Food and Nutrition in the United States 120
Implications for Health Care 122
References Cited 122

Chapter 15 PILIPINO AMERICANS AND PACIFIC ISLANDERS 125

PILIPINO AMERICANS 125
Pilipino World View 126
Family Structure and Interactional Styles 126
Communication 126
Health Beliefs and Practices 127
Health Status in the United States 127
Food and Nutrition in the United States 127
Implications for Health Care 129

PACIFIC ISLANDERS 129
World View 129
Family Structure and Interactional Styles 129
Health Beliefs and Practices 129
Health Status 129
Food and Nutrition 131
Implications for Health Care 132
References Cited 132

Chapter 16 SOUTH ASIANS: ASIAN INDIANS 133

World View 134
Family Structure and Interactional Styles 135
Communication 136
Health Beliefs and Practices 136
Health Status in the United States 137
Food and Nutrition in the United States 137
Implications for Health Care 138
References Cited 138

Chapter 17 MIDDLE EASTERN AMERICANS 141

ARABS and PERSIANS 141
World View 142
Family Structure and Interactional Styles 143
Communication 143
Health Beliefs and Practices 144
Health Status in the United States 144
Food and Nutrition 145
Implications for Health Care 145

JEWS 145
Family Structure and Interactional Styles 146
Health Beliefs and Practices 146
Health Status in the United States 146
Food and Nutrition 147
Implications for Health Care 147
References Cited 148

Discussion Questions 149

Chapter

1. Culture 153
2. Demographics 155
3. Multicultural Communication 157
4. Health Beliefs and Practices 159
5. Food, Culture, and Religion 161
6. U.S. Immigration Policy 163
7. Gender 165
8. Native Americans 167
9. Latinos 169
10. African Americans 171
11. Chinese Americans 173
12. Japanese Americans 175
13. Korean Americans 177
14. Southeast Asians 179
15. Pilipinos and Pacific Islanders 181
16. South Asians: Asian Indians 183
17. Middle Eastern Americans 185

Index 187

List of Tables and Figures

Table: **Page:**

2-1	Racial/ethnic distribution as a percentage of the total population, 1950–1990	13
2-2	Racial/ethnic distribution as a percentage of the total population in selected cities, 1990	14
2-3	Socioeconomic characteristics of racial/ethnic populations in the United States	15
2-4	Children under 18 years old living with mother only, 1991; percent of the population by income	15
2-5	Mean annual number of deaths per 100,000 population from 1986 through 1988; by race, sex, and Hispanic origin	16
2-6	Current smoking among adults, 1991, as percentage of each population by race, ethnicity, and sex	17
3-1	Cultural values	20
9-1	Socioeconomic status of Hispanics in the U.S.	64
9-2	The four humors	67
9-3	Death rates per 100,000 populations by sex and Hispanic origin 1986-1988 based on data from 18 states and the District of Columbia	71
11-1	Asia-Pacific Islander population characteristics	94

Figure:

6-1	U.S. immigration policy — Time line	38

Foreword

Communication is the key to providing culturally competent health care. *Ethnic Americans for the Health Professional* focuses on knowledge and skills needed by health professionals and others to create better understanding of ethnic minority groups living in the United States. Better understanding of these groups should translate into better communication. The author decries cultural stereotyping and with this book gives the reader the kind of information which will make it possible, not only to recognize the potential damage of stereotyping, but to avoid related pitfalls. The book provides alternatives to equip health professionals to engage in crosscultural and multicultural communication that recognizes and respects each individual.

Multicultural communication refers to understanding and empathy with many types of people. Recognizing that there are legitimate styles of communication which differ from those which are common to mainstream culture in the U.S. is an important step toward learning to communicate with ethnic minority patients and clients. The author's organization of the work, which describes universal rules of communication and the importance of context in communication, should be carefully studied by the reader because the concepts are critical to success in crosscultural and multicultural communication.

This book has been crafted with loving care and has been successfully field tested in the classroom. The students with whom the book has been used represent virtually all the ethnic groups described and discussed in the book. The author has carefully delineated the parameters of the knowledge contained within. The reader is cautioned to follow the author's advice to refrain from overgeneralization. For example, the author has carefully delineated the population of Blacks discussed in the book and has delimited the group to African Americans, non-Hispanic Blacks. Therefore, the reader would be ill-advised to then apply the knowledge provided in this very well-written and carefully documented chapter on African Americans and the data provided for non-Latino Blacks to Latino Blacks and Africans.

Unlike many books on multicultural issues in health care, this one includes chapters on gender issues; food, culture, and religion; as well as on culture and health beliefs. Further, the book is richly illustrated by tables which expand the presentation of the text and provide a thoroughly readable volume which will serve as a professional resource long after its introduction in the classroom. In addition to solid, current information, the author gives the reader practical tools for effectiveness as a health professional with ethnic populations such as the interview questions to assist in gaining understanding of the clients' stories of how their illnesses or conditions that brought them into treatment occurred.

It has been a pleasure to observe the creation, nurturance, and continued development of a classroom manual that has emerged as a highly valued, scholarly work. The reader is invited to explore its contents, store the knowledge, heed its advice, practice the skills, and enjoy success in crosscultural, multicultural communication and culturally competent delivery of health care.

Lela A. Llorens, Ph.D., OTR, FAOTA
Professor, Occupational Therapy
Former Co-Director, Division of Health Professions
Associate Academic Vice President for Faculty Affairs (interim)

San José State University

Introduction

Many recent immigrants have little prior knowledge of United States' culture. They bring to the health care setting some unfamiliar communication styles, values, and beliefs about the causes and treatments of illness. In addition, their access to Western health care is decreased because many are struggling for economic survival in this high-tech, industrial society. This book is written with the conviction that improved health care for ethnic minorities will result as health care practitioners gain knowledge of and sensitivity to the experiences, beliefs, values, and behaviors of people outside the dominant White culture.

Early versions of this manuscript have been used as a university/college textbook for students in the health professions and for others studying various cultures as a university "cultural pluralism" requirement. For the health professional, the importance of being culturally sensitive is demonstrated by an experience of a registered nurse who was taking a class that used this book. She was discharging a Vietnamese youth from the hospital into the care of his uncle and sensed that the uncle's responses to her instructions were polite "yes" answers. She told the class that normally she would not have suspected a problem. However, because of the class content, she decided to call in an interpreter who learned that the uncle was terrified. He believed that his nephew was being sent home to die. At this point, the nurse called in the boy's doctor, who, through the interpreter, assured the uncle that his nephew was recovering and would soon be well. It turned out that the boy was the only relative this man had in the United States, and he had been devastated by the fear of losing him.

In addition to university students, this book is also appropriate for health professionals, teachers, and counselors who serve ethnic minorities. There is considerable literature on most of the topics that were selected to provide a broad overview of non-European ethnic groups now living in the United States. The content has been reviewed and validated by numerous first-generation university students whose input was invaluable. An example of their input occurred when students read literature sources that I had cited which described Asians as being very open when communicating about sexual matters (Chang, 1981; Freebairn and Gwinup, 1979). The first generation university students strongly disagreed with this view. A Japanese woman said that Americans confuse the traditional community bathing practices with being sexually open. She assured the class that bathing was to get clean and had nothing to do with sex. Since then, students from Cambodia, China, India, the Philippines, and Vietnam have all reported that Asians are modest and do not openly discuss sex. However, as seen through American eyes, community bathing could suggest sexual freedom. Anthropologists have cautioned researchers about the effects of cultural bias on the interpretation of the actions of others. The same caution applies to health care professionals who practice in ethnically diverse communities, because their clients could have value systems and behaviors that are very different from the United States norm.

Stereotyping

Cultural beliefs and behaviors that differ from those of the dominant society are predominant in this book in order to alert health professionals to possible unexpected behaviors and attitudes among ethnic clients. It is very important to understand, however, that these cultural differences may apply to only some members of a group and are most likely to be observed among the elderly, the poor, and the most recent immigrants. Many people may never have heard of some of the behaviors attributed to their ethnic group.

It is vital to the safe and effective care of clients that health professionals know about beliefs and behaviors which could affect health care. At the same time, the practitioner must be reminded to avoid generalizations (stereotyping) and the assumption that clients will have certain behaviors, values, or attitudes because of their ethnicity. An interaction with a male Southeast Asian student demonstrates the problems elicited by stereotyping. This particular student was receiving very low grades in class and was among several students I asked to see me during office hours. He was very amused by my caution in approaching the subject of his low grades. He had the opportunity to plead poor language skills, lack of support at home, and so on. Instead, he laughed and said he came to the United States in 1975 from Vietnam and had been in U.S. schools since the first grade. The low grade was the result of a typically American problem; he didn't study. This episode identifies the need to evaluate the degree of acculturation in clients as well as the effect of age, because younger people acculturate more readily than older adults. Many other factors (religion, income, occupation, sex, geographical location, education, etc.) also contribute to diversity within ethnic groups.

Terminology

Every attempt has been made to refer to each ethnic group using terms preferred by members of the group. This leads to difficult choices caused by disagreement within some groups and the lack of clarity about what defines a group. For example, many Blacks prefer to be called African American which leads to the problems that not all Blacks come from families originating in Africa, and a Black person might identify with a culture other than African. Many people prefer to be identified by their country of origin, but there can be great diversity of people within one country. For example, Pilipinos are mixtures of many ethnicities; they may be Chinese, but call themselves Pilipino. Despite these and other problems, it is necessary to refer to groups by name. The terms that will be used here include:

African American or **Black** (used interchangeably). Both terms are used in current literature (Tiedt and Tiedt, 1990; Willis, 1992; Frymer, 1992) and are acceptable to most individuals in this group. A few authors have recognized the need to use a capital "B" in Black when referring to people (race) and a lower case "b" when black is used as an adjective to represent color, as in black ball, black robe, or black hole (Frymer, 1992; Greathouse and Miller, 1981; Coner-Edwards and Spurlock, 1988; Benjamin, 1991; Parrillo, 1985). Frymer (1992) reported that Geoffrey Nunberg, a linguist for *The American Heritage Dictionary of the English Language*, prefers to spell Black with a capital "B" when it is used to identify an ethic group.

Asian American. This term replaces "oriental," which is no longer used except in such specific examples as oriental rug or oriental art. Whenever the country of origin is known, the more specific terms, such as Chinese American and Japanese American, are preferred.

Latino. "Latino" is used in preference to "Hispanic" because the latter implies that people in this group are from Spain, which is usually not true. However, federal government publications use the term Hispanic to acknowledge the common Spanish language. When government data are reported, as in some Tables, the term Hispanic is used to reflect federal terminology. This distinction (use of the term Hispanic when referring to government data and Latino at other times) was also made by Furino (1992). When the country of origin is known it is used.

Native American and **American Indian.** These are preferred terms for the indigenous people of the United States. The term Native American includes all natives of Alaska (Inuets and Aleuts) as well as Indians. Hawaiian natives (Polynesians) are not included in this group, but are included with Pacific Islanders.

Pilipino. There is an increasing tendency to change the English spelling of Filipino to Pilipino. This is consistent with the national language of the Philippines (Tagalog) which does not include the letter "f" (Anderson, 1983).

Introduction

White. This term is used almost exclusively in the literature for people of the dominant U.S. culture. Although it is possible to find the terms European American and Caucasian in literature, these names are not common. As with the spelling for Black, a capital "W" is used for White when referring to people (race).

Objectives

Most people are immersed in their own cultures and do not recognize the very different beliefs, attitudes, and behaviors that other individuals bring to an interaction. Even when diversity is recognized, it is very difficult to consider an interaction from the other person's viewpoint. However, it is possible to improve communication; which leads to a statement of the broad goals of this book: (1) to improve rapport between health professionals and their clients; (2) to assist health professionals in identifying some cultural reasons for unexpected behaviors among their clients, and (3) to develop sensitivity and improve communication with people of diverse ethnic groups. Cultures and people change over time, and the reader needs to continue studying the impact of culture on health care.

Specific objectives are stated as competencies which the reader should be able to accomplish as the result of reading this book:

- Describe the beliefs, attitudes, and behaviors of people as the products of their history, lifestyle, family influence, and world view;
- Identify some traditional health beliefs and practices;
- Communicate a willingness to consider the client's beliefs in health care;
- Describe the health status of members of the major ethnic groups in the United States;
- Explain the influence of socioeconomic status, culture, and psychological stressors on health;
- Report on many aspects of culture that may impact on interactions between a health care practitioner and an ethnic client; and
- List cultural barriers to effective communication and optimal health care.

References Cited

Anderson, J. 1983. Health and illness in Pilipino immigrants. *Western Journal of Medicine* 139(6):811-819.

Benjamin, J. 1991. The Black elite: *Facing the color line in the twilight of the twentieth century*. Chicago: Nelson-Hall Pub.

Chang, B. 1981. Asian American patient care, Chapter 17 in *Transcultural health care*, edited by G. Henderson and M. Primeaux. Menlo Park, CA: Addison-Wesley Publishing Company, Inc.

Coner-Edwards, A. and J. Spurlock. 1988. *Black families in crisis: the middle class*. New York: Brunner/Mazel Pub.

Freebairn, J. and K. Gwinup. 1979. *Cultural diversity and nursing practice, instructors manual; #7 Overcoming language barriers, #8 Beyond Language*. Irvine, CA: Concept Media, Inc.

Frymer, M. 1992. What's in a word? A lot of politically correct questions. *San José (CA) Mercury News*, July 25, p. 1C, 5C.

Furino, A. and F. Guerra. 1992. The issues: an overview, Chapter 1 in *Health policy and the Hispanic*, edited by A. Furino. Boulder: Westview Press.

Greathouse, B. and V. Miller. 1981. The Black American, Chapter 4 in *Culture and child rearing*, by Ann Clark. Philadelphia: F. A. Davis Press.

Parrillo, V. 1985. *Strangers to these shores*, 2nd edition. New York: John Wiley and Sons.

Tiedt, P. and I. Tiedt. 1990. *Multicultural teaching - a handbook of activities, information, and resources*, 3rd edition. Boston: Allyn and Bacon.

Willis, W. 1992. Families with African American Roots, Chapter 6 in *Developing cross-cultural competence, a guide for working with young children and their families*, edited by E. Lynch and M. Hanson. Baltimore: Paul Brookes Pub. Co.

PART 1:

OVERVIEW OF CULTURE IN THE UNITED STATES

This section provides background information that sets the stage for the study of ethnic Americans. The Introduction to this book contains important preliminary information regarding terminology and the need to avoid stereotyping. Chapter 1 (Culture) includes definitions of words used throughout the book and introduces some of the characteristics of American culture. Other overview chapters include topics on Demographics (Chapter 2), Multicultural Communication (Chapter 3), Health Beliefs and Practices (Chapter 4), Food, Culture, and Religion (Chapter 5), United States Immigration Policy (Chapter 6), and Gender (Chapter 7).

Chapter 1

CULTURE

Culture is the learned part of human life styles. Things such as language, dress, religion, art, music, health beliefs and practices, family life, values and foods are all part of culture. Culture defines the rules that people live by and makes communication and education possible. Culture guides and protects people; it also places limits on behaviors. If a cultural taboo is violated, the violator will be punished. In a group of people, most believe that their ways are sane and rational, and they usually believe that their way is the only way. Several aspects of culture are important to understand:

- Culture is learned and can be changed (Hall, 1976). An infant has the potential to learn any culture.
- The parts of a culture are related (Hall, 1976). No one part of a culture can be understood by itself. For example, when people learn a new language they may not communicate very well because much of the meaning is conveyed through nonverbal means.
- All cultures are constantly changing. When members of one culture are exposed to other cultures they make changes in their own culture. Discoveries and inventions also change cultures.
- Culture is shared by members of a group; the group can be defined by its culture (Hall, 1976).
- Every culture has a value system. Values are social principles which determine the worth of something. Values are what people believe they ought to do (Lustig, 1988), and determine what is good or bad, right or wrong, just or unjust. Examples of values that vary among various cultural groups are: (1) the relationship of people to nature and the degree to which nature is protected; (2) the decision-making process and whether the individual or the group (family) makes personal decisions; (3) time orientation, from being dependent on the clock as in the dominant United States culture to almost no regard for time because the completion of a task is more highly valued than being on time; (4) preventative actions to protect the individual, as observed in the dominant United States culture, to fatalism, where there is believed to be little point to taking preventative actions; and (5) orientation toward children and the elderly, from care and respect to neglect and disrespect (Hartog and Hartog, 1983).
- Within each culture is great diversity. This occurs because individuals have different histories and experiences; they practice various religions and live in a variety of socioeconomic conditions based on factors such as education and sex. Attitudes, values, and beliefs are influenced by family, friends, and the community. So, geographical location also creates diversity. For recent immigrants, the degree of acculturation varies based partly on the length of time in the new culture and the age of the individual. School age children are more readily acculturated than their grandparents.
- To be culturally different is not deviant or inferior (Herring, 1992).

Definitions

There are a number of terms used throughout this book which need to be defined to assure maximum clarity in communication.

Acculturation. "The process of becoming adapted to a new or different culture..." (Webster's..., 1986, p. 10). Adapting one's own values and attitudes to those of the host society (Brislin, 1981). The degree to which an individual is acculturated varies from one person to another, and some aspects of a person's culture may be more fully acculturated than others.

Assimilation. "To absorb (groups of different cultures) into the main cultural body. To be absorbed and incorporated" (Webster's..., 1986, p. 84). The metaphor for this is the "melting pot" in which immigrants were expected to assimilate and everyone in the United States would form one culture. The melting pot theory did not work, partly because people of color could not melt. Today, the trend in the United States is to value ethnic diversity and encourage a tapestry of cultures.

Culture. "Those aspects of a society that all members share, are familiar with, and pass on to the next generation" (Brislin, 1981, p. 51). "The ideas, customs, skills, etc., of a given people in a given period" (Webster's..., 1986, p. 345). Culture is learned and can be changed (Hall, 1976). "Culture is what guides people in their thinking, feeling, and acting" (Arvizu and Saravia-Shore, 1990, p. 368).

Cultural pluralism. A policy of preserving distinctive ethnic groups and cultures within a society (Webster's..., 1986). This is the concept that replaces the melting pot theory and is commonly described as a tossed salad in which the national culture is made up of various distinct groups (Teidt and Teidt, 1990). In a culturally pluralistic society, diverse cultural patterns are respected and accepted. Arvizu and Saravia-Shore (1990) described American culture to be "like a major river fed by many streams," (p. 365).

Cultural shock. The body's physical and emotional reactions to adjusting to a new culture. "... The accumulated stresses and strains which stem from having to meet one's everyday needs in unfamiliar ways" (Brislin, 1981, p. 13).

Discriminate. "To make distinctions in treatment, show partiality (in favor of) or prejudice (against)" (Webster's..., 1986, p. 403). Discrimination refers to a person's behavior which puts out-group members at a disadvantage (Brislin, 1981). However, discrimination can also include any act based on factors other than individual merit; so, a friend may be given an unfair advantage over someone else.

Egalitarian. The belief that all people "should have equal political, social, and economic rights" (Webster's..., 1986, p. 446). In a family, both mother and father share responsibilities and authority.

Entitlement. Having a right to something. The belief that a group of people has suffered an injustice and that society owes them something (an advantage) in return.

Ethnic. "... Any of the basic groups or division of mankind or of a heterogeneous population, as distinguished by customs, characteristics, language, common history, etc. (Webster's..., 1986, p. 481)." The term ethnic not only includes cultural (learned) characteristics, but also racial (biological) distinctions. "Pertaining to a social group within a cultural and social system that claims or is accorded special status on the basis of complex, often variable traits including religious, linguistic, ancestral, or physical characteristics" (Spector, 1991, p. 51). Green (1982) observed that "members of an ethnic group have a sense of a shared past and similar origins" (p.9).

Ethnocentrism. "Belief in the superiority of one's own ethnic group" (Spector, 1991, p. 52). Health professionals may exhibit ethnocentrism when they are judgmental about the food patterns of another group, or when they reject traditional healing practices because these practices are outside Western medicine. It is essential that health professionals strive to avoid ethnocentrism.

Matriarchy. ". . . The mother is recognized as the head of the family or tribe, descent and kinship being traced through the mother instead of the father" (Webster's . . . , 1986, p. 875).

Matrilineal. A social system in which descent is traced ". . . through the mother instead of the father (Webster's . . . , 1986, p. 875)."

Prejudice. "A judgment or opinion held in disregard of facts that contradict it; unreasonable bias" (Webster's . . . , 1986, p. 1122). Prejudice is a judgment not based on facts; it is an irrational attitude of hostility.

Race. "Any group of people having the same ancestry, family, clan, lineage" (Webster's . . . , 1986, p. 1169). A division of humans distinguished by traits transmitted by biological descent.

Racism. "A claim to find racial differences in character and intelligence without scientific support" (Webster's . . . , 1986, p. 1170). The practice of discrimination against or persecution of people because of race.

Stereotyping. ". . . Allowing for no individuality" (Webster's . . . , 1986, p. 1396). The process of taking characteristics from a small number of individuals and applying them to an entire group; generalization.

Traditional health care. As used in this book, refers to alternative medical methods not recognized by Western medicine. Sometimes called folk medicine, but also includes Chinese medicine, Ayurvedic medicine, Homeopathy, and others.

Xenophobia. "The fear or hatred of strangers or foreigners . . ." (Webster's . . . , 1986, p. 1644).

American Culture

It is very difficult to recognize the characteristics of one's own culture. Many people born in the United States think they lack a culture, and actually envy persons who have a different background. American culture is unique; many of its values are quite commendable. For example, this is one of the few countries in which people are making an effort to understand cultural diversity and help peoples of different cultures co-exist. Within the United States are many subcultures, yet Americans have a number of traits in common.

World view. Every culture has a world view. This is the way a group defines and explains physical objects and living things. World view is a cultural explanation of how the world works. Americans look to the future, seek change, and value progress. In the United States, the dominant culture believes that the universe is governed by scientific laws and explanations. Things are logical and rational. In contrast, in some cultures happiness and success are believed dependent on the will of God, fate, or other supernatural force. Why should an individual work hard if ultimate success is dependent on a supernatural force? "What will be, will be." Some cultures believe in limited good in the universe. In this case, if an individual is successful it is believed to be at the expense of someone else.

Most Americans assume that the earth is material and does not have a soul or spirit. This view is not shared in all cultures. Native Americans and Southeast Asians may think of nature as having "essence" or a soul, and of humans as just another form of life that must integrate with nature. Because of their belief that only humans have souls, Westerners tend to exploit nature and seek material possessions (Stewart, 1972).

Interactional styles. Some characteristics common to Western interactions are informality, assertiveness, directness, and a linear process of thinking. Americans have developed large organizations and institutions to control activities. Sometimes this control isn't very logical. Hall (1976), for example, cited the efforts of the U.S. Park Service police to prevent kite flying around the Washington Monument in Washington, DC. The law they were enforcing was written to keep kite strings from obstructing the Wright brothers' airplanes. Hall suggested that there were many instances in which American institutions could be called insane; yet, society believes they make sense. According to Hall (1976), the Western "linear, step-by-step, compartmentalized way of thinking" (p. 12) is learned. Therefore, it is cultural and not innate.

Time and space. Hall (1976) stated that Americans (and northern Europeans) are captives of cultural beliefs about time and space and have great difficulty in dealing with people of foreign cultures. He coined two terms to represent two classifications of time: monochronic and polychronic.

Monochronic time (M-time) is associated with Western culture. It is characterized by linear thinking, being on time, and doing one thing at a time. M-time people place great value on time; time is saved, wasted, and lost, and it even runs out. It should be noted here that people who have been in the United States for a short time have acculturated to some M-time thinking and behaviors. Hall's second classification for time is Polychronic time (P-time), which is not linear. In P-time cultures, several things happen at once; transactions are completed with little regard for time; that is, people will finish a task and not worry about the time. Thus, P-time people pay little attention to schedules. Rather than pursue an interaction without interruption, P-time people frequently take "timeout" from an ultimate goal and become involved in several transactions. It is very difficult for an outsider to gain recognition in a P-time culture. There are horror stories about people who wait hours for someone to keep an appointment in a P-time culture. The delay is related to cultural values and the need to complete a previous task; it does not reflect on the status of the person who has been kept waiting. Several cultural/ethnic groups are readily identified as P-time, including Middle Eastern (Arabs), Mediterranean, Latino, and African.

Doing business in a P-time culture can be very frustrating for an American on M-time. According to Hall (1976), P-time organizations/businesses tend to be limited in size because they depend on the abilities of one person (man) at the top who needs to know everything that is going on. In contrast, since M-time people concentrate on one thing at a time and schedule tasks and delegate work, organizations can grow very large. Nevertheless, there are disadvantages to M-time businesses. When scheduled time runs out, work is interrupted to go on to the next scheduled activity. As a result, many people have a number of incomplete projects waiting to be finished, and there is little unplanned interaction among people.

M-time also influences the division of space. In business, M-time people prefer to have private offices. The largest offices are assigned to the top level managers. This organization of space separates people, and those at the top tend to lose track of the big picture because contact with the workers is lost. The Japanese have reduced some M-time disadvantages by having everyone in an organization work together in one large room where work space is not divided into offices. This makes it easier to keep track of the big picture, but takes away privacy.

Values. Many American values differ from those of other cultures. Individual success is sought over success of the group/family. Americans expect to work to better themselves, and they believe that hard work will result in success and that personal failure is the result of not working hard enough. In other cultures people may not try very hard because they believe that their destiny is up to fate.

Americans generally place high value on money, prestige, power, material possessions, and education. Some old sayings demonstrate the value on self-reliance: "If at first you don't succeed, try, try again;" and Pull yourself up by your bootstraps." Unfortunately, values can't always guide people. Despite the value on self-reliance, Americans do borrow money and many people rely on Social Security in retirement (Stewart, 1972). When Americans seek expert advice, they still like to make their own decisions. In some other cultures, decisions are made by the family group which conveniently relieves the individual of responsibility for the consequences. However, even though this seems like an advantage from an American's view, it really isn't, because it would be very important to individuals, in cultures where group decisions are made, that the group be successful. Thus, the individual becomes responsible for group success.

Americans believe in majority rule; that is, 50.1 percent of the people can decide for the group. In some cultures, the majority will seek compromises until a consensus is reached. No one is completely defeated and "face" is preserved.

Work and play are separate activities for Americans. When Americans work they are very direct and "to the point." In other cultures it is necessary to become a friend before doing business, and pleasure is mixed with business. Other American values include appreciation for humor, youth, toughness, speed, fair play, generosity, achievement, work, action, material goods, privacy, popularity, physical comfort, and cleanliness. Since Americans have not melted into one culture, not everyone believes in all these values.

Minorities

In the United States, reference to the dominant culture does not mean dominant in numbers. Dominant culture refers to the power of a minority of White males and the social structure that keeps them in power. The non-dominant groups are people of color, women, homosexuals, the aged, and many religious groups. Women are considered among the minority groups because they lack power, not because of numerical deficiencies. Non-dominant people are unimportant and sometimes called invisible (Folb, 1988).

Tradition

Some American traditions don't reflect reality, and these are troublesome. For example, "All men are born equal and have equal opportunities" does not apply to Blacks, Mexican Americans, and other minorities including women. The tradition that hard work and education can overcome most problems is not compatible with the fact that one's ultimate position in society is highly affected by the parents' ethnicity. The tradition of freedom forgets that people are only free as long as they don't step on the toes of someone who is stronger, richer, or superior in other ways. American culture has built up some expectations that haven't been realized.

Poverty

Life styles are shaped by poverty regardless of cultural background. Lewis (1966) described poverty itself as a culture with characteristics of fatalism, helplessness, dependency, and inferiority. He claimed that the values of this "culture" are indoctrinated into children at an early age, and they become unable to take advantage of opportunities which may be offered. The culture of poverty instills a strong orientation to the present with little planning for the future; gratification is not delayed for some future benefit. According to the views of Lewis, many generalizations about ethnic populations in the United States could be related to poverty. However, Green (1982) cautioned that the identification of poverty as a culture allows society to justify an ethnicity's traits as due to poverty, which is "their" problem, and allows society to do little to change the circumstances causing the problems. Green also indicated that the observations of present-time orientation and inability to delay gratification among the poor are not based on rational decisions regarding the uncertainties of the future. Despite the disagreements, poverty remains a significant factor in the lifestyles of many people.

Conclusions

Everyone has a culture, but the characteristics of one's own culture are very difficult to identify. Americans are changing their cultural expectations from the belief that everyone should assimilate into a common culture to the recognition that there is value in maintaining cultural pluralism. This is happening at the insistence of people who do not elect to follow the dominant group in all aspects of its beliefs and behaviors. For the health professional, then, it becomes necessary to be able to successfully cross the boundaries of culture in order to provide safe and effective health care for all clients.

References Cited

Arvizu, S. and M. Saravia-Shore. 1990. Cross cultural literacy. *Education and Urban Society* 22(3):364-376.

Brislin, R. 1981. *Cross cultural encounters: face to face interaction.* New York: Pergamon Press.

Folb, E. 1988. Who's got the room at the top? Issues of dominance and non-dominance, in *Intercultural communication: a reader*, 5th edition, edited by L. Samovar and R. Porter. Belmont, CA:Wadsworth Publishing Co.

Green, J. 1982. *Cultural awareness in the human services.* Englewood Cliffs, NJ: Prentice-Hall, Inc.

Hall, E. T. 1976. *Beyond culture.* Garden City, New York: Anchor Press.

Hartog, J. and E. Hartog. 1983. Cultural aspects of health and illness behavior in hospitals. *The Western Journal of Medicine* 139:910-916.

Herring, E. 1992. Seeking a new paradigm: counseling Native Americans. *Journal of Multicultural Counseling and Development* 20(1):35-43.

Lewis, D. 1966. The culture of poverty. *Scientific American* 215:19-25.

Lustig, M. 1988. Value differences in intercultural communication, in *Intercultural communication: a reader*, 5th edition, edited by L. Samovar and R. Porter. Belmont, CA, Wadsworth Pub. Co.

Spector, R. 1991. *Cultural diversity in health and illness*, 3rd edition. Norwalk: Appleton and Lange.

Stewart, E. 1972. *American cultural patterns: a cross-cultural perspective.* Chicago: Intercultural Press, Inc.

Teidt, P. and I. Teidt. 1990. *Multicultural teaching—a handbook of activities, information, and resources*, 3rd edition. Boston: Allyn and Bacon.

Webster's New World Dictionary, 2nd college edition. 1986. Edited by D. Guralnik. New York: Prentice Hall Press.

Chapter 2

DEMOGRAPHICS

Three *primary* racial groups are identified as Caucasoid, Negroid, and Mongoloid (Webster's ..., 1986). Nine *geographical* races have been identified: African, American Indian, Asiatic, Australian, European, Indian, Melanesian, Micronesian, and Polynesian (Academic American Encyclopedia, 1985). Contrary to these identifications, the 1990 census asked people to designate themselves as belonging to one of five racial categories: (1) White, (2) Black, (3) American Indian-Eskimo-Aleut, (4) Asian-Pacific Islander, or (5) other. After completing their census forms, many people complained that they did not fit into any of these categories. Some wanted a more specific country-of-origin choice such as Chinese, Japanese, or Vietnamese instead of Asian-Pacific Islander. Others found no correct response for their mixed heritages. Many multi-racial people marked their race as White; however, some people marked their race as Black even if only one grandparent was Black (Lewis, 1991). This is consistent with laws which identify Blacks (Negroes) as people who have any Negro blood. No other group of people has such rigid traditions forced upon it.

Because Latino (Hispanic) is not a race but an identification based on culture and use of the Spanish language, Latinos responding to the 1990 census were given the opportunity to identify themselves as "Hispanic" after they had marked their racial category. In California, over half the persons who indicated they were "Hispanic" had previously indicated "other" race (Lewis, 1991). Almost all these people had been expected to indicate that they were White. Clearly, racial data collected in the census are not perfect and need to be interpreted with caution.

The trend that shows an increasing percentage of minorities in the United States population is well documented. The White population as identified in Table 2-1 includes White Latinos. Riche (1991) estimated that if the White population included only non-Latino Whites, the 1990 census would have reported about 75 percent of the U.S. population as White instead of 80.3 percent.

Table 2–1.
Racial/ethnic distribution as a percentage of total population, 1950–1990.

Race/ethnicity	1950[1]	1960[1]	1970[1]	1980[2]	1990[2]
White[3]	89.3	88.6	87.6	83.1	80.3
Black[3]	9.9	10.5	11.1	11.7	12.1
Other[4]	0.7	0.9	1.3	2.3	3.8
Indian	-	-	-	0.6	0.8
Asian	-	-	-	1.5	2.9
Hispanic	-	-	-	6.4	9.0[5]
Non-Hispanic[6]	-	-	-	93.6	91.0

[1] U.S. Bureau of the Census, 1992. *Statistical Abstract of the United States*, 112th ed. Washington, D.C.; U.S. Government Printing Office, Table 15, p. 16.
[2] Ibid., Tables, 14, 15, and 16, p. 16.
[3] Includes Hispanic.
[4] Includes American Indian, Alaskan Native, Asian, and Pacific Islander.
[5] Some authors report that the Hispanic population is actually larger than the Black population because of under-counting of illegal immigrants (see Chapter 9).
[6] Calculated from Hispanic data. Hispancis may be any race.

Because the number of immigrants from Asia and Latin countries greatly exceeds those from Europe and because of high fertility rates among recent immigrants, the percentage of the population that is White will continue to decrease. It is predicted that non-Latino Whites will become a minority group (less than 50 percent of the population) in the United States by the year 2060, in California by the year 2010 (Riche, 1991), and in Texas and New York by the year 2020 (Stern and Haffner, 1992). A number of cities in the United States have populations that vary significantly from the U.S. average population distribution (Table 2-2), and some already have a White minority.

Table 2–2.
Racial/ethnic distribution as a percentage of the total population in selected cities, 1990.[1]

City, State	Black	Am. Indian Eskimo, Aleut	Asian & Pacific Islander	Hispanic Origin[3]
U.S. Average[2]	12.1	0.8	2.9	9.0
Albuquerque, NM	3.0	3.0	1.7	34.5
Atlanta, GA	67.1	0.1	0.9	1.9
Baltimore, MD	59.2	0.3	1.1	1.0
Baton Rouge, LA	43.9	0.1	1.7	1.6
Berkeley, CA	18.8	0.6	14.8	8.4
Birmingham, AL	63.3	0.1	0.6	<0.05
Chicago, IL	39.1	0.3	3.7	18.6
Cleveland, OH	46.6	0.3	1.0	4.6
Denver, CO	12.8	1.2	2.4	23.0
Detroit, MI	75.7	0.4	0.8	2.8
El Paso, TX	3.4	0.4	1.2	69.0
Gary, IN	80.6	0.2	0.2	5.7
Honolulu, HI	1.3	0.3	70.5	4.6
Laredo, TX	0.1	0.2	0.4	93.9
Los Angeles, CA	14.0	0.5	9.8	39.9
Memphis, TN	54.8	0.2	0.8	0.7
Miami, FL	27.4	0.2	0.6	62.5
Newark, NJ	58.5	0.2	1.2	26.1
Philadelphia, PA	39.9	0.2	2.7	5.6
Sacramento, CA	15.3	1.2	15.0	16.2
St. Louis, MO	47.5	0.2	0.9	1.3
San Francisco, CA	4.7	0.7	19.5	26.6
Spokane, WA	1.9	2.0	2.1	2.1
Tulsa, OK	13.6	4.7	1.4	2.6

[1] U.S. Bureau of the Census, 1992. *Statistical Abstract of the United States*, 112th ed., Washington, D.C.: U.S. Government Printing Office, Table 38, pp. 35–37.
[2] Ibid., Table 16, p. 17.
[3] Hispanics may be any race.

In addition to changes in the ethnic distribution, the average age of the population is increasing. Persons who are 65 years old and older now make up about 12 percent of the population. It is estimated that this older age group will increase to 24 percent of the population by the year 2030 and, at the same time, 70 percent of the children and 60 percent of the adults under age 65 will be minorities. Most of the elderly will be White. Hayes-Bautista (1991) expressed hope that the new majority will be willing to provide social services for the elderly White minority.

Socioeconomic Status

Although many racial/ethnic people in the United States are disadvantaged educationally and economically, some are not. Table 2-3 shows the high levels of education and income of Asians compared to Whites. These data hide an increasing population of recent Asian immigrants who have very low incomes. However, a hint of some low-income levels in the data indicates the percentage of Asians with incomes below poverty (12.2 percent) compared to Whites (10.7 percent). The disadvantaged groups include Blacks, Latinos, and Native Americans, with Native Americans having the lowest economic status. The lowest income groups have the largest families to care for. As a result, family incomes can be misleading; for example, family incomes for Latinos are slightly higher than for Blacks (Table 2-3), but because of larger families, the per capita income, in 1989, of Latinos ($8,400) is lower than for Blacks ($8,859). The lowest per capita income in 1989 was among Native Americans ($8,328), only 53 percent of the per capita income of Whites ($15,687) (U.S. Bureau of the Census, 1993).

The percentage of households headed by women is a statistic used frequently to express socioeconomic status (Table 2-3). Black women are much more likely than other women to head households with children. Most of the children in female headed households live in families with incomes of less than $25,000 per year (Table 2-4). There is a substantial decrease in the percentage of children living in female headed households when annual incomes are greater than $25,000. Even though the proportion of Black children living in female headed households remains higher than for other groups, when family incomes are greater than $25,000 the decrease for Blacks, associated with higher incomes, is proportionally equivalent to Latinos and is larger than for Whites.

Table 2-3.
Socioeconomic characteristics of racial/ethnic populations in the United States

Characteristic	White	Black	Hispanic	Asian & Pacific Islander	Indian Eskimo & Aleut
Median family income in dollars, 1991	36,915[1]	21,423[1]	23,431[2]	42,245[3]	20,025[6]
% of population below poverty, 1990	10.7[4]	31.9[4]	28.1[2]	12.2[3]	30.9[6]
% of households headed by women, 1991	13.2[1]	45.9[1]	23.8[2]	12.7[3]	20.5[5]
% of population with 4 or more years of college, 1991	22.2[1]	11.5[1]	9.7[2]	39.0[3]	9.3[6]

[1] U.S. Bureau of the Census, 1992. *Statistical Abstract of the United States*, 112th ed. Washington, D.C.: U.S. Government Printing Office, Table 41, p. 39.
[2] *Ibid.*, Table 44, p. 41.
[3] *Ibid.*, Table 42, p. 40.
[4] *Ibid.*, Table 717, p. 456. 1990 poverty level for a non-farm family of 4 was $13,359.
[5] *Ibid.*, Table 43, p. 40.
[6] U.S. Bureau of the Census, Population Office, racial statistics, 8/2/93. Personal communication.

Table 2-4.
Children under 18 years old living with mother only, 1991; percent of the population by income.[1]

Income	All Races	White	Black	Hispanic
All incomes	23	17	58	28
Annual family income less than $25,000	18	12	48	23
Annual family income $25,000 or more	5	5	10	5

[1] U.S. Bureau of the Census, 1992. Statistical Abstract of the United States, 112th ed. Washington, D.C.: U.S. Government Printing Office. Calculated from Table 68, p. 54.

Health Status

Death rates for racial/ethnic groups show that Asians are the healthiest group in the United States, followed by Latinos, Native Americans, and then Whites. Blacks have the poorest health as measured by mortality rates (Table 2-5). The relatively low death rates and good health status of Latinos make it difficult to accept the thesis that people who have low socioeconomic status are necessarily in poor health.

Compared to Whites, Blacks have high death rates from stroke, diabetes, lung cancer (males only), cirrhosis (males only), injuries (not automobile), cervical cancer, homicide, all infections, and AIDS. The group identified as Asian/Pacific Islander has death rates lower than Whites for all causes except rates for homicide and cervical cancer which are only slightly higher than for Whites. However, subgroups within the Asian/Pacific Islander group do not all have such good health. For example, Native Hawaiians have rates of cancer higher than Whites (Henderson, Kolonal, and Foster, 1982). Latinos are also relatively healthy, but compared to Whites do have excessive deaths due to diabetes, cirrhosis, homicide, cervical cancer, and AIDS. Native Americans (American Indian/Alaskan Natives) have relatively good health except for diabetes, cervical cancer, and deaths related to alcohol abuse as measured by cirrhosis, automobile and other accidents, homicide, and suicide.

Tuberculosis (TB) rates have decreased in the United States in the past 35 years, but the decrease has not been as great among minorities as Whites. There was actually an increase in TB among Blacks and Latinos from 1985 to 1987. Snider, Salinas, and Kelly (1989) reported several reasons for high rates of TB among minorities: (1) non-compliance with treatment regimens, (2) low income, (3) intravenous drug use, (4) HIV infection, and (5) close living conditions including incarceration in correctional facilities. The incidence of TB is also high among

Table 2–5.
Mean annual number of deaths per 100,000 population from 1986 through 1988; by race, sex, and Hispanic origin.[1]

MALE

Cause	Total	Non-Hispanic Whites	Non-Hispanic Blacks	Hispanic	Am. Indian, Alaskan Native	Asian Pacific Islander
All causes	1,104.6	1,053.8	1,439.2	800.3	969.0	619.4
Ischemic Heart Disease	310.9	312.0	299.2	190.6	207.0	158.7
Stroke	62.4	56.7	85.1	44.9	46.7	51.4
Diabetes	16.1	14.2	25.6	20.8	28.2	12.3
Pulmonary Disease	47.1	47.8	34.1	20.0	29.7	18.8
Lung Cancer	84.0	80.7	104.6	36.3	44.1	38.2
Colorectal Cancer	27.7	27.9	30.4	13.6	12.5	17.5
Cirrhosis	15.4	14.5	25.9	29.0	32.9	6.6
Motor Vehicle	29.1	28.0	27.2	30.7	65.8	17.1
Other Injuries	28.4	25.5	42.4	27.2	47.5	12.6
Homicide	13.7	6.5	58.6	27.1	22.8	6.9
Suicide	21.2	22.5	11.9	12.7	23.5	9.7
All Infections	64.4	62.0	112.8	64.9	67.6	42.7
HIV/AIDS	7.5	8.1	25.8	14.0	2.1	1.9

FEMALE

Cause	Total	Non-Hispanic Whites	Non-Hispanic Blacks	Hispanic	Am. Indian, Alaskan Native	Asian Pacific Islander
All causes	704.8	676.3	890.7	518.0	631.2	398.0
Ischemic Heart Disease	189.1	188.3	209.4	131.7	117.2	90.0
Stoke	60.3	55.9	75.9	42.3	43.8	43.4
Diabetes	15.7	12.9	31.1	23.7	36.0	10.8
Pulmonary Disease	19.5	21.0	10.2	8.8	11.1	5.6
Lung Cancer	31.2	32.1	30.3	11.9	20.9	16.7
Cervical Cancer	3.4	2.7	7.6	4.7	6.1	3.3
Breast Cancer	30.2	30.7	32.7	16.6	12.6	12.3
Colorectal Cancer	19.8	19.4	23.3	8.9	11.5	10.5
Cirrhosis	6.9	6.5	11.1	9.7	23.5	3.9
Motor Vehicle	11.4	11.5	8.2	8.7	24.7	10.5
Other Injuries	11.6	10.8	16.3	8.6	14.4	4.5
Homicide	4.2	2.8	12.9	4.4	6.1	3.1
Suicide	5.1	5.8	2.4	2.1	4.7	4.3
All Injuries	39.5	37.7	56.3	36.4	45.5	26.0
HIV/AIDS	0.9	0.5	5.0	1.9	0.2	0.2

[1] Centers for Disease Control and Prevention, 1992 (Nov. 20). *Years of potential life lost before age 65, by race, Hispanic origin, and sex—United States, 1986-1988* by J. Desenclos and R. Hahn in *CDC Surveillance Summaries.* Morbidity and Mortality Weekly Report (MMWR) 41 (No. SS-6): 13-23.

Native Americans living on reservations, probably due to poor living conditions. Recent Asian refugees and immigrants have the highest rates of TB in the United States and usually contract the disease within the first year of residence (Snider, Salinas, and Kelly, 1989).

Smoking contributes to many diseases, such as heart disease, hypertension, and cancer, and is a growing problem among some teenagers who are being targeted by the advertising of tobacco companies. Daily use of cigarettes by high school seniors is highest among Native American males and females; White males and females have the next highest rates. Asian, Black, and Latino students had relatively low rates of smoking (Bachman et al., 1991).

Among adults, wide differences were found between male and female smoking rates for Latinos and Asians. Black and Native American males had the highest rates of smoking. The lowest rates were among Asian and Latino females (Table 2-6). Gillum, Gillum, and Smith (1984) reported much higher smoking rates among urban Native Americans in Minnesota where 77 percent of the men and 67 percent of the women smoked. In Washington state, newly arrived Southeast Asian men had higher rates than those reported in Table 2-6 for Asians-Pacific Islanders. Of the newly arrived Southeast Asian men, 48 percent smoked. This was broken down to smoking rates of 51 percent for Laotians, 42 percent for Vietnamese, and 33 percent for Cambodian men. Only 6 percent of the women smoked (Centers for Disease Control, 1989).

AIDS is increasingly becoming a disease of Blacks and Latinos. In 1991, non-Latino Blacks made up 12 percent of the population and accounted for 30 percent of the cases of AIDS. Similarly, Latinos were 9 percent of the population and had 17 percent of the cases of AIDS. Whites and Asians had fewer cases of AIDS than their representation in the population (Panel sees . . . , 1993).

Non-insulin dependent diabetes mellitus (NIDDM) is increasing rapidly among non-White Americans. A genetic predisposition coupled with environmental factors such as obesity and high fat diets in the United States result in rates of NIDDM that exceed those of U.S. Whites and

Table 2-6.
Current smoking among adults, 1991, as percentage of each population by race, ethnicity and sex.[1]

Race/Ethnicity	Men	Women	Total
White	27	24	26
Black	35	24	29
Asian/Pacific Islander	24	8	16
American Indian/Alaskan Native	35	28	31
Hispanic	25	16	20
Total	28	24	26

[1] Centers for Disease Control and Prevention, 1991. Current Smoking Among Adults, 1991. In CDC Surveillance Summaries, Morbidity and Mortality Weekly Report (MMWR) 42 (12): 230-233.

of people who live in their various countries of origin. In addition to increased risk, diabetic minorities are more likely than Whites to suffer or die from the effects of NIDDM including heart disease, hypertension, stroke, renal disease, and blindness (Pitts, 1991). The incidence of NIDDM in U.S. minorities compared to non-Latino Whites is 1.3 to 3 times greater for Blacks and Asians, 3 times greater for Latinos, and 2 to 10 times greater for Native Americans. The highest rate of NIDDM ever recorded is 49.5 percent of the adult population of Arizona Pima Indians. Other Arizona Indians also have high rates of diabetes (Papago, 42.2 percent; Upland Yuman, 37.6 percent; Maricopa, 29.8 percent; San Carlos Apache, 24.9 percent, and Cocopah 24.4 percent) (Office of Minority Health . . ., ND).

Conclusions

Rapidly changing demographics in the United States are well documented. Ethnic populations, when counted together, will soon become the majority of the population, and in some areas of the United States have already become a majority. The socioeconomic status of this new majority varies from the highest levels of income and education (Chinese and Japanese) to the lowest (recent immigrants and Native Americans). Likewise, there is great diversity in the health statuses of U.S. ethnic groups. Generally, Asians are the healthiest Americans. Native Americans and Latinos are healthier than Whites, but have specific problems such as diabetes and alcohol abuse. Blacks have the poorest health among Americans, with death rates higher than for Whites for almost all causes. Health status of Whites is better than for Blacks, but is lower than for Asians, Native Americans, and Latinos.

References Cited

Academic American Encyclopedia. 1985. Danbury, CT: Grolier, Inc.

Bachman, J., J. Wallace, Jr., P. O'Malley, L. Johnston, C. Kurth, and H. Neighbors. 1991. Racial/ethnic differences in smoking, drinking, and illicit drug use among American high school seniors 1976-89. *American Journal of Public Health* 81(3):372-377.

Centers for Disease Control and Prevention. 1990. Cigarette smoking among Southeast Asian immigrants, Washington State, 1989. *CDC Surveillance Summaries, Morbidity and Mortality Weekly Report (MMWR)* 41(45):854-855.

Gillum, R., B. Gillum, and N. Smith. 1984. Cardiovascular risk factors among urban American Indians: blood pressure, serum lipids, smoking, diabetes, health knowledge, and behavior. *American Heart Journal* 107(4):765-776.

Hayes-Bautista, D. 1991, March. Defining the California Hispanic population: changing trends, *Hispanic diabetes team management*, symposium sponsored by the Diabetes Association of Santa Clara County, San Jose, CA.

Henderson, B., L. Kolonel, and F. Foster. 1982. Cancer in Polynesians; U.S. Department of Health and Human Services, Public Health Service, National Institutes of Health, *National Cancer Institute Monograph No. 62*, NIH Publication No. 82-2438, pp. 73-78.

Lewis, M. 1991. Who's who in California. *San José (CA) Mercury News*, West section, May 12, p. 6-11.

Office of Minority Health, Public Health Services, U.S. Dept. of Health and Human Services. ND. *Closing the gap, diabetes and minorities, fact sheet.*

Panel sees race aspect in AIDS epidemic. New York Times report cited by *San Jose (CA) Mercury News*, Jan 12, p. 8A.

Pitts, T. 1991. Overview of diabetes in ethnic and minority groups. *On the Cutting Edge* 12(6):2-4.

Riche, M. 1991. We're all minorities now. *American Demographics* 13(10):26-34.

Snider, D., L. Salinas, and G. Kelly. 1989. Tuberculosis: an increasing problem among minorities in the United States. *Public Health Reports* 104(6):646-653.

Stern, M. and S. Haffner. 1992. Type II diabetes in Mexican Americans: a public health challenge, Chapter 6 in *Health policy and the Hispanic*, edited by A. Furino. Boulder, CO: West View Press.

U.S. Bureau of the Census. 1993. *Statistical abstract of the United States*, 113 edition. Washington, D.C.: U.S. Government Printing Office, Table 733, p. 468.

Webster's New World Dictionary, 2nd edition. 1986. David Guralnik, editor. Englewood Cliffs, NJ: Prentice-Hall Press.

Chapter 3

MULTICULTURAL COMMUNICATION

It is essential for health professionals to understand and be empathic with different styles of communication, and at the same time to recognize that many individuals within a culture do not exhibit the behaviors attributed to their group. Thus, it is important not to stereotype. However, cultural differences do exist, and in order to provide effective health care it is important to recognize that these differences affect communication.

Communication occurs when someone hears a message or observes a behavior and gives meaning to it (Porter and Samover, 1988). Communication is either verbal or nonverbal. All communication requires a sender, a message, and a receiver. There are a number of ways in which culture affects communication; for example, there are differences in the meanings of words, behaviors vary, rules about who talks to whom differ, and the portion of meaning conveyed by context (nonverbal) differs. Porter and Samover (1988) reported that the meanings of messages are affected by beliefs/values, world view, and social organization.

Beliefs and Values

In order for communication to occur the receiver must accept the beliefs of the sender. For example, a health professional must accept the traditional health beliefs of the client. Part of the message is ignored when a person's beliefs are discounted. Similarly, differences in values affect communication. Americans value honesty, but in other cultures the most important value may be to avoid disagreement (Copeland and Griggs, 1985). An American health professional might assume an honest answer to a health inquiry. However, if the client is Pilipino and an honest response to the question is going to cause the client to disagree with the health professional, the answer may be altered to "go along" with the health professional. The response is intended to be polite, not to answer the question. The care giver has been misled by value differences. Many Asians elect to "save face" and avoid confrontation rather than provide direct responses to questions. A health-care provider may believe that there is a firm agreement with a client to follow certain recommendations or prescriptions, only to discover later that the client had never intended to follow the instructions. Possibly the prescription conflicted with the client's traditional health beliefs. However, the value of "going along with" or avoiding conflict with the professional may have been more important than the value for honesty. For some people, then, saving face and being indirect to avoid negative responses have high value and may not be consistent with dominant White values of being direct, open, and honest.

Another value difference that could disrupt communication has to do with time. The Western health professional works with very little flexibility in an M-time schedule of appointments. If a client arrives late for an appointment, it could be because the P-time client does not place the same value on time as the care giver. Unfortunately, the appointment schedule is disrupted and the anger that ensues could easily affect the relationship. Other value differences could become apparent to a health professional. A dietitian in a Women, Infants, and Children program (WIC) may have difficulty persuading pregnant women to consume food supplements themselves without sharing with other family members. This is because in some cultures, the family is more important than any individual member. It would be very difficult not to share food. Another example is related to fatalism or the belief that what happens to a person is outside the power of the individual to change. Thus, why should people eat a balanced diet to stay healthy if health is not within their control?

Kinebanian and Stomph (1992) reminded health professionals to compare the goals of their professions with those of their clients. In occupational therapy the goal is to help clients become independent. However, in many cultures the welfare of the group/family is valued highly and the independence of individuals is not important. Other value differences are found in Table 3-1.

Table 3-1.
Cultural values.[1]

U.S. Culture	Other Cultures
Individual welfare most important	Family/group welfare predominates
Control over environment	Protect nature, harmony
Individual destiny	Fatalism, God's will
Competition	Cooperation
Materialism	Spiritualism

[1] USDA and DHHS, 1986. Cross-cultural Counseling: A Guide for Nutrition and Health Counselors. FNS-250, Food and Nutrition Service, U.S. Department of Agriculture.

World View

It is less obvious how world view can affect communication. Recall that world view is the way people explain relationships among people, the universe, and nature. World view includes beliefs in gods and other supernatural beings. People assume that their own world view is universal without realizing that other people have different views. In some cultures people believe that they can hear the voices of supernatural beings; so, to hear voices is normal. However, to a Western health professional the person who hears voices is mentally ill.

An American might believe that the ecologic damage of an oil spill can be repaired at some time in the future. Native Americans view themselves in partnership with nature, and damage to nature could create an imbalance that affects a person's health and well-being.

Social Organization

The last of the three values which Porter and Somover (1988) identified as influencing communication is "social organization." Rules of family, schools, and business affect communication and differ from one culture to another. For example, in many cultures the health professional can increase rapport by touching the client. However, if the health professional is male and the client is female, touching would not be acceptable in some cultures.

Rules of Communication

Some universal rules of communication are important to the understanding of the communication process (Harris and Moran, 1987; Porter and Samover, 1988).

- No matter how hard one tries, one cannot avoid communicating, or "we cannot not communicate." All behavior communicates a message.
- It takes two or more people to communicate: sender and receiver.
- Sending a message does not necessarily mean understanding. The sender and the receiver must have the same interpretation of words and gestures.
- Communication is irreversible. We cannot take back something that has been communicated.
- Communication occurs in a context. The situation (physical and social setting) itself has meaning. For example, the message of employer to employee will differ from the message of employee to employer.

- Communication is a dynamic process. It changes.

Context

The rules of communication are valid in all cultures; however, the one rule that is influenced most by culture is the degree to which context influences communication. In American and European cultures, such as German and Swiss, most communication occurs directly through language. Hall (1976) described these cultures, in which words convey most of the meaning of communication and context has minimal impact, as low context. In other cultures, such as Asian, African, Arab, and Native American, languages are less complete and precise, and communication depends on the context in which the words are stated. In these high context cultures, nonverbal cues and subtle "looks" convey considerable meaning (Copeland and Griggs, 1985). Even in low context cultures, high context interactions may occur between individuals who, through years of close relationship, learn to communicate using nonverbal behaviors.

Verbal Communication

Language. Language is a major obstacle in communicating within a diverse society. It would be nice, but not practical, if we could all speak all languages. Even that is not an ideal solution because of context. If we do learn the language, we still may not communicate well except in low context cultures. This is not intended to discourage anyone from learning a foreign language, as any attempt to improve communication is better than nothing. Even a few words in a client's own language can be very comforting.

Interpreters. A possible solution to the language barrier is the use of an interpreter. There is an important distinction between the functions of a translator and an interpreter. A translator puts words into a different language; an interpreter attempts to reproduce someone else's ideas and meanings. The interpreter must be sensitive to culture and social differences as well as language.

When working with interpreters, it is important to prepare them ahead by developing rapport and discussing technical words. The interpreter should be neutral and nonjudgmental in conveying your message. For this reason, it is best not to use children or other family members who may decide to change your message to avoid embarrassment or protect the client from negative information. In families where the social order puts adults in charge of children, the use of a child as an interpreter reverses the order and could cause the child to avoid telling a parent what to do as prescribed or recommended. Also, negative information about a family member could overwhelm a child who needs some protection from bad news (Haffner, 1992; Ramakrishna and Weiss, 1992).

To effectively use interpreters, have the interpreter stand at the client's side. Look at the client while talking to the interpreter. Speak slowly and use simple, short sentences. Do not speak louder than for normal conversation. Use words that the client can understand. Watch for responses that do not fit your questions. Give the interpreter plenty of time. Repeat important information, and don't assume that the message you sent was actually received by the client. Ask the client to repeat important parts of the message.

Nonverbal Communication

Considerable information is communicated by nonverbal behavior. In fact, most (60 to 70 percent) communication is conveyed by body language (Copeland and Griggs, 1985). A handshake, eye contact, gestures, personal space (distance), time, and facial expressions all convey meanings which vary from one culture to another. If a person tells you something verbally, but his or her nonverbal cues conflict, you will most likely believe the nonverbal message.

Space. Proxemics, the distance two people leave between themselves when talking, varies according to culture. Everyone has a personal bubble of space that is comfortably violated only by very good friends. When conversing with someone whose personal space is greater than what is expected, the other person seems cold and aloof. However, the greatest discomfort occurs when the other person seeks a proximity closer than expected. Middle Easterners prefer a very close (two feet) distance, which is definitely too close for people in the United States who prefer an arms-length (three foot) or even a five-foot distance (Hall, 1987).

Time. As described in Chapter 1, M-time is the time system prevalent in the United States, England, Germany, and other Western cultures. The emphasis of M-time is on promptness and doing one thing at a time. Time dominates activities. In other words, if it is time to do something else, Americans will drop their present activities in order to keep on time.

In P-time cultures (Latin countries, Italy, Africa, Middle East, and India) schedules are not as important as the completion of a transaction. P-time is people oriented and promotes interaction with more than one person at a time. Different time orientations can result in misunderstandings and lead to a failure to communicate.

Eye contact. Dominant culture Americans tend to look other people straight in the eye and break eye contact periodically and briefly throughout a conversation. However, this may be impolite in another culture (American Indians, Asians).

Expressiveness. Among others, Mexican American women are very expressive, and a health professional may consider them immature or unable to tolerate pain. Asians, on the other hand, may be totally inexpressive which may be perceived as unfeeling. The difference is cultural and not biological.

Body language and gestures. Similar across cultures are many facial expressions, such as expressions of happiness, fear, and surprise are examples (Muldary, 1983). However, hand gestures and body positions vary by culture. Eckman, Freisen, and Bear (1984) classified gestures into three major categories: manipulators, emblems, and illustrators. Manipulators have no particular meaning. They are habits usually observed in emotional situations. Things such as twisting the hair and rubbing the chin are manipulators. This is not intentional communication, but may convey the fact that there is some emotional stress.

Emblem gestures take the place of spoken words and have specific meanings which may change depending on context and culture. For example, "thumbs up" is a vulgar sign in Iran and Ghana, but means "all right" in the United States. In the former Yugoslavia to shake the head back and forth means "yes."

Illustrator gestures help explain the spoken word. These are especially variable with culture. Italians use many illustrator gestures, while an Asian may use none. Unlike an emblem gesture, the meaning of an illustrator gesture varies depending on the situation.

Posture and gender. Health professionals learn to show their attentiveness by leaning forward, touching, eye contact, and facing a person squarely. However, there are gender differences. Feminine body positions are non-threatening and demonstrate subordination through minimal use of space. It is feminine to keep arms close to the body and keep the legs close together. Small hand gestures add to feminine appearance. Smiling is a non-aggressive, feminine gesture. In contrast, masculine body positions are aggressive with arms and hands held away from the body and legs positioned apart when standing. Men physically occupy more space than women; they move forcefully and abruptly. Men communicate force and appear masculine with serious facial expressions (Devor, 1989).

Other nonverbal behaviors. Other things that communicate meaning include:

- Body type and degree of attractiveness, which communicate information about a

person's characteristics that may not be correct.
- Clothing, jewelry, eyeglasses, etc., communicate messages (stereotypes) about status, sexiness, credibility, and self-esteem.
- Facial expressions communicate emotions. Basic emotions that can be judged by facial expression are fear, anger, happiness, surprise, disgust, sadness, and interest. These are common to all cultures, but people can alter and control facial expressions. Interestingly, people cannot control the muscles around the eyes, which means that eye expressions are more reliable than others. This is one reason that people of some cultures (Arab especially) stand so close when communicating; they are reading the eyes.
- Environmental elements such as lighting and color send messages about us. For example, blue and green are cool and calming colors. Desks and tables send messages. They may act as barriers. The shape of a table and seating location indicate a person's degree of perceived equality or superiority. Where a student sits in a classroom communicates information to the teacher. Students who select front row seats do better on tests and interact more with the teacher than students who choose back row seats. Students on the side don't do as well as students in the center.
- Touching varies with culture, age, and sex. People who like to be touched consider people "aloof" and "cold" when they don't touch. There are accepted rules for touching in every culture, and they vary depending on the situation. For example, a health professional may touch the shoulder of a client to help establish rapport, but wouldn't think of touching the same person if that person is first encountered in an elevator.
- Voice characteristics including the pitch of the voice, the loudness of speech, and the speed of delivery all communicate information. Careful attention to the voice can help the listener detect deception (Malandro, Barker, and Barker, 1989).

Implications for Health Care

Virtually every aspect of communication is influenced by culture. Health professionals of any ethnicity should assume that their own communication styles will differ from those of clients. During initial counseling encounters, it is appropriate to observe the client's preferences regarding seating, touching, and eye contact.

During conversations, it is important to tolerate periods of silence. Care must be used in formulating questions to avoid "yes/no" responses. Many clients will respond in the affirmative rather than disagree with the professional. Frequent nodding may indicate that the client hears you, not that you are understood. Responses may be positive to avoid admitting to the professional that the message has not been stated clearly enough to be comprehended.

Health professionals need to be aware of their own values and those of their professions; they need to recognize that these values affect their interactions with clients. Also, it is necessary to learn the values and expectations of clients without assuming they will be the same as those of the dominant group. With all people, it is essential to develop rapport and a trusting relationship; however, because of cultural barriers, it may take longer and require greater effort when communicating with ethnic clients than with individuals of the dominant culture.

References Cited

Copeland, L. and L. Griggs. 1985. *Going international: How to make friends and deal effectively in the global market place.* New York: Random House.

Devor, H. 1989. *Gender blending.* Bloomington, IN: Indiana University Press.

Eckman, P., W. Freisen, and J. Bear. 1984. The international language of gestures. *Psychology Today*, May, pp. 64-69.

Haffner, L. 1992. Cross-cultural medicine, a decade later: Translation is not enough - interpreting in a medical setting. *The Western Journal of Medicine* 157(3):255-259.

Hall, E. T. 1976. *Beyond culture.* Garden City, NY: Anchor Press/Doubleday and Company, Inc.

Harris, P. and R. Moran. 1987. *Managing cultural differences*, 2nd edition. Houston: Gulf Pub. Co.

Kinebanian, A. and M. Stomph. 1992. Cross-cultural occupational therapy: a critical reflection. *The American Journal of Occupational Therapy* 46(8):751-757.

Melandro, L., L. Barker, and D. Barker. 1989. *Nonverbal communication*, 2nd edition. New York: Random House.

Muldary, T. 1983. *Interpersonal relations for health professionals: a social skills approach.* New York: MacMillan Publishing, Co. Inc.

Porter. R and L. Samover. 1988. Approaching the intercultural communication, pp. 15-30 in *Intercultural communication: a reader*, 5th edition, edited by L. Samovar and R. Porter. Belmont, CA: Wadsworth Pub. Co.

Ramakrishna, J. and M. Weiss. 1992. Cross-cultural medicine a decade later: health, illness and immigration - East Indians in the United States. *The Western Journal of Medicine* 157(3):265-270.

USDA and DHHS. 1986. *Cross-cultural counseling: a guide for nutrition and health counselors.* FNS-250, Food and Nutrition Service. Washington, D.C.: U.S. Department of Agriculture.

Chapter 4

HEALTH BELIEFS AND PRACTICES

In the United States, many people who differ culturally from the dominant White society have low socioeconomic status. Low income affects a person's view of health and care-seeking behaviors; basic needs such as how to obtain food and shelter are more urgent than preventative health care. If a family has been poor for generations there seems to be no possibility of escaping the cycle; self-esteem is low. Thus, low income results in feelings of hopelessness and impossible obstacles to overcome; poverty has no end. It isn't surprising, then, to observe a fatalistic world view among some low income populations. That is, there is a perception that fate has predetermined life's events such as illness; so, there is no point in even trying to improve one's condition (Bloch, 1983). Health promotion and disease prevention are concepts beyond the cultural and financial capabilities of many low income persons. Compared to middle-income Americans, many low income people seek out Western medical care as a last measure and enter the health care system at more advanced stages of illness with less hope of recovery.

There is a clear distinction between illness and disease that presents a communication barrier between Western health care providers and the persons they treat. Modern medicine is geared to treat diseases (biological abnormalities in structure and function); whereas, patients suffer from illness (changes in social function and state of well-being). Illness can occur in the absence of disease, and because illness is a part of the social system it is influenced by culture. Western medicine is concerned with disease and curing, yet almost half the patients treated by Western medicine in the United States are seeking help for illness problems. On the other hand, traditional medicine responds to the social (personal, family, and community) aspects of illness and healing. Cultural healers are usually effective in treating illness, but are not trained to treat disease. As a result, the patient may not be adequately treated by either system (Kleinman, Eisenberg, and Good, 1978).

Harwood (1981) identified two factors that individuals consistently use to determine whether they are ill: "(l) the duration, location, and intensity of symptoms, and (2) the social effects of the symptoms in terms of interference with either valued social activities or the fulfillment of role responsibilities" (p. 490). Diverse behaviors in illness are partly based on culture. For example, Western physicians may have their authority ignored by individuals whose culture identifies a family member as the decision maker. In this event, individuals may take no responsibility for their own health.

Cultural communication values such as touch and space can affect the illness behaviors of clients when they interact with health professionals. Anxiety can be particularly great for an ethnic patient whose symptoms suggest a culturally defined illness with symptoms that are not recognized as serious by the Western health care provider. In many cases, people do not seek Western health care for a culturally defined illness (Hartog and Hartog, 1983).

Etiology of Illness

Despite obvious differences among cultures, there are many similarities in health beliefs and practices. In order to simplify these complex systems for the Western practitioner, cultural beliefs about the etiology of illness will be presented using a model that emphasizes their similarities. There are, of course, some beliefs about the cause of illness that do not fit into this simplified system. The four categories selected to explain illness in traditional medical systems are: (1) imbalance, (2) natural causes, (3) supernatural causes, and (4) scientifically explainable causes (e.g., germs, virus, biological).

Illnesses due to "imbalance" between the individual and the physical, social, or spiritual worlds (or lack of "harmony" with nature) are universal and so important in some cultures that they are identified in a separate category for emphasis. However, these illness beliefs could have been classified as "natural" causes of illness. Among Latinos and Asians the balance of hot (*yang*) and cold (*yin*) are believed important for maintenance of good health. American Blacks may believe in a balance between rich foods and astringent substances to avoid imbalances of the blood.

Snow (1974) described natural illness as pertaining to the world as God intended. A natural or known external force such as food, water, or air (drafts) can cause illness. Psychosocial factors such as stress, worry, racism, and family problems are believed responsible for illness by most ethnic groups.

In contrast, supernatural (unnatural) events are forces of evil which ordinary people are helpless to control. This aspect of traditional medicine can be explained as the belief that the invisible world is inhabited by good and evil spirits (Henderson and Primeaux, 1981). An unnatural illness may occur to a very sinful person when God withdraws His protection and leaves the person prey to demons. Western doctors are not able to cure an unnatural illness; it takes a powerful healer to remove hexes and cure illness caused by witchcraft (Snow, 1974). Supernatural beliefs can be expressed in magic, witchcraft, and religion. Evil eye is an example of illness caused by evil forces. A strong look (also gazing or staring) at another person (especially a child or woman) can cause illness. This belief exists in many areas including the Philippines, the Mediterranean, the Middle East, Mexico, and Germany (Spector, 1985). Most people in the United States have some understanding of the scientific causes of illness. The longer people reside in the United States the more likely it is that some Western medical explanations will be incorporated into their health belief systems. Improved socioeconomic status will also increase reliance on Western medicine.

Treatment of Illness

Every person or family group makes decisions concerning which, if any, health practitioner to consult during illness. The conclusion is depends on a number of variables and may differ from one time to another. Income level is a major factor because the cost of Western medicine may be prohibitive; additionally, many low income people receive no pay if they miss work. Other factors are experiences with medical systems including the attitudes of previous providers, level of education and knowledge about disease symptoms, influence of family and friends, religion, modesty, fear of treatment, generation in the United States, and age. People tend to accept their own cultural medical system (Western medicine in the United States) without question. Any alternative system is viewed as inferior or somehow less appropriate. Many health care providers are ethnocentric in their belief that Western medicine is superior in all aspects of treatment to traditional practices. As a result, the attitude of health providers in this country may produce an additional and unnecessary barrier which reduces the choice of healing systems for ethnic minorities. Clark (1983) identified several cultural barriers to Western health care including communication problems, traditional beliefs and explanations for the causes of illness, and the fear of disease.

Health practice choices include no treatment, self-treatment, traditional practices and healers, and Western health methods. Murray and Rubel (1992) further divide the traditional practices (alternative methods) into four categories of treatment: spiritual/psychological, nutritional, drug/biologic, and physical forces/devices. It has been estimated that from 70 to 90 percent of all illnesses in the United States are managed outside the Western medical system (Zola, 1972).

Murray and Rubel (1992) reported on a survey conducted by Cook and Baisden in rural West Virginia in which 73 percent of the patients reported the use of folk remedies. "There is strong evidence that patients in every social, economic, and educational class seek and use alternative care" (Murray and Rubel, 1992, p. 63). Fennema (1984) indicated that "folk medicines, and practices involving foods, can be observed in all cultures in the world" (p. 63). From these reports, it can be assumed that self-treatment and traditional practices provide a substantial proportion of health care. It is apparent that Western health care providers need to have an understanding of alternative treatments practiced in their own communities.

Persons from the dominant United States culture might argue that cultural practices are not a part of their healing systems. However, self-prescribed health foods, vitamin pills, patent medicines and healing foods are all cultural practices not endorsed by Western medicine. Some people believe that there are harmful combinations of food, such as milk and fish or milk and cherries. A copper bracelet may be worn in the belief that it will cure arthritis. Many Americans rely on television advertised products which are not accepted by Western doctors.

Medical Practices in the United States

Spector (1985) described four types of health care available in the United States.

Allopathic medicine. Allopathic means all therapies. This is the dominant care system used in the U.S. and is the basis of Western medicine. The American Medical Association and medical doctors control allopathic medicine; most have little respect for other methods. Allopathic medicine is based on the view that a disease-free condition is normal and any disease is foreign to the human body. Since disease is foreign, it is treated with something that opposes it (Rosengren, 1980). Allopathic medicine uses a variety of technologies and is continuously changing. Practice/treatment can be outdated very quickly. Methods used may depend on the "experience" of the practitioner. There is no single dogma to guide practitioners as in other medical systems (Rosengren, 1980).

Homeopathic medicine. Homeopathy was practiced in the early 1900s in the U.S. (there are about 1000 practicing Homeopaths in the United States), and it is still practiced in Europe (France, Germany, and Great Britain). Homeopathy is based on the belief that all disorders respond to specific substances and that "like cures like." Homeopathic medicine treats the ill person by using small doses of substances which if given to a healthy person would cause the same symptoms. The purpose is to stimulate the ill persons' natural defenses. The therapeutic substances are named in the text of homeopathy, *Materia Medica*. Homeopathy has rejected change and incorporation of treatments that did not fit its doctrine. As a result, it has failed as a legitimate medical system (Spector, 1985; Rosengren, 1980).

Osteopathic medicine. Osteopathy is based on the belief that diseases are caused by dislocation of small bones in the spinal column and in the muscles surrounding the spine. This happens as the result of nerve and blood supply malfunctions. According to doctrine, treatment for all diseases is based on the manipulation of the spine and its muscular system. However, osteopathy has changed and has incorporated allopathic practices. Doctors of Osteopathy (D.O.) have training similar to the medical doctor (M.D.) and their practices are similar (Rosengren, 1980).

Chiropractic medicine. Chiropractic is based on the theory that disease occurs when "mental impulses" between the brain and the body are blocked by misalignment of the vertebrae. Chiropractic is a surviving and, according to Rosengren (1980), marginal system of medical care that challenges (rather than incorporates) the allopathic monopoly. Manipulation is used in treatment as well as other methods (of diagnosis and treatment) which may be questioned (Spector, 1985; Rosengren, 1980).

Western Medicine in Other Countries

There are other medical beliefs/treatments, but this brief description covers the major choices available to the dominant U.S. culture. Now, what about other technological countries? Payer (1988) studied the Western medicine of European countries and compared their practices with those of the United States. She found that culture (not just science) had a lot of influence on treatment. Doctors responded to what people wanted and would be willing to accept. She found many differences from one country to another, and because of her initial biases was inclined to think that the American way was the right way. Then she realized that life expectancy was as high (if not higher) in the European countries as in the United States. Some of her observations follow:

- A British surgeon treating breast cancer would prefer a lumpectomy to a mastectomy. The reason? British surgeons are paid the same no matter how they treat disease. So, why should they do more than is necessary? Payer commented that the British do less of everything (Pap smears only after age 35 and only once every five years, greater tolerance of obesity, etc.).
- Homeopathic doctors are found in many British cities. The royal family uses homeopathic treatment, which makes it acceptable.
- American doctors use very aggressive treatments and many more diagnostic tests than other doctors. This is partly because Americans expect more tests and associate them with better medicine. Many Americans view the body as a machine that needs to be fixed rather then left to heal.
- West Germans are over-treated for heart disease compared to the standards of other countries. Doctors use six times more heart medication per capita is used than in England or France. In one study, 40 percent of the people were judged to have abnormal electrocardiograms by German standards and only 5 percent by American criteria. West Germans visit the doctor on the average of 12 times a year compared to 5.2 times in France, 5.4 times in England, and 4.7 times in the United States. Germans had the highest number of diagnoses per capita (of course, since they saw the doctor more frequently). Not surprisingly, West German doctors are paid according to the number of "acts" they perform.
- In the U.S., low blood pressure is considered an advantage related to longevity; British doctors are taught that low blood pressure is desirable. However, German doctors say that low blood pressure causes fatigue and they treat it with adrenaline. This goes along with the German obsession with diseases of the heart.
- German doctors use half the antibiotics that French doctors use and less than British or American doctors. Antibiotics are reserved for serious conditions, so antibiotic-resistant germs are less of a problem in Germany. German people and their doctors were inclined to let the body heal itself when they perceived the illness was not serious.
- In France, it is not unusual for an M.D. to use "fringe medicine." Homeopathy is practiced by many French doctors.
- French hospital stays are typically twice as long as those in the U.S. for the same procedures. Note that this was before Medicare cost-containment regulations (DRGs) that now limit U.S. hospital stays; the difference is probably greater now. In French maternity hospitals without operating rooms the average length of stay was 10.6 days in 1981. French people were described as placing great value on vacations and rest.

These are only a few of the examples cited by Payer (1988) to show the effects of culture on Western medicine. Traditional medical systems are based on cultural beliefs; and even though

Western medicine is supposedly based on science, it obviously is influenced by culture.

Traditional Medicine

Traditional medical systems have some common aspects that distinguish them from Western medicine. They usually involve a strong social support system of immediate family, extended family, friends, and church leaders. Families and friends are relied on extensively in emergencies. In addition, cultural medical treatment involves the whole person with no distinction between physical and mental symptoms; mental distress may be expressed by physical symptoms. There are two great medical systems outside Western (allopathic) medicine: Ayurvedic medicine and Chinese medicine. Ayurvedic medicine is practiced in India and surrounding countries (see Chapter 16). The second system is Chinese Medicine which is discussed in Chapter 11. The traditional medical systems described here are less complete and less formal. They don't claim to treat all aspects of illness/disease.

In traditional medical systems the treatment for an illness usually depends on the cause. If an illness is caused by imbalance, then it may be cured by self-treatment and the return to balance or harmony using foods and herbs. Cultural healers may also be consulted for illnesses due to imbalance. Illness resulting from natural causes may require cultural healers who have special curing powers possibly received as a gift from God. Supernatural illnesses usually require a spiritualist for their cure. Of course, disease is appropriately treated by Western doctors. In some cases Western medicine will be used to treat the symptoms of an illness, but the cause is treated by an alternative method. Each culture has a medical system for alleviating the perceived illness. Research shows that most ill people get well no matter what treatment method is used; even if there is no treatment, most people recover. If there is a treatment (of any kind) in which people believe, the placebo effect might be expected to be responsible for satisfactory symptomatic relief of 35 percent of the patients (Fennema, 1984). For these reasons, most people will have their individual treatment methods validated by the fact that they recovered, and as a result cultural health beliefs are strengthened.

In order to assist Western health professionals to learn of their clients' understanding and expectations regarding treatment and healing, Kleinman, Eisenberg, and Good (1978) formulated a series of questions to ask clients. From the responses, a practitioner should learn the patient's perspective and be able to negotiate a treatment compatible with the client's understanding of the illness. The questions include: "(1) What do you think has caused your problem? (2) Why do you think that it started when it did? (3) What do you think your sickness does to you? How does it work? (4) How severe is your sickness? Will it have a short or long course? (5) What kind of treatment do you think you should receive?" (p. 256).

Responses that suggest the use of alternative medical systems may need further exploration to reveal other treatments being used. Alternative health care treatments may delay entry into the Western medical system, and the individual will be sicker on entry than if the first treatment choice had been Western medicine. There are reports that self-treatments and cultural methods of treatment may conflict or compete with Western medicines. Also, alternative care provides a choice and consequently promotes non-compliance with Western prescriptions (Jackson, 1981).

On the other hand, cultural healers provide a valuable service to many ethnic clients in the form of psychosocial counseling. There is evidence that these healers do refer patients to Western health care services and that cooperative treatment can be beneficial (Harwood, 1981).

Many people in an ethnic group do not adhere to traditional beliefs and practices. The tendency to stereotype individuals must be avoided. Not all Mexican Americans consult *curanderos*; not all Black Americans believe in *high blood*. People of higher socioeconomic status tend to have fewer cultural health beliefs than persons of lower socioeconomic standing (Clark, 1983). Additionally, the longer a person has been in the United States the more likely the medical choice will include Western medicine.

Medical Pluralism

People of many cultures use traditional treatments and have beliefs regarding the causes of illness not accepted by Western practitioners. Indeed, many people who practice some forms of alternative medicine acknowledge that Western medicine cannot treat their traditional illnesses. Thus, Western health care providers should expect that their ethnic clients have attempted alternative cures and may still be using them. Further, if Western medicine fails to provide a rapid cure, or relief of symptoms, the ethnic client can be expected to simultaneously use more than one medical system. Since healing methods may not be compatible and some may even be dangerous when used at the same time, it is important that all treatments be identified (Barker, 1992).

Health promotion and disease prevention are concepts familiar to ethnic people who believe in balance of hot/cold or *yin/yang*, harmony with nature, and dietary taboos to avoid illness (Barker, 1992). However, some ethnic clients believe that illness is caused by supernatural forces and is outside an individual's control. For the latter group, efforts to promote health are not understood. Even the notion that food has quality may be foreign, and, in this land of plenty, some people may select foods based solely on flavor.

Implications for Health Care

In order for Western health care providers to effectively treat clients who have some cultural beliefs about illness, it is necessary to have additional time and resources available. Yet, this requisite seems unlikely to be filled because most individuals who need the extra time and resources are low-income and are generally restricted to government sponsored clinics.

Any discrepancies between the Western health care practitioner and an ethnic client who uses traditional treatments may be resolved through patient education, selection of treatments that don't conflict with cultural treatments, and/or negotiation to incorporate treatments from both systems (Harwood, 1981).

Guidelines to help professionals work effectively with ethnic clients were developed by Berlin and Fowkes (1983). They used the mnemonic LEARN as a model to supplement the medical history.

"L   Listen with sympathy and understanding to the patient's perception of the problem.

E   Explain your perception of the problem.

A   Acknowledge and discuss the differences and similarities.

R   Recommend treatment.

N   Negotiate agreement (p. 130)".[1]

Foster and Anderson (1978) indicated that "when effective medical treatment is available in Western systems, is delivered by empathic persons at a price Third World people can afford and at convenient times and places, it will be the first choice of many and perhaps most persons" (p. 253).

---

[1] From *A TEACHING FRAMEWORK FOR CROSS-CULTURAL HEALTH CARE* by Elois Ann Berlin, Ph.D. and William C. Fowkes, Jr., M.D. *The Western Journal of Medicine* 1983 Dec. 139:934-938. Copyright © 1993 by The California Medical Association. Reprinted with permission.

References Cited

Barker, J. 1992. Cross-cultural medicine, a decade later: Cultural diversity—changing the context of medical practice. *The Western Journal of Medicine* 157(3):248-254.

Berlin, E. and W. Fowkes, Jr. 1983. A teaching framework for cross-cultural health care. *The Western Journal of Medicine* 139:934-938.

Bloch, B. 1983. Nursing care of Black patients, Chapter 3 in *Ethnic nursing care*, edited by M. Orque, B. Bloch, and L. Monrroy. St. Louis: C. V. Mosby Co.

Clark, M. 1983. Cultural context of medical practice. *The Western Journal of Medicine* 139:806-810.

Fennema, O. 1984. The placebo effect of foods. *Food Technology* 38:57-67.

Foster, G. and B. Anderson. 1978. *Medical anthropology*. New York: John Wiley and Sons.

Hartog, J. and E. Hartog. 1983. Cultural aspects of health and illness behavior in hospitals. *The Western Journal of Medicine* 139:910-916.

Harwood, A., editor. 1981. *Ethnicity and medical care*. Cambridge, Massachusetts: Harvard University Press.

Henderson, G. and M. Primeaux. 1981. *Transcultural health care*. Menlo Park, CA: Addison-Wesley Pub. Co.

Jackson, J. 1981. Urban Black Americans, Chapter 1 in *Ethnicity and medical care*, edited by A. Harwood. Cambridge, MA: Harvard University Press.

Kleinman, A, L. Eisenberg, and B. Good. 1978. Culture, illness, and care: clinical lessons from anthropologic and cross-cultural research. *Annals of Internal Medicine* 88:251-258.

Murray, R. and A. Rubel. 1992. Physicians and healers: unwitting partners in health care. *The New England Journal of Medicine* 326(1):61-64.

Payer, L. 1988. *Medicine and culture: varieties of treatment in the United States, England, West Germany, and France*. New York: Henry Holt and Co.

Rosengren, W. 1980. *Sociology of medicine: diversity, conflict, and change*. New York: Harper and Row, Publishers.

Snow, L. 1974. Folk medical beliefs and their implications for care of patients. *Annals of Internal Medicine* 81:82-96.

Spector, R. 1985. *Cultural diversity in health and illness*, 2nd edition. Norwalk, CT: Appleton-Century-Croft.

Zola, I. 1972. Studying the decision to see a doctor in Advances in Psychosomatic Medicine, Vol. 8:216-236 cited by A. Kleinman, L. Eisenberg, and B. Good, Culture, Illness and Care: clinical lessons from anthropologic and cross-cultural research. *Annals of Internal Medicine* 88:251-258, 1978.

Chapter 5

FOOD, CULTURE, AND RELIGION

Culture plays a major role in food selection and helps determine what is fit to eat. In order to eat them, foods must be available; however, just because a substance is available does not guarantee that it will be eaten (Grivetti, 1978). Culture may not produce a nutritionally sound diet. Humans do not know instinctively how to select nutritional foods. In fact, people have starved to death in the presence of edible substances which in their cultures were not defined as food.

Some foods not considered edible in the dominant American culture are horsemeat, dog meat, small garden birds, acorns, snakes, ants, grubs, grasshoppers, and termites. In addition to cultural restrictions, some foods are not well liked: parsnips, eggplant, hominy, oysters, turnips, liver, limburger cheese, pig's feet, brains, and tripe. Another limitation on the food supply is due to the tendency to classify foods for certain purposes. For example, Americans tend to think of eggs as a breakfast food. In some cultures, foods may be restricted because of health beliefs; in others, women may avoid some foods during pregnancy because of cultural beliefs (Foster and Anderson, 1978).

Since culture is a learned body of knowledge, it follows that food habits can be "unlearned." This is the basic premise of nutrition education. Culture does change, but is very resistant to change. Thus, food habits are difficult to change. In order to guide individuals toward improved nutrient intake, it is important to understand the cultural reasons for their current eating patterns.

Food Patterns in the United States

During the past 50 years there have been significant changes in the foods that make up the American diet. There has been little change in the total amount of protein consumed, but now much of the protein comes from animal sources rather than from plant foods (beans, peas, legumes, nuts). Saturated fat intake is higher as a consequence of the change in sources of protein. Complex carbohydrate (grains, vegetables, legumes) intake is lower, but sugar intake is higher. A number of influences on family life styles have resulted in changes in eating patterns. Increased technology and availability of processed foods, convenience foods, and fast foods allow many persons to eat more meals away from home. Increased numbers of women in the work force have contributed to the changing food practices.

The American Diet

It is important to note some specifics about the dominant U.S. diet before describing ethnic diets. Originally from England, American foods have been diversified by the influences of many countries. Foods which are not fully integrated into mainstream diets are called ethnic foods. Cassidy (1982) identified a number of foods that are particularly American: hamburgers, hot dogs, pizza, tuna fish salad or casserole, macaroni and cheese, sandwiches, all varieties of corn (maize), fried chicken, cured pork, crab and lobster, turkey, raw salads, country-fried potatoes, sweet potatoes, pies, layer cakes, cupcakes, cookies, ice cream, ketchup, appetizers, alcoholic cocktails, and many packaged and prepared foods.

Probably the most important aspect of the American diet is the central position given to meat which may be the result of the British association between meat and being a good hunter and a good provider. Meat symbolizes masculinity, success, and affluence. Unfortunately, this diet is expensive and researchers have associated it with a number of chronic and degenerative diseases.

Food and Health

Whenever people in a culture lack information about microbes and food safety, they establish "cause and effect" relationships between certain foods and diseases. Observations over several generations may result in a list of harmful foods which is passed on to new generations. Folk medical beliefs develop in this way. Many tribal and peasant people have been able to achieve balanced diets (or at least adequate diets) through trial and error. Unfortunately, some concepts are not learned easily by the trial and error method.

A difficult concept for uneducated people to understand is that poor food quality can result in illness. This problem is made even more critical when some foods are restricted or withdrawn during illness in the belief that a balance needs to be restored. For example, meat and milk may be withheld from the diets of children with diarrhea or intestinal worms because these foods are believed to aggravate these conditions (Foster and Anderson, 1978).

The cultural beliefs in balance/hot-cold/*yin-yang* have an impact on the nutritional quality of some diets. Pregnancy and postpartum are periods when diets are most likely to be controlled, but other stages of life (childhood, old age, and during illness) are also affected. Nutritional deficiencies have been reported among people who follow cultural dietary taboos (Freimer, Echenberg, and Kretchmer, 1983).

Another misunderstood concept has to do with the special dietary needs of children. In some cultures, children are considered to be little adults and their needs are not recognized. Foods classified as "hot" may not be given to children in hot weather or when they are ill. This practice reduces protein intake. The custom of feeding men and older boys before women and children results in poor diets for the women and children because the leftovers are frequently low in nutrition (Foster and Anderson, 1978).

A serious, even fatal, problem for many people in the world is starvation caused by poverty and lack of food. The uneven distribution of food in the world was demonstrated in a hypothetical shrinking of the world population to a small village. Meadows (1990) speculated about what the world would be like if it was a village of 1000 people. She provided data on ethnicity, language, religion, and vocations of the villagers based on actual demographic data. Two hundred seventy of the wealthiest people controlled 40 percent of the crop land and used 83 percent of the fertilizer. The remaining 60 percent of the crop land would receive 17 percent of the fertilizer and produce 28 percent of the grain. This 28 percent of the grain had to feed 73 percent of the people. Obviously, poverty and food distribution have a significant impact on nutrition for many people.

Acculturation

One universal dietary problem exists for immigrants to the United States. Eventually they change their diets to include American foods. If people in the first generation don't change to American foods, their children do. With acculturation, the diets become higher in saturated fats and simple sugar and lower in some vitamins and minerals and fiber. The dietary changes are associated with increased rates of heart disease, some types of cancer, hypertension, obesity, and non-insulin dependent diabetes mellitus. Of course, changes in lifestyle other than diet also occur with acculturation. Decreased exercise and increased stress are also associated with disease rates (Freimer, Echenberg, and Kretchmer, 1983).

Religion

In order to understand the food habits of various cultures, it is necessary to examine some of the less visible roles (context) played by food. Food is used to demonstrate status; it is used for reward, magic, and healing. Religions also stipulate some food rules.

Jewish food customs. Kosher dietary laws pertain largely to the selection, slaughter, and preparation of meat. The only animals allowed for food are quadrupeds with a cloven hoof that chew cud (cattle, sheep, goats, and deer). Pork and pork products (gelatin) are prohibited. Permitted fowl include chicken, turkey, geese, pheasant, and duck. Scavengers and birds of prey are prohibited. All animals, including the quadrupeds and fowl, must be free of disease and killed by a ritual slaughter according to specific rules. Blood is forbidden as a food. The slaughter method and treatment of meat involve removal of blood. Before meat can be consumed, forbidden fat, fat arteries, and blood veins are removed. Then the meat is salted and soaked to remove blood.

Milk and meat must not be consumed in the same meal. Milk may be consumed until half an hour before a meat meal, but after eating meat at least three hours must pass before taking milk. Kosher kitchens keep two sets of dishes, flatware, and cooking utensils to separate milk and meat foods. Fish is allowed if it has scales and fins; this means that shellfish and eels are taboo. Fish and eggs may be eaten with either milk or meat. Other foods are not restricted, but kosher standards are followed. There are some restrictions for holidays; for example, during Passover leavened bread and cake are not consumed (Regenstein and Regenstein, 1983; Krause and Mahan, 1984).

Muslims. The Islamic tradition requires Muslims to fast (not even water is consumed) between sunrise and sunset during Ramadan, the ninth month of the Islamic calendar (see Chapter 17). However, two meals are consumed each day of Ramadan, one before sunrise and the other after sunset. Some of the dietary restrictions for Muslims are similar to Jewish restrictions. Pork and pork products are forbidden as are alcohol and foods containing alcohol. Meat must be slaughtered according to ritual with the letting of blood. Kosher meat is accepted. Some recommended foods are figs, olives, dates, honey, milk, and buttermilk (Krause, and Mahan, 1984).

Christians. Prior to 1966, Roman Catholics abstained from eating meat on Fridays. Fasting was observed on Ash Wednesday (the first day of Lent) and Good Friday (the Friday before Easter), but fasting allowed one meal a day and applied only to people between the ages of 14 and 60. In the United States, most dietary restrictions were abolished in 1966. However, meat is still not eaten on the Friday of Lent and fasting occurs on Good Friday and Ash Wednesdays.

The Eastern Orthodox (Greek) religion observes a number of days of fasting in which no meat or animal products are consumed. Only a few Protestant religions have dietary restrictions. Although their church doesn't require that they be vegetarians, many Seventh Day Adventists are lacto-ovo-vegetarians (they eat no flesh). If meat is consumed it must be from clean animals that have a split hoof and chew cud. Thus, pork, rabbit, horse, dogs, and cats are prohibited as food. Fish must have fins and scales. Adventists also do not use tobacco, alcohol, coffee, or tea. Some do not eat between meals (Bosley and Hardinge, 1992).

The Church of Jesus Christ of Latter Day Saints provides its members (Mormons) with a health code that prohibits tobacco, alcohol, coffee, and tea. Many Mormons also avoid all beverages that contain caffeine. Death rates for heart disease, cancer, and stroke are much lower for Mormons than for the general U.S. population (Krause and Mahan, 1984; Pike, 1992). Mormons are expected to store one year's supply of food and clothing (Krause and Mahan, 1984).

Ethnicity

Additional cultural food and nutrition topics are included with the information on each ethnic group in Chapters 8-17.

References Cited

Bosley, G. and M. Hardinge. 1992. Seventh Day Adventists: dietary standards and concerns. *Food Technology* 46(10):112-113.

Cassidy, C. 1982. Subcultural prenatal diets of Americans, in *Alternative dietary practices and nutritional abuses in pregnancy* - Proceedings of a workshop. Food and Nutrition Board, Commission on Life Sciences, Committee on Nutrition of the mother and preschool child. National Research Council. Washington, D.C.: National Academy of Sciences.

Foster, G. and B. Anderson. 1978. Medical anthropology, Chapter 15 in *Anthropology and nutrition*. New York: John Wiley and Sons.

Freimer, N., E. Echenberg, and N. Kretchmer. 1983. Cultural variation: nutritional and clinical implications. *The Western Journal of Medicine* 139:928-933.

Grivetti, L. 1978. Culture, diet and nutrition: selected themes and topics. *Bioscience* 28(3):171-177.

Krause, M. and L. K. Mahan. 1984. *Food, nutrition, and diet therapy*. Philadelphia: W. B. Saunders, Co.

Meadows, D. 1990. The state of the village. *San Jose (CA) Mercury News*, June 6, p. 7B.

Pike, D. 1992. The Church of Jesus Christ of Latter-Day Saints: dietary practices and health. *Food Technology* 46(10):118-121.

Regenstein, J. and C. Regenstein. 1979. An introduction to the kosher dietary laws for food scientists and food processors. *Food Technology* 33(1):89-99.

Chapter 6

UNITED STATES IMMIGRATION POLICY

There were few restrictions on immigration to the United States before 1882. Most early immigrants were from Europe; however, in the 1850's Chinese laborers traveled to the western United States to work in gold mining and in the 1860's to work on railroad construction. Chinese immigrants also took jobs as farmers, servants, and factory workers, but it was the gold mining and railroad construction work that eventually caused problems with White workers. Both types of employment ended abruptly, and the Chinese sought other work. They were perceived to be taking employment away from U.S. citizens (White). Labor conflicts and racial prejudice led to pressure for legislation to restrict immigration. The Chinese Exclusion Act of 1882 was the first congressional action taken against any race of immigrants (Figure 6-1). Only Chinese laborers were excluded at first; businessmen, students, travelers, and clergy were allowed to enter. Some laborers were subject to deportation, so many of the Chinese changed their work status to businessman by opening small businesses in Chinese communities. Thus, Chinatowns grew. Legislation essentially stopped immigration from China in 1884.

The Chinese who entered the United States prior to 1884 were mostly male laborers. They became socially segregated and many moved together into Chinatowns. In 1890 there were 2,678 Chinese males for every female in the U.S. It shouldn't be surprising to learn that Chinatowns became centers for organized prostitution. In some states, laws were enacted to prevent Chinese males from marrying White women. It wasn't until 1943, when Congress ended the ban on immigration and started a quota system, that legislation allowed Chinese women to enter the United States. However, only 105 people of Chinese descent were allowed to immigrate each year (Parrillo, 1985).

Japanese began entering the United States in significant numbers about 1890. They found racial prejudice against Asians, and many moved to outlying areas where they became agricultural workers and gardeners. In 1913 California passed legislation that prohibited people who were not eligible for citizenship from owning land and allowed them to lease land for only three years. Since long-standing federal legislation stated that citizenship was available to "any alien, being a free white person," the California law meant that only Whites could own land. When Black slaves were freed in 1868, federal law was revised to allow persons of African descent to hold citizenship, but Asians were excluded. Many Japanese escaped the problem by holding land in their children's names, possible because the children were born in the United States and were automatically U.S. citizens. However, in 1920, California legislation prohibited aliens from being guardians of a minor's property and went even further to prevent non-citizens from leasing land. Other states passed similar laws. Japanese immigration was strictly limited in 1908, when the Japanese government agreed to restrict the number of passports issued to the United States (Parrillo, 1985).

A 1917 law required that all immigrants pass a literacy test to be admitted. In 1921 and 1924 immigration quotas, which restricted immigration based on the proportion of residents present in 1890, were set. This law specifically barred entry to Japanese, and restricted entry of Southern, Central, and Eastern Europeans. The intent was to admit only people who were "assimilable" (Bullough and Bullough, 1982).

1880		
	1882–1884.	Chinese Exclusion Act
1890		
	1898.	Philippines became American possession and Pilipinos were designed Nationals
1900		
	1908.	Japan restricted immigration to U.S. by limiting number of passports issued.
1910		
	1913.	California prohibited aliens from owning land: only White persons and Blacks (because of the 1968 federal legislation) could own land.
	1917.	Immigrants required to pass a literacy test; excluded virtually all Asians.
1920	1920.	California prohibited aliens from being guardians of minor's property.
	1921.	Immigration from each country based on proportion of residents present in 1910.
	1924.	Asians were specifically barred. Pilipinos (Nationals) were not affected. Decreased quotas of southern, central, and eastern Europeans, based on proportion present in 1920.
1930		
	1934. 1935.	U.S. Supreme Court ruled that "white persons" meant Caucasian, and excluded Chinese, Japanese, Hindus (East Indians), American Indians, and Pilipinos from citizenship. Quotas were placed on Pilipino entries and some were repatriated.
1940		
	1942.	Bracero program initiated, allowing temporary workers.
	1943.	Quota system charged to allow a few restricted aliens to enter. For example, 100 Chinese a year were allowed. The Chinese Exclusion Act was repealed.
1950	1950.	Aliens required to register.
	1952.	Immigration of a few additional Asians allowed; some refugees were allowed.
1960		
	1964.	End of Bracero program.
	1965.	Old quotas based on country of origin were dropped; Asians no longer restricted and Europeans no longer favored. Preference categories favored entry of family members and of professionals, effective 1968. Allowed admission of refugees.
1970	1970s and 1980s.	In these years most immigrants have been from Latin America and Asia. Many refugees have entered from Vietnam, Southeast Asian, Cuba, and Haiti. In addition, many illegal immigrants enter every year—especially from Mexico.
1980		
	1986.	Amnesty for undocumented workers in U.S. since 1982.
1990	1990.	Immigration ceiling increased from 500,000 to 700,000 annually until 1995.

Figure 6–1. U.S. Immigration Policy—Time Line.

Pilipinos were not classified as aliens because in 1898 the Philippines became an American possession. Pilipinos were designated as "nationals," not citizens. They were allowed to enter the United States and were not affected by the 1924 legislation. In 1934 the United States Supreme Court ruled that "white person" meant members of the Caucasian race and excluded "Chinese, Japanese, Hindus, American Indians, and Filipinos." This action excluded these groups from citizenship. Race riots in California in the early 1930's led to 1935 legislation that placed quotas on Pilipino immigration. The restrictive quota legislation of 1924 (and 1935 for Pilipinos) was modified in 1952 to allow immigration of a few Asians. The 1952 law also allowed refugees from Hungary, Cuba, Vietnam, and Korea to enter the United States.

It wasn't until 1965 that the quota system based on national origin was dropped and Asians were no longer excluded. The 1965 legislation (Immigration and Nationality Act of 1965, Public Law 89-236) made three major changes that became effective in 1968:

- It abolished the quota system by national origin which was started in 1924 and highly favored entry of Europeans.
- It established seven preference categories for admission: four for purposes of family reunion, two for professionals and skilled workers, and one for political refugees. This legislation was the first to place a ceiling on the number of immigrants allowed from the Western hemisphere. Since 1968, most immigrants have entered as family members, students, and undocumented workers.
- It required that the Secretary of Labor certify that entry would not adversely affect wages and working conditions in the United States.

Prior to 1968 about 81 percent of all immigrants were from Europe. After the 1965 Immigration Act, immigration from Europe and Canada decreased while immigration from Asia, Mexico, and Central America increased. The changes have resulted in a shift in the countries of origin of immigrants; with most now coming from Asia and Latin America (Caribbean and Mexico). Compared to the five-year period of 1961-1965, in the five years from 1969 to 1973 the number of immigrants from Asia more than tripled. In addition, a much higher proportion of immigrants are now professionals than before the 1965 act. The number of professionals from Asia increased from 9.7 percent of immigrants in the period of 1961–1965 to 56.7 percent in 1969–1973 (Momeni, 1984).

The immigration of professionals has been criticized from two views. First, it creates a "brain drain" in developing countries that deprives them of needed services. For example, in 1972 nearly 10 percent of India's medical doctors were practicing in the United States and Great Britain. Newer legislation makes it much more difficult for foreign doctors to practice in the United States without U.S. schooling. The second argument is that hiring foreign-trained professionals is not fair to American youths who have fewer job opportunities available and less motivation to undertake professional training. It is then difficult to update and build training facilities in the United States.

In the 1970s and 1980s, many refugees entered the United States. They came (and continue to come) from Vietnam, Southeast Asia, Cuba and Haiti. In addition, thousands of illegal immigrants come into the United States each year, many from Latin America. Legislation in 1984 restricted employers from hiring illegal aliens, but enforcement has been lax.

Recent immigrants include large numbers of people from Latin America who live in poverty, are poorly educated, and do not speak English. The high fertility rate of these immigrants has caused considerable concern over rapid population growth in the United States. One author estimated that by the year 2080, California's population will be double the 1980 population, and 50 percent of the population will be made up of immigrants who arrived after 1980 and their descendants (Kramer, 1989).

In 1989 about 85 percent of all visas were granted to people from Latin America and Asia, most of them coming to join family members. At the present time, countries with backlogs of extended family members wishing to enter the U.S. include the Philippines, Mexico, South Korea, and India. In some cases the wait is as long as 12 years.

References Cited

Bullough, V. and B. Bullough. 1982. *Health care of the other Americans.* New York: Appleton-Century-Crofts.

Kramer, P. 1989. Immigration bill favors the elite, critics charge. *San Jose (CA) Mercury News.* July 15, page 2B.

Momeni, J. 1984. *Demography of racial and ethnic minorities in the United States.* Westport, CT: Greenwood Press.

Parrillo, V. 1985. *Strangers to these shores: race and ethnic relations in the United States.* New York: John Wiley and Sons.

Chapter 7

GENDER

The word "sex" was defined by Segall, et al. (1990) as based on biological differences, the word "gender" as "psychosociocultural . . . as reflected in social statuses, roles, and attitudes regarding the sexes" (p. 240). Thus, "gender" is used to describe cultural influences on whatever differences exist between male and female as the result of genetic inheritance.

In American society, the average man is viewed as dominant, aggressive, competitive, and goal-oriented, while the average woman is considered submissive, nurturing, person-oriented, and passive. However, these descriptions aren't accurate because few people are limited to all-male or all-female characteristics. Usually there is a blending of these characteristics within individuals.

The extent to which male and female behaviors are the result of hormonal differences (sex) or sociological and cultural influences is a matter of debate. There are several opposing theories, each with compelling evidence. Additional information about this discussion can be found in the references cited for Risman and Schwartz, 1989; Leone and O'Neill, 1983; Segall, et al., 1990; Eagly, 1987; and Devor, 1987.

Child Care

Little boys are raised to be physically active and "tough." They are taught that it is "sissy" to cry and cling to their mothers. They play wargames and participate in sports activities. On the other hand, little girls are restricted in physical activity by their parents (and by the need to keep their dresses clean). Girls are treated as fragile and taught to nurture through play with dolls and tea sets.

In American society, children are usually cared for by women (mothers, grandmothers, child-care employees). Children learn early that the more valued sex role is the masculine role. Girls have no trouble identifying with the feminine role even though they recognize the greater value placed on the masculine role; they learn from their mothers. Boys have much less contact with men than with women; their mothers teach them not to be like women but to be independent. Boys have to figure out what their roles should be. This difference in child care has led Chafetz (1983) to propose that the verbal superiority of women and the greater problem-solving abilities of men are based on culture rather than on sex. Boys have to figure out their gender roles and this requires problem-solving skills.

Segall, et al., (1990) also report that little boys learn to fear being feminine (sissy). When boys reach adolescence they attempt to prove their masculinity through aggressive behavior. The result is that 18- to 24-year old males account for a disproportionate number of violent crimes (Segall et al., 1990). This point is important in the study of ethnic groups in relation to the high rates of violence found among inner city males, many of whom were raised in single-parent families by their mothers and had few male role models.

Sex and Gender Roles

In many cultures there is a division of labor based on sex. The need for different labor tasks is explained by the greater physical strength of males and the child rearing responsibilities of women. In societies where women contribute significantly to acquiring food (subsistence), they are more highly valued and have more freedom (Segall, et al., 1990). Women seem to gain more equality as society becomes modernized and women work outside the home. With increased technology the biological differences between males and females become less relevant (Williams and Best, 1989).

Nevertheless, women are expected to nurture and to mother; this is their role. What if men were expected to stay home and raise children? Studies of single fathers who raise their children alone show that men do respond by developing nurturing relationships with their children (Risman, 1989). Men are capable of demonstrating "feminine" child care behaviors despite their training in male gender roles. The distinction between sex roles and gender roles is foggy, and the debate over which behaviors, if any, are biologically determined continues.

The more successful a man is in his work role, the more he is perceived as masculine. Work is seen as the principal family role of men; yet, most work takes place away from the family. When a man marries or becomes a father, his major role (work) doesn't change. This line of reasoning suggests that a man's work activities cause him to place little emphasis on the family. Cohen (1989) reported that many men wanted to be more involved with their families, but work wouldn't allow it. Most men fit their family lives around their jobs.

A major pressure on gender roles is the very real need of many families to increase their incomes by having the mother work outside the home. Over 50 percent of the mothers of school age children now work (Spade, 1989). The family adapts its standard of living to two incomes. Then, the woman, like the traditional male, has no choice. She must work in order to maintain the family's income level. So, she takes on a new role and assumes the pressures of the workplace. As women become involved in careers, their family roles change, and this has an impact on the roles of men. In some families both husband and wife become more androgynous (both male -*andro* — and female -*gyne*).

Bem (1983) theorized that allowing people to be androgynous would make them more flexible in new situations compared with people who have rigid sex roles. In her research, Bem identified androgynous males and females and found they were much more comfortable doing a task associated with the opposite sex than people who had rigid sex roles. She contends that every adult needs to use a variety of behaviors, such as the masculine abilities to be assertive and self-reliant and the feminine sensitivity to the needs of others. Because American society is complex, there is an increasing need to be androgynous.

Communication

Many aspects of communication are nonverbal, and there are some interesting differences based on sex/gender. Researchers believe that when receiving nonverbal messages the lower status person in a communication is able to "read" the nonverbal cues better than the higher status person. Thus, when reading nonverbal messages employees are superior to the boss, Blacks to Whites, and women to men. The lower status person has a need to understand the higher status person. Researchers have also found that when a man and a woman are talking, the man talks more and the woman listens more. In addition, the listener has been found to "look" more than the speaker. Although women hold eye contact more than men, they are more likely to break eye contact. Averting the eyes is a submissive gesture and reduces aggressive behavior. Men are more likely to stare to establish dominance (Eakins and Eakins, 1988).

It doesn't take a lot of research to learn that women smile more than men. Smiling among women, however, occurs not because they are happy, but because they want to please others. Body positions and gestures also vary. Women hold arms close to the body with legs close together, while men are more relaxed and open in body position. Men demonstrate authority by sprawling and taking more room. Women have a smaller personal body space (territory) than men and their space is more likely to be violated. People of both sexes touch women more than men. The authority figure is more likely to touch the subordinate. Thus, when a woman (subordinate) touches a man (authority) the message is likely to be interpreted as an intimate approach because she is subordinate. Eakins and Eakins (1988) believe that for women to gain equal status they need to control their nonverbal behaviors.

Sexism

Men are in charge of culture in the United States; masculine values and traits are generally considered superior. Despite some improvements, discrimination against women continues. When men and women perform tasks with identical behaviors, the woman's behavior is valued lower. Both men and women are prejudiced against women. For minority women, the discrimination could be described as double jeopardy. Some examples of sexism include:

- Women buy half the cars that are sold in the U.S., but few women are employed in management positions or in sales by automobile companies (Nauman, 1992).
- Women pay more money to have garments dry cleaned than men when the garments are the same fabric and style (Whittelsey, 1993).
- Women pay more for clothes purchases when the garments are similar (Whittelsey, 1993).
- Teachers give girls less attention than boys. Girls are not encouraged to study math and science (Girls face heavy . . ., 1992).
- Of all unpaid work in the world, 90 percent is done by women (Scott, 1984).
- Banks are reported to require women to put up collateral five times the amount of their business loans, but men put up equal amounts of collateral (Rhodie, 1989).
- Only five percent of the top executives in the 50 largest American-owned companies are women (Rhodie, 1989).

- Among government workers, women earn an average of $15,579 and men $30,553 (Rhodie, 1989).

Employment and income. Income levels for U.S. women increased slightly in 1991, but women made only 70 cents for every dollar earned by men. Women had median incomes of $21,245 compared to $30,332 for men (U.S. Bureau of the Census, 1993A). At all educational levels, women receive significantly lower income than men. For example, in 1991 women with bachelor's degrees earned average annual incomes of $33,144 while men earned $50,747. A man with a high school diploma earned an average of $28,230 and a woman earned $19,336 (U.S. Bureau of the Census, 1993B). Women are underrepresented in high paying jobs and overrepresented in low paying jobs. This holds true when comparing employment of women and men for all racial/ethnic groups (Gordus and Oshiro, 1986). Racial segregation does exist in women's employment, with White women more often found in white collar jobs than minority women. However, sexual discrimination has greater impact on a minority woman's economic success than racial discrimination (Almquist, 1986). The income advantage of being White applies almost entirely to men. In 1989-90, White men 25 years old and older with four years of high school had average annual incomes of $26,510. Black men with similar backgrounds had average annual incomes of $20,280. The difference reflects the effects of racial discrimination. The average annual incomes ($16,910) of White women with backgrounds similar to the men were only slightly higher than the incomes ($16,440) of Black women. Women's incomes were lower because of sex with very little difference related to race. Almquist (1987) studied gender inequality among U.S. ethnic minorities. She found the greatest gender inequality was among the most affluent ethnic groups. She concluded that there is a greater sharing between men and women in the most disadvantaged groups (Native Americans, Blacks, Mexican

Americans, and Puerto Ricans). In groups with the highest incomes (Koreans, Chinese, Japanese, and Cubans) men had the highest educational levels and the greatest income; women were more likely to have low educational levels, be married, and work at low paying jobs.

Medical care. Very little money is spent on research for women's health issues. For example, in 1990, the National Institutes of Health spent 80 million dollars on research related to breast cancer which was expected to kill 44,500 women in 1991. In five years breast cancer has increased 37 percent; it kills more people than AIDS, but most of the research money ($742 million) goes to AIDS. Of the reported cases of AIDS, women make up 11 percent (Huckshorn, 1991).

Heart disease has decreased among U.S. males since 1950, but increased among women. Ananian and Epstein (1991) reported that women hospitalized for heart disease were significantly less likely to receive diagnostic and therapeutic procedures than men. Denke (1992) stated that because heart disease is primarily a disease of old women, it has been given a low research priority due to both sex and age discrimination. Ananian and Epstein (1991) also cited studies that showed women are less likely than men to receive kidney dialysis and kidney transplantation when they have kidney disease. In a second study the physician authors concluded that, "it is disturbing to note that by all measures employed, women reported more cardiac disability than men before their infarction but were less likely to undergo procedures that are known (at least in men) to lessen symptoms and improve functional capacity" (Steingart, et al., 1991, p.230).

In the United States, medical practitioners are sex-segregated: 84 percent of physicians are male and 97 percent of nurses are female. In 1987, male doctors with one to four years of experience had average annual incomes of $110,600 compared to the average annual income of female doctors with the same experience of $74,000. Overall, women doctors earned 62.8 cents for every dollar earned by male doctors in 1988 (Women in medicine . . ., 1991).

In countries where females have access to adequate resources, female life expectancy is five to seven years greater than for males. This is explained as a genetic difference. However, in third world countries, female life expectancy is five years less than for males. Excessive deaths of females occur during the childbearing years for lack of medical care and in early childhood because of cultural values and lack of resources (Sivard, 1985). Especially in Asia and Africa, male children are valued and female children are neglected and not cared for. Many of the female children die. In China where there is a policy of only one child per family, there is evidence that female children are deliberately killed (Sivard, 1985). In India, for every 100 male infants aged one to four years who die, 300 girls die (Seager and Olson, 1986).

Implications for Health Care

Women must be treated seriously and with respect. Davis and Proctor (1989) reported that professionals have been shown to display impatience when women talk, and they interrupted women more often than men, used first names more frequently, and were more likely to comment on women's appearance than men's.

Male practitioners may need to work hard to develop friendships and trusting relationships with women clients. Caring and trusting relationships must be clearly differentiated from sexual advances which cannot be tolerated.

Health care practitioners (both male and female) must increase their own awareness of sexual prejudice and of the institutionalization of sexism. In many cases, women are not aware that they are the victims of discrimination; they don't know that men are treated differently. Sometimes minority women blame racial discrimination for their unequal treatment, when the real problem is sexual bias. Health professionals can make a difference by asking themselves whether they are providing equivalent care for everyone.

References Cited

Almquist, E. 1987. Labor market gender inequality in minority groups. *Gender and Society* 1(4):400-413.

Almquist, E. 1986. Further consequences of double jeopardy: The reluctant participation of racial-ethnic women in feminist organizations, in *Ethnicity and women*, edited by Winston Van Horne. University of Wisconsin System, Institute on Race and Ethnicity.

Ananian, J. and A. Epstein. 1991. Differences in the use of procedures between men and women hospitalized for coronary heart disease. *New England Journal of Medicine* 325(4):221-5.

Bem, S. L. 1983. Traditional sex roles are too restrictive, pp 31-35 in *Male/Female roles: opposing viewpoints*, edited by B. Leone and M. O'Neill. St. Paul, MN: Greenhaven Press.

Census Bureau study of 110,000 people in 1989-90. 1991. *San José, (CA) Mercury News*, Sept. 20, p. 12D.

Chafetz, J. S. 1983. Society determines sex roles, pp 21-26 in *Male/Female roles: opposing viewpoints*, edited by B. Leone and M. O'Neill. St. Paul, MN: Greenhaven Press.

Cohen, T. 1989. Becoming and being husbands and fathers: work and family conflict for men, in *Gender in intimate relationships: a microstructural approach*. Belmont, CA: Wadsworth Publishing Co.

Davis, L. and E. Proctor. 1989. *Race, gender, and class: guidelines for practice with individuals, families, and groups*. Englewood Cliffs, NJ: Prentice-Hall, Inc.

Denke, M. 1992. Diet and disease. *Food and Nutrition News* 64(5):31-33.

Devor, H. 1987. *Gender blending: confronting the limits of duality*. Bloomington, Indiana: Indiana University Press.

Eagly, A. 1987. *Sex differences in social behavior: a social-role interpretation*. Hillsdale, NJ: Lawrence Erlbaum Associates, Publishers.

Eakins, B. and R. Eakins. 1988. Sex differences in nonverbal communication, in *Intercultural communication: a reader,* 5th edition, edited by L. Samovar and R. Porter. Belmont, CA: Wadsworth Publishing Co.

Girls face heavy bias in school, report says. 1992. *San José (CA) Mercury News*, Feb. 12, p. 1A, 14A.

Gordus, J. and M. Oshiro. 1986. Ethnic-minority women in the private corporation, in *Ethnicity and women*, edited by W. Van Horne. University of Wisconsin System, Institute on Race and Ethnicity.

Huckshorn. K. 1991. Women say they're sick of unequal health funds. *San José (CA) Mercury News*, June 2, p. 8A.

Leone, B. and M. T. O'Neill, editors. 1983. *Male/Female roles: opposing viewpoints*. St. Paul, MN: Greenhaven Press.

Nauman, N. 1992. Industry discounts, degrades women. *San José (CA) Mercury News*, Feb. 7, p. 1H, 2H.

Rhodie, E. 1989. *Discrimination against women - a global survey*. Chapter 16, Case study: the United States. Jefferson, NC: McFarland and Co., Inc.

Risman, B. and P. Schwartz. 1989. *Gender in intimate relationships: a microstructural approach*. Belmont, CA: Wadsworth Publishing Co.

Risman, B. 1989. Can Men Mother?" Life as a single father, pp.155-164 in *Gender in intimate relationships: a microstructural approach*. Belmont, CA: Wadsworth Publishing Co.

Scott, H. 1984. *Working your way to the bottom; the feminization of poverty*. Boston: Pandora Press.

Seager, J. and A. Olsen. 1986. *Women in the world, an international atlas*. New York: Simon and Schuster.

Segall, M. H., P. Dasen, J. Berry, and Y. Poortinya. 1990. *Human behavior in global perspective: an introduction to cross-cultural psychology*. New York: Pergamon Press.

Sivard, R. 1985. *Women - a world survey*. Washington, D.C.: World Priorities.

Spade, J. 1989. Bringing home the bacon, pp 184-192 in *Gender in intimate relationships: a microstructural approach*. Belmont, CA: Wadsworth Publishing Co.

Steingart, R., M. Packer, P. Hemm, M. Coglianese, B. Gersh, E. Geltman, J. Sollano, S. Katz, L. Move, L. Basta, S. Lewis, S. Gottlieb, V. Bernstein, P. McEwan, K. Jacobson, E. Brown, M. Kukin, N. Kantrowitz, and M. Pfeffer. 1991. Sex differences in the management of coronary artery diseases. *New England Journal of Medicine* 325(4):226-30.

U.S. Bureau of the Census. 1993A. *Statistical abstract of the United States*, 113th edition. Washington, D.C.: U.S. Government Printing Office, Table 728, p. 465.

U.S. Bureau of the Census. 1993B. *Statistical abstract of the United States*, 113th edition. Washington, D.C.: U.S. Government Printing Office, Table 731, p. 467.

Whittelsey, F. 1993. *Why women pay more.* Washington, D.C.: Center for Study of Responsible Law.

Williams, J. E. and D. L. Best. 1989. *Sex and psyche: self concept viewed cross-culturally.* Newbury Park, CA: SAGE Publishing.

Women in medicine lag behind in status, pay. 1991. *San José (CA) Mercury News*, Sept. 10, p. 3C.

PART 2:
INDIGENOUS GROUPS, IMMIGRANTS, AND REFUGEES

This section includes topics about non-White, ethnic Americans. Each chapter is introduced with background information which provides some basic understanding of the group's experiences prior to and after their arrival in the United States as well as demographic data. Additional chapter topics include World View, Family Structure and Interactional Styles, Communication, Health Beliefs and Practices, Health Status, Food and Nutrition, and Implications for Health Care. The ethnic groups included in this section are Native Americans (Chapter 8), Latinos (Chapter 9), African Americans (Chapter 10), Chinese Americans (Chapter 11), Japanese Americans (Chapter 12), Korean Americans (Chapter 13), Southeast Asians (Chapter 14), Pilipinos and Pacific Islanders (Chapter 15), South Asians: Asian Indians (Chapter 16), and Middle Eastern Americans (Chapter 17). There is considerable variation between acculturated members of a group and recent immigrants and refugees. However, length of residence in the United States is only one of many factors that affect acculturation. Once again, the reader is cautioned about the dangers in making assumptions based on knowledge that applies to some members of a group.

Chapter 8

NATIVE AMERICANS

The term "Native American" is used here to refer to American Indians and Alaskan Natives. Native Hawaiians are included among Pacific Islanders in Chapter 13. Alaskan Natives include Eskimos (Inupiat and Yupik), Aleuts, and Indians (Athabascans and Tlingits) (Book, Dixon, and Kirchner, 1983). Some authors prefer the term American Indian because it excludes Pacific Islanders (Kramer, 1992); however, it does not include all of the indigenous people of Alaska.

There is great diversity among Native Americans; they reside in widely different geographical areas and speak many native languages (Kramer, 1992). Throughout the entire United States, there are over 500 different Native American tribal groups that are recognized by the Bureau of Indian Affairs (Moss, 1992). In 1990, 0.8 percent of the United States' population was Native American, and the states with the highest proportions of Native Americans were Alaska (15.6 percent), New Mexico (8.8 percent), Oklahoma (8.0 percent), South Dakota (7.3 percent), Montana (6.0 percent), and Arizona (5.6 percent) (U.S. Census 1992A). The 1990 census reported the largest numbers of Native Americans are in Oklahoma (252,000), California (242,000), Arizona (204,000), and New Mexico (134,000) (U.S. Census, 1992A). However, ten years earlier the 1980 census reported that California had the greatest number of Native Americans of any state. The decrease to second position in the 1990 census could be related to the undercount of minority populations. Few Native Americans in California live on reservations; urban residents would be more likely subject to the problem of undercounting than reservation residents.

Native Americans were living in North America long before the first Europeans arrived in the 1400s (the Vikings arrived about 1010, but did not settle). Upon the arrival of Europeans, Native Americans became in danger of extermination. Communicable diseases (introduced by Whites), natural disasters, genocide (the systematic killing of an ethnic group), and wars wiped out entire tribes.

Joe and Malach (1992) reported that the English viewed the natives as "savages" which "served as a justifiable excuse for removing them from their land, dispossessing them, even killing them" (p. 93). As the number of Europeans grew, Native Americans were forced to move west. One of the "ugliest episodes in this country's history followed" (Parrillo, 1985, p. 212). During the eight years (1829-1837) in which Andrew Jackson was president, 125,000 American Indians were forced to move from the Atlantic states to Oklahoma territory. Over 40,000 lives were lost (Richardson, 1981). In the winter of 1838–39, the entire Cherokee Nation of 13,000 people was forced to move at gunpoint from Georgia to Oklahoma territory. Fewer than 9000 people survived the long march in snow and cold weather. Later called the "Trail of Tears" by the Cherokee, this move was forced on peaceful people who were the original land owners and who were willing to adapt to European lifestyles. On December 3, 1838, President Van Buren announced to Congress that the removal of the Indians to their new homes had the "happiest effects" and they emigrated without apparent reluctance (Parrillo, 1985).

The Wounded Knee Massacre of 1890 symbolized the end of Native American resistance. They had been killed, moved, and starved; they could fight no longer. After that, it was only a matter of time before all Native Americans were moved to reservations where their lives were segregated and poverty became established. They were then dependent on Whites for their survival. Native Americans were forced to give up their various cultures. Even much of their reservation land was taken from them by squatters who moved into their unfenced property (Marden, Mayer, and Engel, 1992). Traditional healing practices were threatened due to the death of Native practitioners and restrictions placed on those who survived. White officials sent American Indian children to distant boarding schools to acculturate them. As many as 25 to 35 percent of the children were separated from their families (Herring, 1992). The children were unable to learn the traditional ways of health care. The traditional methods of treating illness were also threatened by the lack of medicinal herbs and minerals on many reservations (Wilson, 1983). Without their traditions, their lives had no meaning (Marden, Mayer, and Engel, 1992). It wasn't until 1934 that Native Americans were encouraged to revive their customs and traditions (Parrillo, 1985). In 1933, Franklin D. Roosevelt's administration appointed Harold I. Ickes as Secretary of Interior and John Collier as Commissioner of the Bureau of Indian Affairs. Their interests were in preserving American Indian culture and making American Indians self-sustaining. Legislation in 1934 supported these views, and Native Americans were given more control over their reservation land and their lives. The United States government retained the power and responsibility of providing education and health care. Distant boarding schools were eliminated and children attended schools in their own communities. The teaching of native culture and language was encouraged.

Gradually, Native Americans have gained more control over education and health care through federal legislation (Marden, Mayer, and Engel, 1992). Today, about 38 percent of Native Americans live on reservations, trust lands, tribal areas, and in Alaskan villages which are mostly rural and isolated (U.S. Bureau of the Census, 1992B). Advantages to reservation life include the security of having family and friends nearby and the ability to maintain tribal customs. Educational and medical resources are also available.

However, increasing numbers of Native Americans are moving to cities in search of better employment opportunities. They have difficulty in adjusting to an urban lifestyle, and the resulting stress may be expressed in the form of social and/or physical problems (Wilson, 1983). Over half the Native Americans in the United States live in urban areas; some health clinics have been established in cities by the Indian Health Services (Kramer, 1992).

California is home to the second largest number of Native Americans, at least half of whom are not indigenous to California. They were forced into the state during the 1950's by the federal government in an attempt to force assimilation. Most of California's Native Americans live in urban areas of San Francisco and Los Angeles. California receives little money to provide services for these displaced Native Americans because federal aid is specific for rural Indians living on or near reservations. California would receive three or four times the money it does if it were treated equitably based on its Native population (Ewell, 1990). Lack of money means that many Native Americans living in various areas do not receive adequate health care.

Government sponsored health services for Native Americans were initiated in the early 1800's, primarily to stop the raging epidemics of contagious diseases such as measles, influenza, smallpox, and tuberculosis which had been introduced by White settlers. In 1955, the responsibility for Native American health services was given to the United States Public Health Service. This action resulted in a reduction of communicable diseases and infant mortality rates (Wilson, 1983). Federal services to Native Americans should not be considered charity because, unknown to most Americans, the federal government agreed to provide services to Native Americans in exchange for land and resources (Ewell, 1990). The Bureau of Indian Affairs (BIA), which administers programs for Native Americans, has been criticized for mismanagement of money. According to a *New York Times* report cited by Marden, Mayer, and Engel (1992), only 11 cents of every dollar actually went to the reservations.

In the 1970s, there was a movement to establish greater local control over health programs. It was proposed that tribal groups could best organize and manage culturally appropriate programs within their own communities. The federal government provided funding to initiate these programs (Wilson, 1983). Consideration of tribal health plans and of Native American opinions are required by law. As a result, Alaskan Natives are served by 12 regional, locally controlled health agencies. The local health agencies provide housing for families of patients who must be hospitalized away from their villages, environmental health services, eye care, dental care, alcohol treatment programs, mental health services, health education, and many other programs (Dixon, et al.,1983). The strength of the Alaskan system is its cultural sensitivity. Traditional health care practices are studied, preserved, and integrated into the services of the health care agencies. Since it is not possible to have a physician in every community in Alaska, health aides provide primary medical and emergency care in most villages. The aides are Native residents of the communities in which they serve. They are given extensive training and continuing education in modern medicine and are able to combine their medical knowledge with cultural understanding (Dixon, et al., 1983).

American Indians are the most poverty stricken of all ethnic groups in the United States (Holmes, 1983). For example, on reservations in 1980, 50 percent of their houses lacked indoor toilets, 46 percent lacked electricity, and 79 percent lacked telephones (Kuntz and Levy, 1981). In 1990 the median family income was $20,025 compared to the median family income of Whites of $36,915 (Table 2-3). The 1990 per capita income of $8,328 was 53 percent of White per capita income ($15,687) and was lower than the per capita income of Latinos ($8,400) and Blacks ($8,859) (U.S. Bureau of the Census, 1993).

A report on unemployment indicated that official figures significantly underestimate the degree of unemployment (Indian Unemployment . . ., 1991). The problem is that most unemployed Native Americans give up looking for jobs and are not counted in official figures. A study by the Lutheran Council USA found a rate of unemployment for Indians on the Pine Ridge reservation in South Dakota of 87 percent in 1985. The Bureau of Indian Affairs estimated 78 percent unemployment for the same group in 1989, but the South Dakota Labor Market Information Center reported approximately 3 percent and 5 percent unemployment in the two counties that make up the reservation. The U.S. Labor Department estimates that 20 percent of Arizona Navajos or Dine (pronounced din-NAY), as they prefer to be called, are unemployed, but the Lutheran Council USA reported unemployment at 75 percent (Indian Unemployment . . . , 1991). An unemployment rate of 50 percent for all American Indians was estimated by Rhoades, Reyes, and Buzzard (1987). California Indians have an unemployment rate of at least 49 percent (Ewell, 1990). Educational levels are also low, with only 9.3 percent of the population having four or more years of college (Table 2-3).

World View

Although there is wide variation among Native American groups in their traditional values and beliefs, several characteristics are common. Spirituality is a part of life, not something to be practiced separately as other groups practice religion. Religion is the universe; it is present in all things. Existence is circular, not a straight line with a beginning and an end. In their cultural beliefs, many Native Americans hold a circular world view in which everything returns to its beginning. Spiritual beliefs aren't contained in a building (church), but are represented by harmony among all things (Ethnic diversity . . . , ND).

The belief in harmony between man and nature is most important. The environment is highly respected; its resources are to be conserved by taking from it only that which is necessary to sustain life. Land is especially valued for its role in supporting and nurturing human life. The phrase "Mother Earth, Father sky" illustrates this viewpoint. The earth is considered the body of a higher individual which possesses a will and a desire to be well. When people harm the earth they harm themselves, and when they harm themselves they harm the earth (Spector, 1991). Since Native Americans believe that everything is alive, they also believe that everything is connected, including religion, medicine, and culture (Moss, 1992; Richardson, 1981). They accept others and are not critical of differences. Harmony among individuals and respect for others are highly valued, as are generosity, sharing, wisdom, bravery, happiness, and cooperation; competition is discouraged (Wilson, 1983; Herring, 1992; Richardson, 1981). People are valued above material goods; ownership of things is held in common and even success is shared (Primeaux, 1977). Values are very different from the dominant U.S. values of competition, personal property and wealth (materialism), verbal skills, manipulation of the environment, progress, and postponed gratification for future benefit (Laramine, 1989).

The religions of American Natives are associated with nature and animals. All living things (plants and animals) are viewed as having a spiritual side. Native Americans "do not make the marked contrast between humans and animals that others do. They find the animal capable of planning, thinking, loving, and caring; and they have many legends to emphasize the wisdom and greatness of animals" (Richardson, 1981, p. 221). Mythology and stories are passed from one generation to another and include beliefs in reincarnation, spirits, and supernatural beings. Religious practices include the use of charms, amulets, omens, taboos, and songs.

Time orientation is generally directed to the present. That is, many traditional Native Americans live for today rather than being concerned with the future (Primeaux, 1977), and strict adherence to schedules and "watching the clock" are not common. Rather, completion of the task at hand is emphasized (Primeaux, 1977). Age and experience are respected in many Native American communities. Positions of authority and leadership are usually given to the elders rather than the young (Wilson, 1983).

Family Structure and Interactional Styles

Native American tribes are extremely diverse. John (1988) challenged the view that Native American families are always extended families. He said that many different forms of family life existed before Native Americans were in contact with Europeans and that many differences remain. Some researchers believe that extended families are common among rural and reservation residents, and nuclear families among urban Native Americans. Others believe that family structure varies among tribes, and the ideas of family cannot be generalized (John, 1988). When there is an extended family, it is not limited to a three-generation family of kin, but includes a wide support network of cousins, grandparents, aunts, uncles, and non-relatives (McWhirter and Ryan, 1991). Farris and Farris (1981) indicated that the support system of the extended family is decreasing because fathers do not have marketable skills and are no longer role models.

Children. Traditional Native American society is very family oriented. Family decisions are made by group consensus, a practice that devalues aggressive and individualistic behaviors (Joe and Malach, 1992). Social and, in some cases, economic needs are met by the extended family members who frequently live in the same household (Wilson, 1983). Alaskan Natives (both Eskimos and Indians) are also family oriented. Three or four generations may live together in small houses. Everyone, including aunts and uncles, makes decisions about child rearing. Because women bear children at a youthful age, they tend not to be prepared for the responsibilities of child care. Grandmothers, who are only 30 and 40 years old themselves, frequently care for their daughters' children, and it isn't unusual for children to live with their grandparents (John, 1988), who hold a respected leadership position within the family unit (Wilson, 1983). They are particularly valued for storytelling which teaches values and traditions to their children. To be old is to be wise (Jackson and Mead, 1990).

Indian children are considered very special (Farris and Farris, 1981). They are not disciplined physically, but they are expected to learn by observation and by being told the consequences of their actions. Children are taught to be independent and to care for themselves. American Indian children may appear to be spoiled, shy, and withdrawn (Primeaux, 1977; Farris and Farris, 1992). When they are among other Indians, the children are competitive and excel in school, but they may have low self-esteem and not do well outside the culture because they do not assert themselves. Studies show this has a serious effect on the performance of Native American children in integrated schools. Reading skills of children are poor because Native American languages are oral, not written. Because of poor performance, the school dropout rates are very high (McWhirter and Ryan, 1991). Low self-esteem is also related to poor health status, inadequate education, and poverty. The children are torn between the traditional culture and the culture of the dominant society (McWhirter and Ryan, 1991). Lamarine (1989) believes that it is important for Native American children to be taught cultural traditions while they learn to live in American society. Schools should avoid competitive learning and, most importantly, be operated by tribal authorities (Lamarine, 1989; Joe and Malach, 1992).

Because of alcohol abuse and the breakdown of some families, many American Indian children have been removed from their homes and placed in non-Indian homes by various state welfare agencies. This practice has been reduced by federal legislation, which now gives reservations the right to protect their children and limits the ability of states to intervene. Most children are now placed in other American Indian homes if they must be removed from their own homes (John, 1988).

Gender roles. Before White European intervention, many Native American tribes recognized a cross-gender role (berdache) for men and women. In most studies the berdache have been identified as males who assumed the roles, activities, dress, and occupations of females. However, Blackwood (1984) reported that in the 33 tribes she studied, the berdache role was as viable for women as for men. Callender and Kochems (1983) indicated that there were probably only a few berdaches in any one tribe. Many individuals who became berdache did so as the result of a dream or vision. A second way to become a berdache was to assume the cross-gender role after a childhood in which the child elected to learn the roles of the opposite sex. Blackwood (1984) reported that one Kaska (subarctic region) family which had no male children selected one daughter to take the cross-gender role.

Berdache were allowed to marry people of the same sex. Although the cross-gender person (the berdache) may have been a homosexual, the persons they married were not. The berdache have been described variously as asexual, heterosexual, homosexual, and bisexual (Callender and Kochems, 1983). There was no stigma to the cross-gender role, and it did not imply a particular sexual role. However, in most tribes, homosexuals were considered an asset (Farris and Farris, 1981). Because male berdache were physically stronger than women, they were more productive. Families that included a berdache were very prosperous (Callender and Kochem, 1983). Some tribes believed the berdache had supernatural powers and consequently the goods they made were more valuable. Female berdache took the hunting roles of men, but did not participate in war. Male berdache seldom fought in wars, but they had other roles in war time (Callender and Kochem, 1983). The demise of the cross-gender roles occurred with the increasing disapproval of White culture.

Communication

Native languages have played an important part in the maintenance of cultural traditions through the ages. Although languages spoken by the various tribes are distinctly different from one another, the value attached to the spoken word is shared by all. Many older Native Americans still speak an Indian language in addition to English. Traditional values which reflect the Native American's world view are incorporated into language patterns. Communication is designed to encourage generosity, compassion, bravery, respect for elders, and tribal unity (Wilson, 1983).

Since few native languages were written, oral communications traditionally depended heavily on nonverbal communication. In many tribes, children were trained to observe the environment using all of their senses. Today, children are frequently disciplined using nonverbal behavior (Primeaux, 1977). Not surprisingly, silence is valued. Instead of viewing silent periods among people as awkward, the Native American believes that silent time should be used to organize thoughts so that the spoken words will be more meaningful.

Health Beliefs and Practices

Each tribe has its own unique health beliefs and practices; traditional healing systems have been influenced over the years by interactions among tribes, Christianity, and Western education and technology. Many Native Americans continue to have strong faith in their traditional healing systems.

Harmony with nature. Health and illness are viewed holistically by most Native Americans; an individual's psychological and spiritual well-being are intertwined with physical well-being. Health is possible only when there is harmony with family, friends, nature, and the universe. Because of the parallel between man and nature, it is believed that people harm the earth when they harm themselves, resulting in illness. If they respect themselves and nature through proper care, harmony and health will result (Spector, 1985).

Causes of illness. There are many possible causes of illness, but all are believed to be influenced by the supernatural and result from a violation of nature's laws. One such cause of illness may be witchcraft or sorcery. Navajos (Dine), for example, may carry special objects to protect themselves against supernatural powers. Another possible cause of illness is violation of taboos or rules. Many tribes have restrictions regarding behaviors; illness is believed to be punishment for breaking these rules (Wilson, 1983; Spector, 1991).

Intrusion of the body, either by an object or by spirits, may also result in illness. Worms, snakes, insects, or other small animals may lodge in the body, sometimes as the result of witchcraft. Similarly, spirits of humans or animals may "possess" a person and cause physical or emotional illness. In this case, native healers may perform exorcism ceremonies. The loss of soul is also believed to result in sickness and may occur during a dream. When the soul leaves the body it may be captured by witches or evil spirits, and death could result if the soul is not recovered (Wilson, 1983). Displeasing a holy person or annoying the elements will also cause disharmony and result in illness (Spector, 1985). In North Dakota, Sioux Indians believe disease is caused by failing to keep a promise or by leading a bad life (Lang, 1985).

Healers. Healing is based on the belief in a great spirit. Medicine, religion, and harmony with nature are tied together (Adams and Knox, 1988). Healing practices vary among tribes, but the ultimate goal is to restore harmony between the patient and nature. Healers among Native Americans are known as medicine men. They are believed to possess psychic powers which allow them to perceive causes of and remedies for illness. There are several different types of medicine men. One type is capable only of positive forces and cannot do evil. They are important to the maintenance of the group's cultural identity. Another type is able to do good and evil; they may use witchcraft or poisoning to harm the group's enemies. Diviner-diagnosticians are a third type of medicine men. They are able to diagnose illnesses and their causes, but are unable to perform treatments. Diagnostic methods include sand painting, hand motions, star-gazing, and listening (Spector, 1991).

Treatment. Specialist medicine men use herbs to treat illness. Some medicine men specialize in the care of the soul, performing such feats as the recovery of "lost" souls. "Singers" are able to cure by song or by laying on of hands and have received their power from supernatural beings (Wilson, 1983). Other methods of treatment include massage, heat treatment, and sweat baths. Healing and religion are closely interrelated in traditional Native American society. Many rituals and ceremonies contain both healing and worship components. The healing power of medicine men is based on faith. Similarly, the patient's motivation to get well is considered vital for recovery.

Native American men use sweat baths (both dry and steam heat) for ritualistic cleansing as well as for socializing. Sweat baths bring relief from many conditions such as rheumatism, arthritis, colds, sinus infections, dry skin, insect bites, and psychological stress. In addition, an enhanced feeling of general well-being is noted, as well as a feeling of intoxication, upon leaving the intense heat. It is believed that Alaskan natives used hot springs for the same purposes with similar results (Book, Dixon, and Kirchner, 1983). Today, groups of patients travel to Serpentine Hot Springs in Northwest Alaska under the sponsorship of one of Alaska's regional native health care corporations. They seek relief from many conditions including arthritis, back and hip pain, headaches, rashes, and muscle strain. Many have already sought help from Western physicians and Native Alaskan healers. At the springs, days are centered on bathing, eating, and sleeping. Eskimo healers monitor patients' tolerance of the baths and perform therapeutic massage. Algae found near the springs is used in a poultice for cuts and infections (Book, Dixon, and Kirchner, 1983).

Treatment at the hot springs has been found to be beneficial in many cases. This has been attributed to several factors, including the heat and minerals in the spring water and the associated traditional treatments such as exercise and massage. The psychosocial experience is also believed to play a major role in the efficacy of this regimen. The patients (mostly Inupiat Eskimos) are treated within an environment where traditional cultural patterns are allowed to flourish. Meals contain traditional foods, the native language is spoken, and the style of social interaction is characteristically Inupiat. Although removed from their families, the patients become an extended family and provide mutual support. This program illustrates the potential benefits to be gained from the restoration of traditional ways among Native Americans. Treatment (in this case, physical therapy) is provided in a culturally appropriate manner (Book, Dixon, and Kirchner, 1983).

Although Native Americans living on reservations usually have access to traditional medical treatment, those living in cities do not. The cultural healing beliefs of urban patients must be respected by health professionals and integrated with Western medicine whenever possible. If a person who believes in traditional ways is not allowed to utilize them, complete healing (psychological and spiritual, as well as physical) will not occur (Wilson, 1983).

Health Status

Early deaths from infectious diseases have been reduced significantly by efforts of the Indian Health Service (Lamarine, 1989). Behaviorally based health problems (accidents, heart disease, cirrhosis, suicide, and homicide) are among the leading causes of death of Native Americans (Spector, 1991). Together they cause 25 percent of all Native American deaths. Alcoholism is the number one health problem (Spector, 1991; Mail and Wright, 1989). Native American youths have high rates of crime and delinquency. Compared to Whites, Native Americans commit 10 to 20 times more crimes; many are related to drug and alcohol abuse (Marden, Mayer, and Engel, 1992). In addition, heart disease, diabetes, and mental illness are leading health problems (Rhodes, et al., 1987).

Alcohol was introduced to Native Americans by Europeans. The stereotype of alcohol abuse among American Indians pictures them as wild and out of control when drinking. However, much of the alcohol behavior attributed to Native Americans has not been studied. From 1832 until 1953 the U.S. government prohibited sale of alcohol to Native Americans. Tribal governments were given permission to prohibit the sale of alcohol on their reservations, and most reservations do prohibit alcohol. Prohibition of alcohol may have led to abusive drinking patterns in which binge drinking on the outskirts of the reservations became popular. In other words, the prohibition of alcohol did not allow Native Americans to learn to control social drinking but led to a drinking pattern which became enculturated. Native Americans are frequently classified among Asian groups as having reduced ability to metabolize alcohol. However, May (1989) contends that there is no scientific evidence that Indians metabolize alcohol differently than other ethnic groups. In fact, most studies show that alcohol is metabolized faster by Native Americans than by Whites. May's position is that as long as prohibition exists on reservations, Indians will drive to the border towns to drink, will become intoxicated, and will be at increased risk of death.

Death rates for Native Americans under 45 years old are especially high and are related to unintentional injuries, cirrhosis, homicide, suicide, pneumonia, and diabetes (Wilson, 1983). Alcohol abuse is responsible for most of these early deaths among youths and is associated with families that abuse alcohol and students who do not do well in school and who do not identify with Indian culture. Adult males are more likely to drink than females. Drinking is most likely to occur within the ages of 16 to 29 years (May, 1989). Almost all male suicide victims among Alaskan Natives were under the influence of alcohol when they committed suicide. The suicide rates among males ages 20 to 24 per 100,000 population are 26 deaths for the general U.S. population, 44 for Alaskan White males, and 257 for Alaskan Native males (A people in peril, 1988).

Recreational drinking patterns are characterized by periodic drinking in which alcohol is consumed rapidly in large amounts over a long period of time. Intoxication is tolerated in many tribes and may even be encouraged. Some Native Americans fit the drinking patterns of typical skid-row alcoholics. Many who abstain are former drinkers. Drinking patterns vary depending on socioeconomic status; acculturation into the dominant society is accompanied by moderate social drinking (May, 1989). Mail and Wright (1989) commented that alcohol abuse among women may be greater than suspected. They stated that little is known about factors that permit some Indians to be social drinkers while others must abstain or they become abusers. May (1989) reported that Native Americans who have successfully integrated into modern culture and who have meaningful values in their traditional cultures are least likely to abuse alcohol. Native Americans who cannot cope in both worlds are lacking in social support and personal skills, thus, increasing their chances of abusing alcohol (May 1989). The solutions to the problem of alcohol abuse must come from within the Native American communities (Mail and Wright, 1989).

For those Native Americans over 45 years of age, the death rate is less than for Whites due to lower rates of heart disease, cancer, and stroke (see Table 2-5) (Heckler, 1985). Non-insulin dependent diabetes mellitus (NIDDM) is a significant problem, with an incidence 2.3 times higher than in the general population, and this problem is increasing along with obesity and hypertension (Kramer, 1992; Welty, 1991). American Indians have varying rates of diabetes depending on their tribal affiliation. The general U.S. rate for diabetes is 5.3 percent for ages 35 years and over; the highest known rate is among Pima Indians of Arizona at 49.5 percent. This is an incidence of diabetes that is many times higher than that of the general population (Heckler, 1985; Groziak and Diemand, 1989). One study found the rate of diabetes among New Mexico Indians to be from 9.8 percent to 28.2 percent in persons over 35 years of age (Carter, et al.,1989). The high incidence of diabetes among Native Americans is explained by a genetic predisposition, stress, low levels of exercise, dietary changes (which result in high sugar and fat diets with low intake of fiber), and increasing rates of obesity. A small group of obese Indian women in Arizona had diets similar to non-obese women except for a high energy intake from alcoholic and non-alcoholic beverages (powdered mixes, canned fruit drinks, and sweetened drinks) (Teufel and Dufour, 1990). Treatment for NIDDM involves an attempt to reverse these conditions.

A return to traditional diets is not possible because there is a short supply of foods which were used in the past. Another serious problem in preventing and treating diabetes is the perception among Native Americans that diabetes is imposed on them by Whites. The westernized lifestyle is undoubtedly responsible, but, unfortunately, the recommended changes in lifestyle are perceived as another attempt by Whites to control their lives (Lang, 1985).

For the Native Americans who live in urban areas, health problems include high rates of diphtheria, tuberculosis, inner ear inflammation (otitis media), alcohol abuse, iron deficiency anemia, depression, and dental problems (Spector, 1985). More than 50 percent of Native American children suffer from baby-bottle tooth decay that occurs when the infant is put to bed with a bottle of milk or juice (Bruerd, Kinney, and Bothwell, 1989). The incidence of tuberculosis has been dramatically reduced among American Indians and Alaskan Natives. However, the rate is still higher among these populations than among the general population (Rieder, 1989). Marital problems are caused by low income, unemployment, and alcoholism. Domestic violence is a serious problem that is not a traditional part of the culture (Spector, 1991).

Food and Nutrition

Before the arrival of White people in North America, Native Americans obtained their food either by hunting and gathering or by farming, depending on their geographical location. They ate when hungry, not according to the time of day (Farris and Farris, 1981). Today, American Indians value traditional foods (Jackson and Mead, 1990); however, the increased availability of processed and convenience foods sold in stores in nearby towns and on reservations has altered their food patterns. Many of the purchased foods are high in fat, sugar, and sodium (Pelican and Bachman-Carter, 1991).

Traditional Native American foods still consumed by many include the staples corn, berries, roots, squash, and beans (Farris and Farris, 1981). Other native foods are chili peppers, bread (fried or baked in outdoor ovens), fruit, vegetables, wild berries (Jackson and Mead, 1990), fowl, wild rice, venison, fish, and buffalo (Farris and Farris, 1981).

Most of the calories in traditional Eskimo diets come from protein and fat foods: reindeer, bearded seal, seal oil, and fireweed tops (Book, Dixon, and Kirchner, 1983). Although dietary habits vary among tribes, food is commonly associated with social and religious activities. Sharing of food with others including extended family members, friends, and visitors, is valued. Prayers are frequently an integral part of the meal (Wilson, 1983).

Because of low income, many Native Americans who live on or near reservations receive food from the Food Distribution Program of the federal government. Also, low-income Native Americans are eligible to receive Food Stamps (Jackson and Mead, 1990). Diets lacking in protein and calories have been documented among some reservation children who have been diagnosed with kwashiorkor (protein deficiency) or marasmus (inadequate calories, starvation). Economic problems and lack of transportation, running water, refrigeration, and fuel contribute to malnutrition (Jackson 1986). Acculturated diets of Native Americans are high in carbohydrates, fat, sugar, and sodium; dietary intake of calcium is low (Groziak and Diemand, 1989).

Many other cultural food patterns and restrictions have been observed among Native Americans. Especially common are those involving women before and after childbirth. Foods such as liver, rabbit, milk, cabbage, onions, huckleberries, salt, and certain fish may be forbidden. During illness, some foods, including meat and eggs, may be restricted. Corn has religious significance as well as medicinal and nutritional uses among American Indians. It is used in several rituals for illness prevention and healing. Postpartum Navajo women may drink blue cornmeal gruel in order to improve milk production and help the recovery from childbirth (Wilson, 1983).

Lactose intolerance is common among Native Americans, and probably has led to the belief held by Papago and Pima Indians that illness results from the consumption of undiluted cow's milk (Wilson, 1983). Persons with lactose intolerance do not produce an enzyme (lactase) necessary for the digestion of milk sugar (lactose). If milk is consumed in significant quantity, the undigested lactose will remain in the intestine promoting bacterial fermentation. The result is abdominal gas, pain, cramps, nausea, and diarrhea. Many adults who are not of Northern European heritage are lactose intolerant, by small amounts of milk may be tolerated by individuals.

Implications for Health Care

Poverty influences many aspects of health care for Native Americans. Health care providers need to understand the barriers that low income presents and be able to show empathy and genuine concern for Native American clients. Many American Indians live off reservations and use urban clinics for their health care. Barriers associated with low income which have been identified as reasons for not using clinic services include high cost, no transportation, no child care, long waits in clinics, impersonal attention, distance to clinics, and inconvenient hours (Miller, 1982).

If a Native American manages to get past the barriers and makes a clinic appointment, the health care agency should extend an invitation for family members to accompany the ill person. Family members should be encouraged to discuss medical treatments because the patient may need their approval before making decisions (Kunitz and Levy, 1981). In matrilineal tribes, the elder women (grandmothers) may be consulted in health care decisions (Primeaux, 1977).

During illness, the family is a primary source of support for the Native American patient. Therefore, many relatives can be expected to visit the hospitalized family member and sit for long periods of time with their hospitalized relative. It is important to accommodate the Native American who requests a diagnostic or healing ceremony in the hospital room. The patient's family may use cornmeal in private healing ceremonies; hospital staff should be alerted to the sacred meaning of the cornmeal and not remove it without the family's permission (Primeaux, 1977).

Nonverbal communication plays a major role in decision making in families. Native Americans learn by observation and seem able to sense each other's needs without discussion (John, 1988). Health care providers need to develop nonverbal skills and reflect (mirror) nonverbal behaviors (Herring, 1992).

It is best to be casual, natural, and relaxed. Do not be devious; get to the point. White practitioners could have a disadvantage because Native Americans may be suspicious of White people.

Eye contact should be periodic because continuous eye contact may be considered disrespectful (Primeaux, 1977); some Native Americans believe that staring into one's eyes is an invasion of privacy equivalent to controlling a person's spirit (Farkas, 1986). A Native American may show respect by downward glances and by lack of eye contact (McWhirter and Ryan, 1991). Other nonverbal behaviors that may be expected include a relaxed body position and absence of gestures and facial expressions (Farkas, 1986).

After introductions and a light handshake, it is important to develop a trusting relationship before getting down to business (Freebairn and Gwinup, 1979: Kramer, 1992). Unfortunately, it may be difficult to develop rapport with Native American clients. They may believe in the family as the sole support when there are problems, and may not be willing to accept outside help (McWhirter and Ryan, 1991).

Native Americans may feel that Western medicine is very impersonal (Adams and Knox, 1988), and is not effective because so little time is spent with the patient and too much time is taken in diagnosing and recording medical histories. Expectations regarding time are developed from experiences with Native healers who diagnose rapidly through magic and who are already familiar with the culture if not the individual (Kunitz and Levy, 1981). Also, because of diagnostic methods used by Native healers, the health care provider may be expected to know what is wrong without recording a medical history. It is desirable to obtain as much information as possible through friendly conversation and then record the data after the interview.

Traditional Native Americans value silence and speak only when they have something to say. They are usually shy and may converse in a very soft voice that requires complete attention to understand. It would be impolite to ask them to repeat their comments. A long period of silence may mean that the question requires time to formulate an answer, not that the question is misunderstood (Farkas, 1986; Miller, 1982). Since it is not polite to interrupt a speaker or a silent period, the usual counseling technique of encouraging responses by using feedback messages, such as "uh-huh," could be interpreted as discourteous (Farkas, 1986). Richardson (1981), a Native American, suggested that White counselors should "minimize their authoritarian role, be cautious about giving advice, and avoid stereotyping" (p. 230). Health care providers need to "listen" with all their senses and speak with a soft voice.

Some sources (Green, 1982; Freebairn and Gwinup, 1979; Kniep-Hardy and Burkhardt, 1977) report that Native Americans are reluctant to reveal personal information about another person; however, Miller (1982) did not observe this trait. Differences in behaviors could be due to the diversity among people in this group.

When treating Native Americans, health care providers need to recall that "time" for them may not be regulated by clocks and that meal times vary from day to day and cannot be used reliably when giving instructions (Primeaux, 1977). In summary, the health care provider needs to be aware of and sensitive to traditional beliefs and values and to allow adequate time in counseling. Health care professionals would benefit from attending workshops and learning to accept Native American values without attempting "to solve the cultural conflicts but rather to make it more acceptable for the Natives to have one foot in both cultures" (Richardson, 1981, p. 231).

References Cited

A people in peril. 1988, January. *Anchorage (AK) Daily News*, Special report reprint.

Adams, L. and M. Knox. 1988. Traditional health practices: significance for modern health care, in *Ethnicity and health*, edited by Winston Van Horne. The University of Wisconsin System, Institute on Race and Ethnicity.

Blackwood, E. 1984. Sexuality and gender in certain Native American tribes: the case of cross-gender females. *Signs: Journal of Women in Culture and Society* 10(1):27-42.

Book, P., Dixon, M., and Kirchner, S. 1983. Native healing in Alaska. *The Western Journal of Medicine*, 139(6):923-927.

Bruerd, B., M. Kinney, and E. Brothwell. 1989. Preventing baby bottle tooth decay in American Indian and Alaska Native communities: a model for planning. *Public Health Reports* 104(6):631-640.

Callender, C. and L. Kochems. 1983. The North American berdache. *Current Anthropology* 24(4):443-462.

Carter, J., R. Horowitz, R. Wilson, S. Sava, P. Sinnock, and D. Gohdes. 1989. Tribal differences in diabetes: prevalence among American Indians in New Mexico. *Public Health Reports* 104(6):665-669.

Dixon, M., W. Myers, P. Book, and P. Nice. 1983. The changing Alaskan experience. *The Western Journal of Medicine* 139(6):917-922.

Ethnic diversity and the care of the terminally ill in Santa Clara County: a handbook. ND. San José, CA: Hospice of the Valley.

Ewell, M. 1990. History, politics shortchange state of millions in Indian aid. *San José (CA) Mercury News*, Sept. 9, p. 15A.

Farkas, C. 1986. Ethno-specific communication patterns: implications for nutrition education. *Journal of Nutrition Education* 18(3):99-103.

Farris, E. and L. Farris. 1981. The American Indian, Chapter 3 in *Culture and child rearing*, edited by Ann Clark. Philadelphia: F. A. Davis Co.

Freebairn, J. and K. Gwinup. 1979. *Cultural diversity and nursing practice, instructors manual; #8, Beyond language.* Irvine, CA: Concept Media, Inc.

Green, J. 1982. *Cultural awareness in the human services.* Englewood Cliffs, NJ: Prentice-Hall, Inc.

Groziak, S. and L. Diemand. 1989. Diet and nutrition related diseases of ethnic minorities. *School Food Service Journal* 43(6):82.

Heckler, M. 1985. *Report of the Secretary's Task Force on black and minority health. Volume 1, Executive Summary.* Washington, D.C.: U. S. Department of Health and Human Services.

Herring, E. 1992. Seeking a new paradigm: counseling Native Americans. *Journal of Multicultural Counseling and Development* 20(1):35-43.

Holmes, L. 1983. Other cultures, elder years, Chapter 8 in *Minority aged in America*. Minneapolis, MN: Burgess Publishing Co.

Indian unemployment under-tallied, study says. 1991. *San José (CA) Mercury News* report on a study "Native American unemployment: statistical games and cover-ups" by George Tinker and L. Bush. Denver, CO; Feb. 15, p. 8A.

Jackson, M. and M. Mead. 1990. Nutrition education for Indian elders. *Journal of Nutrition Education* 22(6):311-313.

Jackson, M. 1986. Nutrition in American Indian health: past, present, and future. *Journal of the American Dietetic Association* 86(11):1561-1564.

Joe, J. and R. Malach. 1992. Families with Native American roots, Chapter 5 in *Developing cross-cultural competence: a guide for working with young children and their families*, edited by E. Lynch and M. Hanson. Baltimore: Paul H. Brookes Pub. Co.

John, R. 1988. The Native American family, in *Ethnic families in America*, 3rd edition, edited by C. Mindel, R. Haberstein, and R. Wright, Jr. New York: Elsevier.

Kneip-Hardy, M. and M. Burkhardt. 1977. Nursing the Navajo. *American Journal of Nursing* 77(1):95-96.

Kramer, J. 1992. Cross-cultural medicine, a decade later; Health and aging of urban American Indians. *The Western Journal of Medicine* 157(3):281-285.

Kunitz, S. and J. Levy. 1981. Navajos, in *Ethnicity and medical care*, edited by Alan Harwood. Cambridge, MA: Harvard University Press.

Lamarine, R. 1989. The dilemma of Native American health. *Health Education* 20(5):15-18.

Lang, G. 1985. Diabetics and health care in a Sioux community. *Human Organization* 44(3):251-260.

Mail, P. and L. Wright. 1989. Point of view: Indian sobriety must come from Indian solutions. *Health Education* 20(5):19-22.

Marden, C., G. Meyer, and M. Engel. 1992. *Minorities in American society*, 6th edition, Chapter 5. New York: Harper Collins Publications.

May, P. 1989. Alcohol abuse and alcoholism among American Indians: an overview, in *Alcoholism in minority populations*, edited by T. Watts and R. Wright, Jr. Springfield, IL: Charles C. Thomas Publisher.

McWhirter, J. and C. Ryan. 1991. Counseling the Navajo: cultural understanding. *Journal of Multicultural Counseling and Development* 19(2):74-82.

Miller, N. 1982. Social work services to urban Indians, Chapter 8 in *Cultural awareness in the human services* by J. Green. Englewood Cliffs, NJ: Prentice-Hall, Inc.

Moss, R. 1992. We are all related. *San José (CA) Mercury News*, Parade Magazine, Oct. 11, p. 8, 10.

Parrillo, V. 1985. *Strangers to these shores: race and ethnic relations in the United States*, 2nd edition. New York: John Wiley and Sons.

Pelican, S. and K. Bachman-Carter. 1991. Ethnic and regional food practices series; *Navajo: food practices, customs, and holidays.* Chicago: The American Dietetic Association, and Alexandria, VA: American Diabetes Association, Inc.

Primeaux, M. 1977. Caring for the American Indian patient. *American Journal of Nursing* 77(1):91-94.

Rhoades, E., J. Hammond, T. Welty, A. Handler, and R. Amler. 1987. The Indian burden of illness and future health interventions. *Public Health Reports* 102(4):361-368.

Rhoades, E., L. Reyes, and G. Buzzard. 1987. The organization of health services for Indian people. *Public Health Reports* 102:352-356.

Richardson, E. 1981. Cultural and historical perspectives in counseling American Indians, Chapter 9 in *Counseling the culturally different*, by D. Sue. New York: John Wiley and Sons.

Rieder, H. 1989. Tuberculosis among American Indians of the contiguous United States. *Public Health Reports* 104(6):653-657.

Spector, R. 1991. *Cultural diversity in health and illness*, 3rd edition. Norwalk: Appleton and Lange.

Spector, R. 1985. *Cultural diversity in health and illness*, 2nd edition. Norwalk: Appleton-Century-Crofts.

Teufel, N. and D. DuFour. 1990. Patterns of food use and nutrient intake of obese and non-obese Hualapai Indian women of Arizona. *Journal of The American Dietetic Association* 90(9):1229-1235.

U.S. Bureau of the Census. 1993. *Statistical abstract of the United States*, 113th edition. Washington, D.C.: Government Printing Office, Table 733, p. 468.

U.S. Bureau of the Census. 1992A. *Statistical abstract of the United States*, 112th edition. Washington, D.C.: Govt. Printing Office, Table 26, p. 24-25.

U.S. Bureau of the Census. 1992B. *Statistical abstract of the United States*, 112th edition. Washington, D.C.: Govt. Printing Office, Table 43, p. 40.

U.S. Bureau of the Census. 1992C. *Statistical abstract of the United States*, 112th edition. Washington, D.C.: Govt. Printing Office, Table 714, p. 454.

Welty, T. 1991. Health implication of obesity in American Indians and Alaska Natives. *American Journal of Clinical Nutrition* 53:1616S-1620S.

Wilson, U. 1983. Nursing care of American Indian patients, Chapter 9 in *Ethnic nursing care: a multicultural approach*, edited by M. Orque, B. Bloch, and L. Monrroy. St. Louis: C.V. Mosby.

Chapter 9

LATINOS

The term "Latino" refers to the people of Latin America. Although most individuals prefer to be identified according to their country of origin (e.g., Mexican American, Cuban American), the term Latino is commonly accepted. Latinos include Mexicans/Chicanos, Central Americans, South Americans, Spanish, Puerto Ricans, and Cubans. The commonly used term "Hispanic" is misleading, because a person of "Spanish" heritage is a Caucasian. Many Latinos, including most Mexican Americans, are of Spanish and Indian descent. The Spanish intermarried with American Indians and produced mixed race children known as *mestizos*. A heritage of Spanish, American Indian, and African American is referred to as *mulatto*.

When possible, the country of origin is used here to identify individuals or groups. When more than one group is discussed, general information is reported, or the country of origin is unknown, the term Latino(s) or the feminine Latina(s) is used. The term "Hispanic" is used in Tables that report federal government statistics because this is the word used by the source.

Usually, Latinos are identified within a population by locating Spanish surnames. This method has been criticized for its inability to distinguish between descendants of colonial times and more recent immigrants from Mexico and other countries. A Mexican American may be a descendant of ancestors who have lived in the U.S. for over 300 years (Chicano), or may have entered the U.S. more recently as a legal "green card" holder (Bracero), or entered illegally ("Wetback"). Bradfield and Brun (1970) suggested that the predominant language used in the home (Spanish vs. English) should be the method used to identify Latinos.

Many Mexicans inhabited the southwestern United States before this area was settled by White Europeans. They lived in the areas now known as Texas, New Mexico, Arizona, and California when this territory was part of Mexico. The Mexican-American War ended with the Treaty of Hidalgo in 1848, which transferred all this territory and its Mexican inhabitants to the United States (deValdez and Gallegos, 1982). Mexican Americans subsequently provided inexpensive labor in farms, railroads, factories, mines, and food processing plants. As with Native Americans, the Mexican American people, indigenous to the southwest, had much of their land confiscated; they were arrested, beaten, and even repatriated.

Mexican laborers were encouraged to enter the United States during World War II when there was a serious need for agricultural workers. Active recruiting of farm laborers (the Bracero program) was discontinued in 1964, but high migration continued because of poor economic conditions in Mexico (Bacerra, 1988). Immigrants from Mexico continue to enter the U.S. (legally and illegally) in search of employment opportunities. Mexican Americans make up 62 percent of all U.S. Latinos; incomes are low compared to most other groups (U.S. Bureau of the Census, 1992A).

Puerto Ricans were granted U.S. citizenship in 1917. The culture of Puerto Rico has been influenced by the Spanish, Native Indians, African slaves, and the United States. The world depression beginning in 1928 severely affected Puerto Rico, whose major exports were sugar and tobacco. A program of industrialization did little to help the economic situation because as industrial jobs were added there were continuing losses in agriculture. The major migration of Puerto Ricans to the United States occurred in the 1950s when United States industries were looking for cheap labor, and Puerto Ricans were seeking jobs at higher pay. Most were unskilled farm laborers. They settled in urban areas (usually inner cities), particularly in New York City. More recent Puerto Rican immigrants are found in New York, New Jersey, Illinois, California, and other states. In 1990 Puerto Ricans accounted for 13 percent of the Latino population in the United States (U.S. Bureau of the Census, 1992A). Compared to Mexicans and Cubans, Puerto Ricans have less education, lower incomes, and the women more out-of-wedlock children (Sanchez-Ayendez,1988). Puerto Ricans tend to return to their homeland frequently, which helps them retain cultural identity but works against acculturation into United States society (Ruiz, 1985).

Cuban culture has been influenced by Spain, West African slaves, the United States, and, more recently, by the former Soviet Union. Major immigration of Cubans began with the Marxist revolution of Fidel Castro in 1959 (Szapocznic and Hernandez, 1988). Cubans continue to flee their homeland for political reasons; most settle in southern Florida (Miami area). Five percent of U.S. Latinos are from Cuba (U.S. Bureau of the Census, 1992A). Because of the high numbers of professional and upper income people in the early wave (1959) of refugees, Cubans have been more successful economically than other Latino groups.

California cities are home to large populations of Central and South Americans. Latinos entering the U.S. commonly move to urban areas where their relatives or friends can assist them in locating housing and jobs.

The income status of the Latino population in the United States is generally poor in comparison to that of non-Latinos. Fifty percent live in the inner cities of metropolitan areas. In 1990, 28 percent were living below the poverty line (Table 9-1). Puerto Rican family incomes are substantially lower than incomes of Mexican Americans and Cubans (Table 9-1) (Sanchez-Ayendez, 1988). In 1991, Latinos had median family incomes of $23,431 compared to the incomes of Whites of $36,915 (Table 2-3). This difference is even greater when considering the larger sizes of Latino families (Montes, 1989). In 1990 the per capita income of Latinos was $8,425 or 55 percent of the per capita income of Whites ($15,265). Low income is related to a lack of education; for example, only two out of five Mexican Americans complete high school (Bacerra, 1988), and in 1991 only 10 percent had completed four or more years of college compared to 22 percent for Whites and 39 percent for Asian-Pacific Islanders (Table 9-1).

Table 9–1.
Socioeconomic status of Hispanics in the U.S.

Country of Origin	1998, Median Family Income, $[1]	1990, % of Population Below Poverty[2,3]	1991, % of Population with 4 or More Years of College[3]
Total Hispanic	20,306	28.1	9.7
Mexico	19,968	28.1	6.2
Puerto Rico	15,185	40.6	10.1
Cuba	27,294	16.9	18.5
Central/South America	22,939	25.4	15.1

[1] U.S. Bureau of the Census, 1990. *Statistical Abstract of the United States*, 110th ed. Washington, D.C.: U.S. Government Printing Office, Table 45.
[2] U.S. Bureau of the Census, 1992. *Statistical Abstract of the United States*, 112th ed. Washington D.C.: U.S. Government Printing Office, Table 717. Poverty level for a non-farm family of four was $13,359.
[3] Ibid., Table 44.

In 1990, the states with the highest percentages of Latinos in their populations were New Mexico (38.2 percent), California (25.8 percent), Texas (25.5 percent), Arizona (18.8 percent), and Colorado (12.9 percent) (U.S. Bureau of the Census, 1992B). Most Mexican American families (85 percent) live in urban areas (Bacerra, 1988). The U.S. Latino population is growing very rapidly; in 1990 Latinos made up 9.0 percent of the population compared to 6.4 percent in 1980. Murillo-Rohde (1979) reported that, unofficially, Latinos are already the largest ethnic minority group in the United States because illegal immigrants are not counted in official records. In 1985 the Census Bureau estimated the Latino population at 17.3 million. Estimates regarding the population of illegal immigrants in the United

States range from 2 million to 40 million. Weyr (1988) estimated the total population of Latinos in the United States as 25 to 30 million including illegal immigrants. This is consistent with the statement that Latinos are the largest minority group in the United States.

World View

Although the term Latino encompasses many cultural subgroups, some values and beliefs are shared. People with low incomes and educational levels tend to have more traditional beliefs than high income people (Schreiber and Homiak, 1981). Other factors associated with adherence to ethnic beliefs include rural residence, first generation in the U.S., and living in ethnic communities (Clark, 1959). However, many Latinos in the U.S. have adopted some beliefs and values of the dominant society.

As in several other cultures, the concept of balance or harmony is central to traditional Latino values and beliefs. Physical, psychological, emotional, and social aspects of life must be balanced in order to promote a sense of well-being. Imbalance or disharmony result in illness. High value is placed on harmonious human social relations. It may be believed that disruption of social harmony results in illness (Maduro, 1983).

The world is perceived as a dangerous place; humans may be the victims of evil forces such as witchcraft, spirits, and magic (Maduro, 1983). This may be a factor in the great importance placed on religion by many Latinos. The majority of Latinos are Roman Catholics; many place their trust in God, believing their health or illness is His will (Monrroy, 1983). Perhaps related to this strong religious belief is the concept that body and soul may be separated. Therefore, the soul (one's psyche or self) may be "lost" from the body; it may get lost when it travels in dreams. Loss of soul from the body may also be due to changes in life which are disturbing (Maduro, 1983). Related to beliefs of the soul is the belief that a person's destiny is under the control of outside forces (fatalism), which can lead to disinterest in the consequences of ones actions accompanied by more risk taking than would otherwise occur (Harris and Moran, 1987).

In the traditional Latino world view, the natural and supernatural worlds are united, not separate. Therefore, practices such as prayers, sacrifice, penance, and vows are included in the cultural healing system. Gods, spirits, and saints may be asked to grant favors, and miracles can occur. Humans can control the supernatural by two types of magic. Imitative magic is based on the laws of similarity: "Like produces like." The voodoo doll is an example of this. The doll represents the victim and (supposedly) injury to the doll will affect the victim. Contagious magic is based on the belief that an object that was once physically associated with a person will continue to influence that person even after it is taken away. Hair, fingernails, clothes, and teeth may exert power over individuals. As an example of this belief, girls may drink chocolate containing the ground fingernail clippings of their boyfriends to ensure that they will remain faithful (Maduro, 1983).

Traditional Latino values regarding time are present oriented. In other words, individuals are concerned with what is happening now, rather than what will happen in the future. It has been suggested that this orientation is changing in the U.S., because adapting to changes in a new country requires a high degree of future orientation (Monrroy, 1983). However, the mañana concept (tomorrow may never come) in which it is permitted to promise anything that makes the other person happy, is a value that could affect communication (Harris and Moran, 1987).

Family Structure and Interactional Styles

The family unit is the most important social influence in the lives of most Latinos, and children are the central reason for marriage (Zuniga, 1992). Roles are well-defined in the traditional Latino family. The father is the head of the household, and although he is considered the primary decision-maker, women are gaining influence as they work more outside the home and earn additional income (Monrroy, 1983; Zuniga, 1992). Forty-nine percent of U.S. Latinas are in the work force (Heckler, 1985). Contrary to the stereotypes of traditional gender roles among Mexican Americans, in one study the women were reported to be involved in money decisions and the men in food purchase decisions (Yetley, Yetley, and Aguirre, 1981).

The extended family structure of Mexican Americans grew out of economic needs in Mexico. Every family generation was assigned tasks to perform to assure survival. Mutual support was necessary and became a way of life (Bacerra, 1988). The needs of the family come before those of its individual members and each member's behavior is a reflection on the entire family. Pride in these close family ties results in a reluctance to seek help from outside the extended family. There is a sense of obligation to provide support for members of one's immediate and extended family (Monrroy, 1983), and interdependency in the family is valued above independence of the individual (Maduro, 1983).

Puerto Rican families retain the traditional Latino pattern. The mother's world centers on family and home. The father's obligations are to provide for and protect the family. The principal religion of Puerto Ricans is an unorthodox version of Catholicism which includes beliefs about spiritualism (Sanchez-Ayendez, 1988).

Cuban American families are less dominated by males, and family responsibilities are not as clearly defined as in other Latino families. Among immigrant families, women are significant contributors to family income. This has led to a decrease in the traditional patriarchal family structure. In the process of acculturation, Cuban adolescent children become alienated from their parents who attempt to restrict and control them. These intense conflicts erode the traditional family relationships (Szapocznik and Hernandez, 1988).

The teachings of the Catholic church are factors in the high fertility rate of many Latino women who frequently reject the practices of contraception and abortion. Women are expected to refrain from sexual relations outside of marriage, but men are permitted, even encouraged, to be promiscuous (deValdez and Gallegos, 1982). There is a high regard for having many children in the Latino culture. A man's degree of *machismo* (the term is derived from a belief in the biological superiority of men) is indicated by the number of children he fathers (Monrroy, 1983). Although the stereotype of the *macho* male is that of a loud, domineering person, the traditional *macho* figure is a strong, brave individual who is a caring provider for his family and is just and fair in the use of his authority (Maduro, 1983; Bacerra, 1988).

Male children are highly valued in the Latino family because they will carry on the family name. They are socialized from an early age to take on the traditional male role and are allowed more freedom than girls. Outside the home, they are expected to protect their sisters, who are generally more sheltered in their upbringing. Girls are taught to care for the home and the younger children. Education may not be considered important for girls. Siblings are taught to share and cooperate, producing less competition and rivalry than among White children (Monrroy, 1983).

The extended Latino family includes numerous family and non-family members. Grandparents (*abuelitos*) hold a respected position. As they interact with their grandchildren, they pass history and traditions from generation to generation. Aunts, uncles, and godparents may raise children if death or other situations so require. Most (75.7 percent) Mexican American families are headed by married couples, but only 52 percent of Puerto Rican families are headed by married couples. For Mexican Americans, family structure continues to be strong because it provides security and promotes the values of sharing and cooperation (Bacerra, 1988).

Since the 1970s, political refugees from Central and South America have entered the United States. Their family structures and values are generally similar to those described for other Latin Americans. The father is the family protector and the mother is dependent on him. Extended family members are important and many traditional beliefs are followed.

Communication

Many Latinos in the United States speak Spanish. Although accents vary depending on country of origin, most words and definitions are the same. The ability to speak and read Spanish is a source of pride. Those who are bilingual may revert to their first language, Spanish, when under the stress of illness. Therefore, interpreters may be of great assistance in communicating in a medical setting. Although it is important in all counseling situations to develop rapport with the client, with Latinos it is very important to make small talk before getting down to business. Latino clients who may have poor English language skills may appear to understand spoken English by answering in the affirmative. Adding to this tendency, Latinos are very careful of others' feelings and may be reluctant to respond negatively to questions or directions (Monrroy, 1983).

Nonverbal communication, especially touch, is important among Latinos. Hugs, kisses, and hand holding between two individuals of the same sex are all acceptable behaviors that demonstrate affection. Direct eye contact may be avoided especially by women and children. It is disrespectful to have direct eye contact with persons in authority. Latinos are generally talkative, but modesty and privacy are also valued, especially in the health care setting. For example, undressing for a physical exam may cause embarrassment (Freebairn and Gwinup, #8, 1979).

Interactions with elders reflect traditional family values of courtesy and respect for the elderly and adults. Since most Latino adults prefer this, the health care worker should address patients by their last names and titles (Mr., Mrs.) (Monrroy, 1983; Freebairn and Gwinup, #8, 1979).

Health Beliefs and Practices

Causes of illness. The beliefs and practices discussed in this section are generally from Mexican American culture, and those specific to other Latino cultures are identified. Illness may be caused by various factors. Commonly, illness is believed to be punishment by God for one's transgressions. Health and disease are viewed as "His will." In such cases, *curanderos* may be consulted for treatments which include prayers and other rituals (Monrroy, 1983). Faith in the healing power of the Catholic saints is also strong (Scheper-Hughes and Stewart, 1983).

A second cause of illness is imbalance. Whether physical, emotional, or social, balance needs to be maintained by avoiding excesses in all areas of life including work, play, eating, and drinking (Scheper-Hughes and Stewart, 1983). The most obvious application of this emphasis on balance is the "hot/cold" theory of illness and curing. Based on ancient Greek pathology, this system attributes illness to an imbalance of "hot" and "cold" substances in the body. Hippocrates classified four liquids, or humors, within the body as hot or cold and wet or dry (Table 9-2).

Table 9-2
The four humors

Humor	Hot/cold	Wet/dry
Blood	Hot	Wet
Phlegm	Cold	Wet
Black bile	Cold	Dry
Yellow bile	Hot	Dry

If illness is caused by imbalance, then curing involves return to balance by adding or subtracting heat, cold, wetness, or dryness. These ideas were brought to Latin America by the Spanish in the sixteenth century. They were blended with the beliefs and remedies of the Indian shamans (medicine men) who thought illness was caused by loss of soul due to fright, possession by evil spirits, and injury through witchcraft (Sanjur, 1982).

Today, many foods, beverages, and medications (including herbs) are classified as either "hot" or "cold." This refers to the effect the substance is believed to have on the body, not to taste or temperature. Foods and medications classified as "hot" are prescribed for "cold" illnesses and vice versa. "Cold" foods include many fresh vegetables, tropical and citrus fruits, and dairy products. "Hot" foods include chile peppers, beef, oils, hard liquor, and beverages such as coffee and tea. Beans, rice, wheat, pork, and peaches may be considered "hot" or "cold." These designations vary among different populations (Monrroy, 1983). As a result of these beliefs, hospitalized Latino patients may request cilantro (coriander greens, or Chinese parsley), which is a "cold" food, to balance a "hot" illness. Postpartum women may refuse foods classified as cold because in childbirth heat is lost and the woman is susceptible to cold illness (Maduro, 1983).

A third possible cause of illness is magic or witchcraft. For example, evil eye (*mal ojo*) is a common disorder affecting infants and young children who have been looked at (often admiringly), but not touched, by someone with powerful eyes. Necklaces or medallions may be worn to keep evil spirits away from children and pregnant women. Magical illnesses may also be caused by witches, who cast spells on their victims. Often a spiritualist (*espiritualista*) will be called on to provide a cure through counter-magic. Puerto Ricans have a strong belief that spirits cause and cure illness. Their folk healing system is known as *espiritismo* and the healers as *espiritistas* (Monrroy, 1983; Spector, 1991).

For Mexican Americans, the dislocation of internal organs is another possible cause of illness. Most common is fallen fontanel (*caida de la mollera*). The cause is believed to be rapid removal of the nipple from an infant's mouth, resulting in difficulty sucking. Dehydration from diarrhea is the usual underlying physiological problem in this situation (Monrroy, 1983; Spector, 1985).

Illness may also be due to natural causes. *Empacho* is a traditional illness described as a gastrointestinal obstruction caused by a large ball of undigested food stuck in the abdomen. Symptoms include nausea, vomiting, diarrhea, and fever. Exposure to drafts or night air may cause *mal aire* (bad air) resulting in symptoms of nausea, vomiting, headaches, and dizziness.

For this reason, postpartum women may avoid bathing after delivery because "bad air" may enter the vaginal cavity and cause abdominal bloating (Monrroy, 1983; Spector, 1991; Freebairn and Gwinup, 1979).

Finally, disease may be due to emotional, mental, or interpersonal difficulties. Strong emotions may trigger illness. Fright or emotional trauma may cause *susto*, an illness in which the soul is believed to separate from the body. Symptoms may include fatigue, loss of appetite, and insomnia. Another emotionally triggered state is *bilis*, which is the result of feelings of rage. Other strong emotions, such as envy and loss, are believed to result in physical illness. This illustrates the Latino world view of the oneness of mind and body. Because they are inseparable, it is common to experience emotional problems as physical ailments (Maduro, 1983).

Mental illness. Among Latinos, mental illness is believed to result from emotional or supernatural causes or to be inherited. Usually *curanderos* or family physicians are consulted rather than psychiatrists. There is often reluctance to expose personal problems or to solve them using outside help (Monrroy, 1983). It has been reported that the incidence of mental illness is surprisingly low among Latinos in the U.S., as evidenced by their underrepresentation as psychiatric patients. This may be due to the warm, supportive atmosphere within the extended family, as well as the holistic practice of *curanderismo* (Maduro, 1983), or it may be that mental illness is not reported. Others find that underutilization of mental health care is due to barriers to care, not less need (Morris, et al., 1989).

Treatment. Health beliefs and practices of Latinos vary among and within cultural groups. Traditional healing practices may be used in conjunction with Western medicine. However, several factors have combined to result in an under-use of Western medical services by many Latinos in the U.S. These include strong family ties, a religious (rather than secular) world view, and mistrust of White institutions

(Scheper-Hughes and Stewart, 1983). Hospitals and clinics, where Spanish is not spoken or where negative attitudes and discrimination occur, will be avoided. The presence of Spanish-speaking staff who are culturally aware could improve this situation (Monrroy, 1983). In addition, Western health care may be under-used for practical reasons such as the economic need to work, lack of transportation, and problems with child care.

Mexican Americans are the less likely than Cubans, Puerto Ricans, or Blacks to use health care services. It is believed the reasons include their low access to health care resulting from factors such as language barriers and lack of health insurance. Cubans are more likely to have private health insurance; Puerto Ricans, because of their low economic status and high number of households headed by women, are more likely to qualify for Medicaid through the Aid to Families with Dependent Children program (Solis et al., 1990). Mexican men have the lowest use of health care of all racial/ethnic/sex groups in the United States (Higgenbotham, Trevino, and Ray, 1990).

In this setting, it is not surprising that *curanderismo*, the folk healing system of Mexican Americans, has been maintained. Although there are many regional variations, they share several common premises, values, and beliefs. *Curanderismo* is based on the Latino world view and provides a holistic view of healing. Not only physical, but also psychological, spiritual and emotional well-being are considered (Maduro, 1983). One study found, surprisingly, that use of folk medicine is not correlated with age, education, or socioeconomic status among Latinos. Rather, the patient's knowledge of the folk healer (*curandero*) as a friend, neighbor, or relative is a major determinant in the use of the *curanderismo* system (Scheper-Hughes and Stewart, 1983).

Folk medical beliefs were brought to Cuba by African slaves, and the concepts filtered throughout Cuban society. A common belief is that illness is caused by natural or supernatural forces. In either case the symptoms are similar. As with the Mexican American *curandero*, folk healers (*santeros*) may be used at any time (before, during, or after) in relation to Western medicine. Most Cubans are familiar with American medicine because they came from urban areas that were greatly influenced by the United States before Castro took power. In addition, some traveled to the U.S. for medical treatments. Cuban immigrants have adapted quickly to the American medical system and have introduced their own type of prepaid medical clinic to the Miami area (Ruiz, 1985).

The presence of folk healers within a community may be discounted by Western practitioners because persons outside the culture do not know of their existence. One reason for this invisibility has to do with laws against the practice of medicine without a license. In California, the practice of medicine is defined as "diagnosing or treating any disease or physical or mental condition" (Salner, 1985, p. 1A). A newspaper report of a Palo Alto, California holistic healer, who was arrested for practicing medicine without a license, stated that an estimated 5,000 to 10,000 alternative healers (unlicensed) are practicing in California (Salner, 1985). Mull and Mull (1983) reported an estimate of 1000 *curanderos* practicing in Orange County, California. The extent to which Latinos use folk healers is unknown. One study in the southwestern United States found that only 4.2 percent of Mexican Americans reported they had visited a folk healer in the previous 12 months. In this study the authors reported that the use of *curanderos* did not delay entry into Western medicine, as has been suggested in the literature (Higgenbotham, Trevino, and Ray, 1990).

An Orange County, California physician (J. D. Mull) made a professional visit to a *curandero* and reported on his experience (Mull and Mull, 1983). The *curandero* practiced treatments to cure folk illnesses and chronic conditions such as headache, fatigue, and infertility. He frequently referred clients to Western practitioners when he couldn't help them. He stated that his success was a gift from God and dependent on the patient's faith in God and in himself; God did the healing.

This *curandero* was licensed as a "Christian Health Healer." A visit to his office in 1983 would cost from $5 to $10.

There are many precautions in the use of folk healers. They can do more harm than good, and they can cause a delay in seeking a Western practitioner. However, Mull and Mull (1983) concluded that "with few exceptions, *curanderos* would seem to be talented healers whose efforts often benefit their patients and whose continued popularity has important implications for physicians, especially those serving large numbers of people of Mexican descent" (p. 30).

Family support as well as religious faith are the patient's major resources during recovery. Religious and magical practices common among Mexican Americans include 1) making promises, 2) visiting shrines, 3) offering medals and candles, and 4) prayers (Spector, 1985). Folk illnesses, such as *susto* or *bilis*, may serve a positive function because treatment and recovery serve to reintegrate patients into their native culture; community ties are renewed, traditional values are reclarified, and the stresses of acculturation to the dominant society are reduced (Maduro, 1983).

The traditional healer has a warm and personal relationship with the patient. Rapport is established early on, and active communication and interaction between the healer and patient are expected (Maduro, 1983). The healing methods of *curanderos* include herbs, prayers, laying on of hands and massage. Latinos in the United States may use both traditional and Western medicine. Studies have found that *curanderismo* is not the primary method of care in many locations today; rather, it is an alternative method used in cases of chronic illness or psychosomatic and stress-related conditions which are not successfully treated by "modern" medicine.

Health Status in the United States

For Mexican Americans and Cuban Americans, the risk of death from heart disease, cancer, and stroke is lower than for non-Latino Whites. Of the various Latino countries of origin, Puerto Ricans have the poorest health (Table 9-3). Data regarding the incidence of disease and death among Latinos are not consistent. There is no standard method for collecting data and some states do not yet identify "Hispanic" as a separate group. Thus, careful comparison of data in Table 9-3 shows unexplained values when compared with the total "Hispanic" values in Table 9-2. Deaths for the total population (Table 9-2) from motor vehicle accidents, HIV/AIDS, stroke, and others are not explained by the individual countries of origin in Table 9-3. In addition, since these are mortality rates, care must be taken to distinguish them from morbidity (disease) rates found in some studies.

The incidences of high serum cholesterol and hypertension are reported to be lower for Latinos than for non-Latino Whites (Fanelli-Kuczmarski and Woteki, 1990; Diehl and Stern, 1989). This is consistent with lower death rates from heart disease. However, the Council on Scientific Affairs of the American Medical Association (1991) cited two studies that reported higher levels of cholesterol and triglycerides in Mexican Americans than in Whites, and three sources reported higher rates of hypertension.

Latinas have less osteoporosis than non-Latino White women (Groziak and Diemond, 1989). Death from stomach cancer is twice the rate for Latinos as for Whites (Council on Scientific Affairs, 1991). Literature sources report that Latinas are more likely to die from cervical cancer than non-Latinas (Morris, et al., 1989; Council on Scientific Affairs, 1991), but Table 9-3 data differ except for Puerto Rican women. Morris, et al. (1989) reported a high rate of cervical cancer among Mexican American women and suggested the cause is related to the high numbers of sexual partners and high smoking rates of Latino men. An additional problem for Latinas is the underutilization of health care which results in delays in detection of cervical cancer (Morris, et al., 1989).

Morbidity data indicate that Latinos have high rates of diabetes (Maxwell and Jacobson, 1989), gallbladder disease, and obesity (Morris, et al., 1989; Council on Scientific Affairs, 1991)

Table 9–3.
Death rates per 100,000 populations by sex and Hispanic origin 1986–1988 based on data from 18 states and the District of Columbia.[1]

MALES

Cause	Non-Hispanic Whites	Mexican	Puerto Rican	Cuban
All causes	1053.8	448.2	1165.0	644.9
Ischemic heart disease	312.0	109.9	290.7	169.5
Stroke	56.7	21.7	49.2	30.2
Diabetes	14.2	10.0	31.6	9.8
Pulmonary disease	47.8	12.0	32.8	15.2
Lung cancer	80.7	20.1	42.3	40.6
Colorectal cancer	27.9	8.3	18.9	13.7
Cirrhosis	14.5	17.7	50.6	10.6
Motor vehicle	28.0	11.9	17.8	14.5
Other injuries	25.5	14.1	36.1	14.7
Homicide	6.5	15.9	35.0	32.6
Suicide	22.5	7.0	11.7	14.9
All infections	62.0	44.6	146.6	60.6
HIV/AIDS	8.1	15.7	57.2	24.2

FEMALES

Cause	Non-Hispanic Whites	Mexican	Puerto Rican	Cuban
All causes	676.3	319.1	703.3	323.8
Ischemic heart disease	188.3	85.1	217.0	92.0
Stroke	55.9	22.6	41.3	24.2
Diabetes	12.9	12.3	32.7	11.1
Pulmonary disease	21.0	6.4	15.5	5.4
Lung cancer	32.1	7.1	15.8	6.8
Breast cancer	30.7	10.8	18.5	15.3
Cervical cancer	3.4	2.8	5.4	2.2
Colorectal cancer	19.8	6.7	13.8	10.6
Cirrhosis	6.9	5.7	12.0	4.5
Motor vehicle	11.4	4.8	5.4	3.6
Other injuries	11.6	5.9	10.9	6.1
Homicide	4.2	3.4	6.5	6.2
Suicide	5.1	1.3	1.2	2.3
All infections	39.5	25.4	64.2	19.5
HIV/AIDS	0.9	2.7	10.0	1.2

[1] Centers for Disease Control and Prevention, 1992. *Years of potential life lost before age 65 by race, Hispanic origin, and sex, United States, 1986–1988* by J. Descencles and R. Hahn in CDC Surveillance Summaries, Nov. 20. *Morbidity and Mortality Weekly Report* (MMWR) 41 (No. 6): 13–23.

which are associated with a genetic predisposition related to American Indian heritage. American Indians have very high rates of these conditions compared to other ethnic groups. Diehl and Stern (1989) reported that the incidence of these conditions among Mexican Americans is directly related to the percentage of Indian ancestry and may be triggered by an environmental factor, probably diet. Since many cases of diabetes are not reported, the real prevalence of diabetes is probably much higher than the reported two to three times the non-Latino White rate. Data from the San Antonio Heart Study show that increased acculturation among Mexican Americans resulted in a decline in obesity and diabetes, suggesting that these conditions have an environmental basis as well as a genetic basis (Hazuda, et al., 1988).

Most Central Americans are familiar with Western medicine; the greatest obstacle to its use is lack of money (Boyle, 1991). Because many Central Americans are refugees, they are subject to stress related problems which may be expressed as somatic conditions. There is a social stigma to mental illness, and health professionals need to be cautious about terminology when treating post-traumatic stress disorders. Some Central Americans are in the United States illegally, which adds to the stress and may keep them from seeking health care in fear of being deported (Boyle, 1991).

As Latinos become more acculturated, their rates of heart disease and cancer are increasing. The reasons are related to increased use of alcohol, tobacco, and foods high in saturated fats. Maxwell and Jacobson (1989) cited many studies which show high levels of alcohol consumption among male Latinos. The effect of alcohol abuse on the health of Latino males is demonstrated by death rates for cirrhosis and homicide (Table 9-3). Alcohol drinking patterns differ in Mexico compared to the United States. The total amount of alcohol consumed by men in Mexico is less than that consumed by Mexican Americans; also, the frequency of alcohol consumption is less for Mexicans in Mexico than for Mexican Americans. However, when Mexican men do drink, they drink more at one time than Mexican Americans. The increased frequency of drinking in the United States has been associated with more money, more education, and fewer family ties to help moderate the drinking (Caetano and Mora, 1988; Caetano, 1990). White males who consume alcohol tend to drink more heavily through their 20s, but then they decrease alcohol consumption. In contrast, Mexican American drinking continues into middleage (Maxwell and Jacobson, 1989).

Latinas are more likely to abstain from alcohol use than Black or White women. The present problem of abuse is among males. However, the sex difference in drinking patterns is less among Latino youths. This means that alcohol consumption among Latinas will increase as the young people become older and more acculturated (Marks, Garcia, and Solis, 1990). Drinking among Puerto Ricans and Cubans seems to be lower than in the general population. The patterns of alcohol consumption among Latinos are complex and varied according to sex, age, income, education, marital status, and employment status (Caetano, 1990).

Tobacco smoking by Latino males has increased over the last 20 years and is now estimated to be similar to that of all other males in the general population. Haynes, et al. (1990) reported 1982–84 rates of smoking among Latino men of 42.5 percent, 39.8 percent, and 41.6 percent respectively for Mexican America men, Cuban American men, and Puerto Rican American men. The 1981–83 rates were Black males 39.7 percent, Black females 26.4 percent, White males 35.3 percent, and White females 28.5 percent (Remington, et al., 1985). A recent increase in lung cancer among Latinos and the trend is expected to continue. Until the mid-1980's, Latinas smoked much less than other females. With recent increased smoking among young females, increases in lung cancer can be expected. Deaths from heart disease can also be expected to increase (Maxwell and Jacobson, 1989; Montes, 1989).

The influence of advertising on increased use of alcohol and tobacco among Latinos should not be discounted. These products are advertised much more in Latino and Black neighborhoods than in White neighborhoods. Advertising is found on billboards, in newspapers, and in magazines directed to minority populations. The concentration of liquor stores is also greater in ethnic neighborhoods. Many events in Mexican American communities are sponsored by tobacco and alcohol companies. According to Maxwell and Jacobson (1989), the major reason for the promotions is to get "free samples into the hands of potential customers" (p. 50). The community organizers refuse to accept messages which would alert the public to the adverse health effects of tobacco and alcohol because this would offend the industries which support their events. The results of this advertising and financial support are distortion of known facts regarding adverse health effects and the undermining of educational efforts of schools and non-profit health organizations. Many Latinos and Blacks are not aware that smoking cigarettes is a risk factor for heart disease (Blum, 1989). The effect of advertising and marketing of alcohol on Latino communities has not been studied (Caetano, 1990).

Infections and deaths due to HIV/AIDS for Latino males and females are double the expected rates based on the proportion of Latinos in the population. Health education regarding the transmission of HIV does not seem to reach Latino communities. Other factors in the high rates of HIV infection include drug use and failure to use condoms because of religious beliefs and the cultural importance of producing children (Council on Scientific Affairs, 1991).

Food and Nutrition

Food within the Latino culture is valued as a sign of hospitality and friendship as well as a means of maintaining balance within the body. Socioeconomic status influences the dietary habits of many Latinos in the United States today. Poverty, which affects 28.1 percent of the Latino population (Table 2-3) in the U.S., requires that the diet consist of affordable foods. For example, staples in the Mexican American diet include pinto beans, corn or flour tortillas, rice, and chili (garlic, onion, peppers, and tomatoes). Beans are the major source of protein. Depending on economic status, meat may not be consumed daily. Green leafy vegetables, fruits, and dairy products (milk and cheese) are not consumed frequently (Groziak and Diemond, 1989). Although meat intake may be low, many foods are fried in lard or bacon fat which increases dietary saturated fat.

The Hispanic Health and Nutrition Examination Survey (HHANES) conducted from 1982 to 1984 found that Mexican American children consume adequate meat group foods, but inadequate amounts of fruits and vegetables (only 33 to 47 percent of recommendations). Teenagers had the poorest diets, low in milk as well as fruits and vegetables and high in fats and sweets (Murphy, et al., 1990). The HHANES study also found that Hispanics (Mexican Americans, Puerto Ricans, and Cubans) did not have a higher rate of iron deficiency than non-Latino Whites or Blacks (Fanelli-Kuczmarski and Woteki, 1990). Latinos are less likely to avoid dietary fat than Whites (Frank, et al., 1991). In their study, Romero-Gwynn, et al. (1993) found that diets of Mexicans changed significantly after immigration. There was a decrease in some traditional foods which resulted in decreased consumption of fruits and vegetables in the United States. Non-traditional foods which were substituted for traditional foods included sodas and high sugar fruit-flavored drinks for homemade fruit drinks, vegetable oil for lard, and toast, butter, and marmalade for Mexican sweet bread. Of particular concern was the increase in fat from higher consumption of margarine, butter, vegetable oils, mayonnaise, salad dressings, sour cream, and peanut butter (Romero-Gwynn, 1993).

Lactose intolerance is common among many Latino adults, although it is rare in infants and children. Dairy foods are not consumed in large quantities in traditional diets, contributing to possible calcium and riboflavin deficiencies (Monrroy, 1983). The low rate of osteoporosis among Latinas could be the result of genetic factors or other dietary advantages such as low protein consumption. Central American women may be confused by encouragement to breast-feed their babies. This is contrary to custom in Central American countries, where infant formula companies have convinced women that infant formulas are superior to breast milk (Gleave and Manes, 1990).

A nutrition-related phenomenon involving pregnancy in Latinas is pica, the craving for and consumption of non-food substances. Ice, dirt, clay, and laundry starch may be eaten (see Chapter 10).

Implications for Health Care

When first meeting with a Latino client, the professional needs to develop rapport and become a friend by engaging in small talk before getting down to business. Don't be in a hurry. Assess the client's literacy in both Spanish and English. Spanish language educational materials are of no use if the client doesn't read Spanish. Because Latino clients may be reluctant to discuss personal matters, health care professionals need to develop warm, sharing relationships.

The degree of acculturation and the economic status of the client could have a major impact on health status and barriers to care, such as lack of transportation and child care. These need to be assessed.

If a family comes in to the clinic together, address the father first. Provide an opportunity for family decisions regarding health matters, and assess beliefs regarding use of traditional medicine. Because of the possibility of present-time orientation, it is suggested that practitioners set small, short-term goals that can be reached quickly (Locke, 1992). Some Latinos may object to direct eye contact; follow their lead.

Because of somatization, severe depression may not be diagnosed or treated. Patient's complaints might include dizziness, aches, fatigue, and headaches, but all tests will be negative. Health care providers need to be alert to the possibility of depression because it could result in suicide (Ruiz, 1985).

Puerto Ricans may display a group of symptoms that resemble epilepsy (convulsions, trembling, falling to the ground). This condition is cultural and not based on a pathological problem. Health professionals need to acknowledge these beliefs and not attempt to change them. Working within the traditional belief system, health professionals are able to use Western medicine effectively (Ruiz, 1985).

The health professional may learn that a Latino client is an illegal immigrant, it is important to know about resources available to illegal immigrants. This status will, of course, add to the stress of being ill. Latinos are generally healthy, and should be encouraged to retain many of their traditional customs.

References Cited

Bacerra, R. 1988. The Mexican American family, in *Ethnic Families in America*, 3rd edition, edited by C. Mindel, R. Habenstein, and R. Wright, Jr. New York: Elsevier.

Blum, A. 1989. The targeting of minority groups by the tobacco industry, in *Minorities and Cancer*, edited by L. Jones. New York: Springer-Verlag.

Boyle, J. 1991. Transcultural Nursing Care of Central American Refugees. *National Student Nurses Association Inc./Imprint*, April/May, p. 72.

Bradfield, R. and T. Brun. 1970. Nutritional status of California Mexican Americans, a review. *The American Journal of Clinical Nutrition* 23(6):798-806.

Caetano, R. 1990. Editorial: Hispanic drinking in the U.S.: thinking in new directions. *British Journal of Addiction* 85:1231-1236.

Caetano, R. and M. Mora. 1988. Acculturation and drinking among people of Mexican descent in Mexico and the United States. *Journal of Studies in Alcohol Abuse* 49(5):462-471.

Clark, M. 1959. *Health in the Mexican American culture*. Berkeley: University of California Press.

Council on Scientific Affairs. 1991. Hispanic health in the United States. *Journal of the American Medical Association* 265(2):248-252.

deValdez, T. and J. Gallegos. 1982. The Chicano *familia* in social work, in *Cultural awareness in the human services*, by J. Green. Englewood Cliffs, NJ: Prentice-Hall, Inc.

Diehl, A., and M. Stern. 1989. Special health problems of Mexican Americans: obesity, gallbladder disease, diabetes mellitus, and cardiovascular disease. *Advances in Internal Medicine* 34:73-96.

Fanelli-Kuczmarski, M. and C. Woteki. 1990. Monitoring the nutritional status of the Hispanic population: selected findings for Mexican Americans, Cubans, and Puerto Ricans. *Nutrition Today*, 25(3): 6-11.

Frank, G, M. Zive, J. Nelson, S. Broyles, and P. Nader. 1991. Fat and cholesterol avoidance among Mexican-American and Anglo preschool children and parents. *Journal of The American Dietetic Association* 91:954-958, 961.

Freebairn, J. and K. Gwinup. 1979. *Cultural diversity and nursing practice, Instructors manual: #8, Beyond Language*. Irvine, CA: Concept Media, Inc.

Gleave, D. and A. Manes. 1990. The Central Americans, in *Cross-cultural counseling*, edited by N. Waxler-Morrison, J. Anderson, and E. Richardson. Vancouver, BC: University of British Columbia Press.

Groziak, S. and L. Diemond. 1989. Diet and nutrition related diseases of ethnic minorities. *School Food Service Journal* 43(6):82.

Harris, P. and R. Moran. 1987. *Managing Cultural Differences*, 2nd edition. Houston: Gulf Publishing.

Haynes, S., C. Harvey, H. Montes, H. Nickens, and B. Cohen. 1990. Hispanic Health and Nutrition Examination Survey, 1982-84: VIII, Patterns of cigarette smoking among Hispanics in the United States: results from HHANES 1982-84. *American Journal of Public Health* 80 (Supplement): 47-53.

Hazuda, H., S. Haffner, M. Stern, and C. Eifler. 1988. Effects of acculturation and socioeconomic status on obesity and diabetes in Mexican Americans, The San Antonio Heart Study. *American Journal of Epidemiology* 128(6): 1289-1301.

Heckler, M. 1985. *Report of the Secretary's Task Force on black and minority health, Volume 1; Executive summary*. Washington, D.C.: U.S. Department of Health and Human Services.

Higgenbotham, J., F. Travino, and L. Ray. 1990. Hispanic Health and Nutrition Examination Survey, 1982-84; V: Utilization of *curanderos* by Mexican Americans: prevalence and predictions, findings from HHANES 1982-84. *American Journal of Public Health* 80 (supplement): 32-35.

Locke, D. 1992. *Increasing multicultural understanding*, Chapter 9 Mexican Americans. Newbury Park, CA: SAGE Pub., Inc.

Maduro, R. 1983. *Curanderismo* and Latino view of disease and curing. *The Western Journal of Medicine* 139(6):868-874.

Marks, G., M. Garcia, and J. Solis. 1990. Hispanic Health and Nutrition Examination Survey,

1982-84; III: Health risk behaviors of Hispanics in the United States: findings from HANES, *1982-84*. American Journal of Public Health 80 (supplement): 20-26.

Maxwell, B. and M. Jacobson. 1989. *Marketing disease to Hispanics: the selling of alcohol, tobacco, and junk foods*. Washington, D.C.: Center for Science in the Public Interest.

Monrroy, L. 1983. Nursing care of Raza/Latina patients, Chapter 4 in *Ethnic nursing care: a multicultural approach*, edited by M. Orque, B. Bloch, and L. Monrroy. St. Louis: C.V. Mosby.

Montes, J. 1989. Specific concerns affecting Hispanics in the United States, in *Minorities and cancer*, edited by L. Jones. New York: Springer-Verlag.

Morris, D., G. Lusero, E. Joyce, E. Hannigan, and E. Tucker. 1989. Cervical cancer, a major killer of Hispanic women: implications for health education. *Health Education* 20(5):23-28.

Mull, J. and D. Mull. 1983. A visit with a *curandero*. *The Western Journal of Medicine* 139:730-736.

Murillo-Rohde, I. 1979. Cultural sensitivity in the care of the Hispanic patient. *Washington State Journal of Nursing* (supplement): 25-32.

Murphy, S., R. Castillo, R. Martorell, and F. Mendoza. 1990. An evaluation of food group intakes by Mexican-American children. *Journal of the American Dietetic Association* 90(3):388-393.

Remington, P., M. Forman, E. Gentry, J. Marks, G. Hogelin, and F. Towbridge. 1985. Current smoking trends in the United States: the 1981-1983 Behavioral Risk Factor Surveys. *Journal of the American Medical Association* 253(20):2975-2978.

Romero-Gwynn, E., D. Gwynn, L. Grivetti, R. McDonald, G. Stanford, B. Turner, E. West, E. Williamson. 1993. Dietary acculturation among Latinos of Mexican descent. *Nutrition Today* 28(4):6-12.

Ruiz, P. 1985. Cultural barriers to effective medical care among Hispanic-American patients. *Annual Review of Medicine* 36:63-71.

Salner, R. 1985. Palo Alto holistic healer on trial on charge of practicing medicine. *San José (CA) Mercury News*, November 21, p. 1A, 13A.

Sanchez-Ayendez, M. 1988. The Puerto Rican American Family, in *Ethnic families in America*, 3rd edition, edited by C. Mindel, R. Habenstein, and R. Wright, Jr. New York: Elsevier.

Sanjur, D. 1982. *Social and cultural perspectives in nutrition*. Englewood Cliffs, NJ: Prentice-Hall, Inc.

Scheper-Hughes, N., and Stewart, D. 1983. *Curanderismo* in Taos County, New Mexico—A possible case of anthropological romanticism? *The Western Journal of Medicine* 139(6), 875-884.

Schreiber, J. and J. Homiak. 1981. Mexican Americans, Chapter 5 in *Ethnicity and medical care*, edited by A. Harwood. Cambridge, MA: Harvard University Press.

Solis, J., G. Marks, M. Garcia, and D. Shelton. 1990. Hispanic Health and Nutrition Examination Survey, 1982-84; II: Acculturation, access to care, and use of preventive services by Hispanics: findings from HHANES 1982-84. *American Journal of Public Health* 80 (supplement):11-19.

Spector, R. 1991. *Cultural diversity in health and illness*, 3rd edition. Norwalk, CT: Appleton and Lange.

Spector, R. 1985. *Cultural diversity in health and illness*, 2nd edition. Norwalk, CT: Appleton-Century-Crofts.

Szapocznik, J. and R. Hernandez. 1988. The Cuban American family, in *Ethnic Families in America*, 3rd edition, edited by C. Mindel, R. Habenstein, and R. Wright, Jr. New York: Elsevier.

U.S. Bureau of the Census. 1992A. *Statistical abstract of the United States*, 112th edition. Washington, D.C.: U.S. Government Printing Office; Table 45, p. 42.

U.S. Bureau of the Census. 1992B. *Statistical abstract of the United States*, 112th edition. Washington, D.C.: U.S. Government Printing Office; Table 26. p. 24-25.

Yetley, E., M. Yetley, and B. Aguirre. 1981. Family role structure and food-related roles in Mexican-American families. *Journal of Nutrition Education* 13(1) supplement: S96-101.

Weyr, T. 1988. *Hispanic USA, Breaking the melting pot*. New York: Harper and Row Publishers.

Zuniga, M. 1992. Families with Latino roots, Chapter 7 in *Developing cross cultural competence: a guide for working with young children and their families*, edited by E. Lynch and M. Hanson. Baltimore: Paul Brookes Pub. Co.

Chapter 10

AFRICAN AMERICANS

Most African Americans are the descendants of West Africans brought to the United States as slaves beginning in 1619 (Herskovitz, 1966). During the period of slavery, the health care of Blacks (with the exception of health care for free Blacks) was the responsibility of their masters, but after slavery was abolished Blacks became responsible for their own health care. Life after the Civil War was very difficult. Little was done in the 1880s to help freed slaves obtain education, housing, and employment. They grouped together in cities, forming inner city slums (Willis, 1992). Because of low income, Blacks (and poor Whites in the South) turned to folk healers such as *root doctors* and *hoodoo men*. Also, because of poverty and racism, Western medicine was largely unavailable to Blacks. There were few Black doctors since most medical schools refused admission to Blacks no matter how well they were qualified. At the same time, White doctors and hospitals usually refused to care for Blacks. So Blacks had little choice but to turn to folk healers and self-medication. These factors account for the prevalence of traditional medical treatments among Blacks even today (Jackson, 1981).

Poverty among African Americans has increased since the 1960s. In 1990 almost one-third (31.9 percent) of all Black Americans lived in poverty despite rising incomes for the general population (Table 2-3). The poverty rate for Black children ages 18 and under was 45.6 percent in 1987, and for children under age three was 49.1 percent (Incomes decline . . . , 1988). At the same time that many African Americans are becoming increasingly poor, the upwardly mobile are finding more employment opportunities, widening the gap between middle class and low income Blacks (Jackson, 1981). Middle class Black families usually adopt some characteristics of the dominant White group. They have worked very hard to accomplish their income status, and usually demonstrate pride in being Black and have high self-esteem. Many are involved in activities that increase their quality of life. Unfortunately, greater involvement in White society means less involvement in the Black community. This sometimes leads to feelings of guilt at leaving family and friends behind in a lower socioeconomic status (Conner-Edwards and Spurlock, 1988).

In her research, Benjamin (1991) personally interviewed 100 highly successful Blacks. Her subjects had a median annual income greater than $50,000 and 76 percent had either a Ph.D., master's, medical, law, or bachelor's degree. She found that despite their success, they continually faced institutional racism. Benjamin described racism as "a process of justification for the domination, exploitation, and control of one racial group by another" (p. xxvii). This definition seems to indicate that racism is intentional, but Benjamin explained that it is also unintentional. A *Newsweek* magazine special report indicated that the Black middle class (incomes greater than $20,000 a year) had grown to nearly 56 percent of Black wage earners in 1980 (Gelman, 1988); much of this chapter is about the other 44 percent and the non-wage earners.

Blacks are about 12 percent of the U.S. population. This makes them the largest minority group (although some authors believe that the Latino population is larger because of illegal immigrants; see Chapter 9). About 98 percent of the Black population is native born (Jackson, 1981). In 1980, 59 percent of all Blacks lived in central cities; the largest populations were in New York City, Chicago, Detroit, Philadelphia, and Los Angeles (Heckler, 1985).

Most demographic literature on Black families compares all Whites with all Blacks or subdivides these into age and sex groups. There is little attempt to compare ethnic groups within similar socioeconomic levels. Thus, data are influenced by the many African Americans who live in poverty. For example, when statistics show that 38 to 55 percent (sources do not agree on this) of Black households are headed by women, it is apparent that this problem is associated with low income (Table 2-4). The percentage of male headed households (this would be married couples) is similar to Whites when considering only families with incomes of $20,000 and over (Staples, 1989). Data which report the total Black population tend to hide the substantial middle class. Nevertheless, in recent years, Black family life has been plagued by divorce, single heads of families (Heckler, 1985), and low employment rates. Gardner and Herz (1992) associated the low income of Blacks with fewer years of education, racial discrimination, and single worker families. They indicated that only 14 percent of Blacks in the work force had completed college, compared to 25 percent of Whites.

World View/Life Experiences in the United States

The traditional African world view included the belief that things influence each other and people could influence their own futures (and the futures of others) through behavior and knowledge. Health was believed related to harmony with nature and illness to disharmony caused primarily by demons and evil spirits. The treatment of illness centered on removal of evil spirits from the body (Spector, 1985). From African cultural beliefs, some United States Blacks believe that spirits are real with the ability to communicate. Discussions with the spirits of deceased relatives are considered normal (Bowser, 1992; Willis, 1992).

The concept of *soul* is often used to describe the sense of Black solidarity and racial pride originating from the experiences of slavery and the hard times that followed. *Soul* may also refer to communication (*soul talk, soul music*) or to a "down home" association (as in *soul food*). The feeling of oneness among Blacks is characteristic of Black culture. Familial terms such as *brother* and *sister* are used to address other Blacks who could even be strangers. Diversity within Black culture may be caused by factors such as socioeconomic class, age, region of residence within the U.S., and individual experiences.

Many Blacks are poor; they react to their low socioeconomic status in predictable ways. Medical help may not be sought until the condition interferes with daily activities, especially the ability to work. They may be present-oriented, meaning that attention and resources are focused on present, day-to-day necessities (food and shelter). Preventative medicine and health promotion may be seen as irrelevant in the struggle to meet basic needs. A fatalistic attitude toward illness ("It's going to happen anyway," "It's my lot"), as well as a flexible adherence to schedules (P-time orientation), may also delay the initiation of health treatment (Bloch, 1983).

Intergenerational (age) differences are apparent where health care attitudes are concerned. Influenced by the early Black life experience in the U.S. (slavery, racism), elderly Black patients may exhibit patience and passivity, and resign themselves to institutional health care practices which they feel powerless to challenge. On the other hand, young Blacks (influenced by the Black civil rights movement) may be more assertive and outspoken in the clinical setting (Bloch, 1983).

The African American life experience in the U.S. fostered the development of religion as an escape or haven from the difficulties of daily life. Black churches were built, financed, and controlled by Blacks. The churches provide spiritual support and have many additional positive functions: they provide aid and support, strengthen family ties, guide moral behaviors, serve as gathering places, support social programs, and allow members to assume leadership roles. Church members may become extended family.

Most Blacks are Baptist; Methodists are the second largest religious group and Roman Catholics the third largest. Fewer than 11 percent have no religious preference (Jackson, 1991). Cultural features such as the Black spiritual, supernatural and religious healing beliefs, and a tradition of mutual aid have been preserved in the church (Bloch, 1983). Health care practitioners should remember that religion may provide vital psychological support in the face of illness; religious practices must be respected.

Family Structure and Interactional Styles

To gain an understanding of interactions among Black family members requires a background on family life during the period of slavery in the United States. Most Black Americans were brought to the U.S. from West Africa where they were members of very strong kinship groups (extended families). The present extended family structure of Blacks evolved from traditional African culture. The concepts of tribe and family survival (doing whatever is necessary to maintain the family) are expressed today in deep kinship ties (Heckler, 1985). Green (1982) described the extended families of African Americans as a network of households that connect family units, even across geographical distances; there is usually a "dominant" senior family figure who is the authority for all the households in the network.

Because of slavery, families were separated and most Blacks were placed in situations without any kin present. Marriages and separations of slaves were not legally sanctioned, but were controlled by the slave owners whose purpose was the breeding of additional children who would become slaves. Most of these marriages were stable, unless one spouse was sold by the owner (Taylor, 1986). Since men and women worked side-by-side in the fields, children were cared for by older women. In a sense, the extended family was continued despite the separations.

After emancipation (1860) many Black couples were legally married, and, by 1917, 90 percent of Black children were born into two-parent families. Black men tried to copy White family lifestyle by discouraging their wives from working for their former owners. Many of the Black men did this because they believed their wives deserved as much respect as White women who did not do this kind of work (Taylor, 1986). Unfortunately, Black men had trouble finding employment, and many Black women had to work. Out of necessity, men shared in rearing children and women provided some outside income. Thus, family responsibilities were shared more equally in the early African American families than in White families. Black males were unable to assume a superior role because the women were never dependent on them in the United States (Greathouse and Miller, 1981; Staples, 1989).

Black values often differ from those of Whites. Wilson and Stith (1991) identified Black values as sharing, obedience to authority, spirituality, and respect for elders and heritage. Values for Whites were stated to be independence, material assets, planning, youth, and power. The differences and similarities are important to acknowledge. Based on African world view, the group is more important than the individual and this fosters values for cooperation and interdependence (Todisco and Salomone, 1991). Greathouse and Miller (1981) described five major strengths of Black families: strong kinship bonds, work orientation, achievement orientation, religious orientation, and adaptability of family roles.

During and after World Wars I and II a number of Blacks from the South moved into urban areas in the North and West. In 1977, 47 percent of U.S. Blacks lived outside the South (Jackson, 1981). Employment of urban Blacks was high during World War II, but the problems of today's Black males began in the 1960's when industrial jobs started a steady decline (Staples, 1989). Some Blacks blame the influx of illegal immigrants (from Mexico) for loss of job opportunities.

Modern problems for African Americans are greatly influenced by racism and the resulting feelings that can lead to low self-esteem. Two African American psychologists (White and Parham, 1990) explain that Black children do not see their own images in movies, TV, newspapers, or magazines. They see White Americans with power and beauty, but not Black Americans. They learn from their parents that Blacks have little control over their social conditions, and they are taught to cope with and to expect racism from Whites and White institutions (Willis, 1992; Benjamin, 1991). Black youths find that reality conflicts with the teachings of liberty, justice, and equality. White and Parham (1990) conclude that Black youths "seem to have been overwhelmed by oppressive conditions to the point that they feel powerless to change, affect, and/or influence their present conditions" (p. 153). Black youths are involved in daily survival and do not develop skills to compete in White society. The high numbers of young African American males who are caught up in the criminal justice system (25 percent in the United States and 33 percent in California) reflect the deterioration of families (Cohn, 1990). It undoubtedly also reflects racism within the criminal justice system and in police departments. Bloch (1983) stated that parental influence is especially important in the development of racial self-esteem. This includes factors such as the presence of Black cultural objects in the home and family discussions about well-known Blacks and the treatment of Blacks in society.

In order to explain the experiences of Black children growing up in the United States, Llorens (1971) used a model of four lifestyles which were originally describe by Cole (1970): (1) *street*, urban poor, stylized speech, walking cool, and possession of weapons; (2) *down-home*, traditional rural, southern, gatherings on front porches and in kitchens, church attendance, extended families, poor to well off, and well-cared-for children; (3) *militant*, revolutionary, African styles of hair and clothing, lifestyles of Black heroes, willing to die to change Black oppression, separate from the dominant culture, political activists, and with high values for education; and, (4) *upward bound*, Black middle-class professionals, most like the White middle class, integrated socially, attend church regularly (Llorens, 1971).

The variety of lifestyle combinations is large. For health professionals who are not Black, the greatest difficulties will occur in communicating with Blacks who follow the street and militant lifestyles.

Education is highly valued in African American families. Most aspire to higher educational levels, especially for their children. Despite traditional values, only 46 percent finish high school compared to 67 percent of Whites. In addition, college enrollments of Black men declined from 1982 to 1986 as enrollments of other groups (including Black women) increased (Black men's college.., 1989). Black women receive more education than Black men but, compared to Black men, even well-educated women are found in the lowest paying jobs. Recall that gender differences have more impact on income than racial differences (Chapter 7). Black women perceive their economic problems as being racial not gender related even though statistics indicate otherwise (Staples, 1989). Within Black communities, the most respected members are the most highly educated and are also the most likely to have high-paying jobs (Bloch, 1983).

Because of a lack of marriageable men, due to violent deaths, incarceration, unemployment and unequal educational levels, many Black women cannot find mates with comparable backgrounds. Jackson (1991) reported that Black men believed it was necessary for men to assume the gender roles of White males (dominance) in order for Blacks to gain racial equality. Black women did not agree. Thus, there is an increasing tendency toward single life that results when women want to be independent and men are unable to provide economically for a family. Black women are likely to be single mothers. In 1991, 54 percent of African American children under 18 years old lived in single parent households headed by their mothers (U.S. Bureau of the Census, 1992). Willis (1992) indicated that members of extended families may not live together and the statistical depiction of "female headed households" fails to recognize the kinship support they receive. Jackson (1991) reported that female headed households were more likely to have kinship ties and to receive outside help than other families, but this did not make up for the economic disadvantages. Staples (1989) explained that the increase in single motherhood is due to a number of factors. Young Black women (under age 30) do not usually marry, and older women are likely to be divorced. When deciding on marriage, a Black woman considers the benefits and the costs. Most (98 percent) who do marry, marry African American men. In order for marriage to be an advantage over single motherhood for the woman, the male needs to have steady employment. Many Black men do not have this opportunity. Welfare requires that men not be present in the home which also encourages women to remain single. When they do marry, only one in three Black couples remains married for 10 years (Staples, 1989).

An interesting point of view in defense of African American women was expressed by Martin and Martin (1986). This has to do with the common stereotype of the Black woman as domineering, emasculating, and (because of matriarchy) the cause of instability in some Black families. To explain, it is necessary to refer to family role changes that occurred as a result of slavery. Black males lost their roles as family patriarch. The White slavemaster became the authority figure. Black men and women were equally subjected to oppression, hard work, and brutality. Black women did the same work that Black men did, and then they did "women's" work as well. In addition, Black women were frequently raped by White men, and Black males were powerless to intervene. Out of slavery grew a gender equality among Blacks that does not exist for Whites (Jackson, 1991). Because of slavery, Black men and women worked side-by-side, and men were not women's protectors. Black women became self-sufficient. Their strength has certainly been a factor in the growing number of middle class Black families. Today, African American children are not taught stereotypic gender-traits such as male aggressiveness and female dependence (Green, 1982). Outsiders sometimes label Black women as domineering and suggest that the problem with inner city Black families is that they don't follow the White pattern of patriarchy. Since many women of all ethnicities seek equal status with men, this would appear to be a step backward. Possibly more important, to expect to blame inner city problems of drugs, homicide, and teenage pregnancies on the breakdown of the traditional family structure does not consider that these problems exist within a segment of society where resources are limited and there are few opportunities to change. The strength of the African American woman is not a negative influence on Black men (Green, 1982).

Communication

Communication patterns reflect Black life experiences in the United States. Black English may be used to prevent outsiders from understanding a conversation, but usually it is used to increase in-group solidarity. Black English developed out of necessity. Africans were purposely separated from people who spoke their same language when they were brought to the United States by slave traders. In order to communicate with Whites and other Blacks, they had to invent a pidgin language, developed by two people who have no common language. A simplified form of one or more languages. Black children grew up using pidgin English, but they needed a more complete language so they developed the pidgin into creole, the language that results when children of pidgin-speaking parents make their language complete. Black English is a creole language with its own recognizable style. It is similar to other high context languages; the way something is said (tone, word order, speed) conveys as much meaning as the words themselves. Some of the characteristics of Black English are carried over from West African languages. For example, if an English word starts with *th*, a *d* sound will be substituted (*de, dose*). If a word ends in *th*, the final sound will be *f* (*bof, mouf*). Some other final sounds are dropped (for example, *d*, *s*, *t* and sometimes *r*). The West African languages had no verb "to be," and Black English reflects this grammatical difference; for example, "He tell me he busy" (Bloch, 1983, p. 87). Another characteristic of Black English is the use of multiple negatives in a sentence (Freebairn and Gwinup, 1979).

During a performance, such as at a church or social event, the audience is usually participatory. That is, there is a constant stream of interactive dialogue between the speaker and the audience. Black English is highly contextual, with hidden meanings which are more than the sum of the words, and reflects the Black experience of hardship and hopes. Some words and expressions may be difficult for non-Blacks to understand. The oral tradition of Black communication emphasizes the ear, memory, spontaneity, and audience participation. Black slaves were not allowed to keep written records, so the oral tradition was developed out of necessity. In contrast, the literate tradition of Whites utilizes the eye and the written word, is less flexible in terms of expression, and does not encourage memorization or audience participation. In the clinical setting, an understanding of the characteristics of Black communication may be helpful. Blacks are more perceptive of nonverbal cues than Whites (Wilson and Stith, 1991).

Kochman (1981) described a difference in communication styles between Blacks and Whites that could lead to misunderstandings. Black culture encourages assertiveness and open expressions of feelings and ideas. Thus, when African Americans disagree, they have an obligation to express their objections. White people who remain silent on a topic in which they are known to disagree will be judged as not honest or as cheating. According to Kochman, Blacks use argument to persuade, not to vent anger. Whites are taught self-restraint and believe in avoiding arguments. For Whites, the truth in a dispute is dependent on the facts, not on the passion of the argument. Whites do not understand that Black argumentative behavior is intended to persuade. To a White person, the use of emotional arguments actually inhibits the ability to reason. A White person is likely to present an idea in an impersonal manner with less intensity and conviction than a Black person (Kochman, 1981).

Blacks may view Whites as the oppressor and interact accordingly. One expression of this is in the use of derogatory terms to suggest that a minority individual is actually *white* inside (Uncle Tom). Terms used for members of various ethnic groups are banana for Asians, oreo for Blacks, and apple for American Indians (Freebairn, J. and K. Gwinup, #7 & #8; 1979).

Health Beliefs and Practices

The approach toward health is holistic: body, mind, and soul are considered one. Today's cultural healing system is a combination of the African influence, last century's folk medicine, modern science, Christianity, and magic (Bloch, 1983). Snow (1983) described three major themes that seem to shape the cultural health beliefs of today's African Americans of lower socioeconomic status: (1) The world is unfriendly and dangerous; (2) a person is likely to be attacked by outside forces (e.g., nature, God, other people); and (3) the individual is helpless and therefore must rely on outside assistance. This fearful view of the world is a natural reaction to an environment of racism and chronic poverty (Snow, 1983).

Causes of illness. There is a widespread traditional belief that illness is either natural or unnatural. This dichotomy is closely related to religious beliefs of good versus evil. Natural illness is part of God's created world and is the result of neglect of the body (such as sitting in a draft or eating a poor diet) or of God's punishment for sin. Unnatural illness does not follow nature's laws and is caused by the evil influences of people with special powers (witchcraft, voodoo, and hexes). It is believed that unnatural illness cannot be cured by Western physicians, that only specialized healers can be effective (Snow, 1983; Green, 1982; Willis, 1992).

Natural illness is believed to have several common causes. The first of these is entrance of coldness into the body. Thickness of the blood is thought to change according to outside temperatures and with age. Blood should thicken in the winter (to provide protection against the cold), and thin in the summer. The elderly and the young have thinner blood and therefore are prone to illness. Illnesses commonly attributed to cold exposure include flu, bronchitis, pneumonia, and arthritis. Women are especially susceptible to cold during menstruation and postpartum bleeding, and may be advised to avoid getting chilled, taking a bath, or walking in the rain during these times (Snow, 1983).

Dirt is a second common cause of natural illness in Black folk medicine. The body may be unclean due to inadequate bathing, irregularity in bowel function, impeded menses, and sexual excess. Dirt or impurities in the body are associated with "hot" conditions: fever, inflammation, and skin eruptions (e.g. measles and skin cancer). One consequence of this focus on dirt is a preoccupation with digestion and elimination. Laxative dependence is common. Menstruation is also believed to be a means of expelling dirt from the body and deviation from the normal pattern (especially light flow) is worrisome. Contraceptives that affect menstruation patterns may therefore be unacceptable to some Black women (Snow, 1983).

A third commonly mentioned cause of natural illness is improper diet. Dietary factors are seen as determinants of the conditions "high blood" and "low blood." High blood commonly indicates that there is too much blood in the body, but may also refer to too much blood in the upper body. High and low blood are seen as acute conditions and are usually treated by diet and home remedies. High blood is believed to be caused by "rich" food: red foods (blood builders) such as beets, carrots, grape juice, red wine, and red meat. Symptoms of high blood include dizziness, headache, "swimming in the head," and falling out (sudden collapse) (Jackson, 1981). Treatments include substances which "thin" the blood and are often white or colorless. Examples include astringents such as vinegar, lemon juice, olive or pickle juice, garlic, and Epsom salts (Snow, 1983). Obviously, confusion of the term high blood with high blood pressure (hypertension) could be a problem if the patient self-treats hypertension with pickle juice or fails to take medications because of the belief that traditional cures will correct high blood pressure. Other blood conditions include bad blood, unclean blood, and thin blood (Jackson, 1981). An illness may be attributed to any of a number of causes, depending on which aspects of the patient's life have been neglected. For example, a stroke may be blamed on improper diet or witchcraft. Illness is seen as an "attack" on the individual by outside forces, and cures are often instantaneous (Snow, 1983).

Beliefs regarding unnatural illnesses reflect the world view of a hostile environment in which there is little control over life. In this setting, belief in magic is not surprising. Charms, spells, fixes, and hexes may be used to control undesirable situations; the most common are those dealing with problems of love and envy. Symptoms of unnatural or magical illness are generally gastrointestinal or behavioral. Commonly the hex or poison is hidden in the victim's food or drink. It is believed that animals (such as snakes and lizards) can be deposited in the body, thrive within, and cause illness. Some people are so fearful of being poisoned that they won't eat away from their own homes. Only traditional healers (not physicians) have the power to cure such unnatural illnesses (Snow, 1983; Freebairn and Gwinup, # 2, 1979).

Traditional treatment practices. Many Blacks are described as present oriented with a fatalistic outlook. Traditionally, self-treatment is the predominant method of health care. Jackson (1981) reported that illnesses most often treated in the home were either those perceived as not serious, those not recognized as having other treatments, or those recurring illnesses where the individual felt able to resume the treatment. Health care professionals need to be aware of some dangerous methods of self-treatment: for example, laxative abuse and oral doses of kerosene, turpentine, and mothballs (Snow, 1974).

Maintenance of health is based on moderation, including proper diet, rest, and exercise. In addition to care of the body, a healthy lifestyle includes care of one's soul and relationships with God and other human beings (Snow, 1983). Besides such practical measures, health maintenance may include magical practices. For example, it is important to observe and heed messages in nature (the signs; moon and planet positions and seasons) which may be believed to affect the functions of the human body. Other customs, found especially in the south, include use of roots, herbs, oils, powders, tokens, amulets, and burning candles. Black cultural healers (spiritualists, voodoo priests) provide psychological support (Bloch, 1983). Jackson (1991) found that 9 percent of Blacks used traditional healers not including friends, family, and ministers. It is likely that successful healers share the world view of their clients and apply treatments that allow them to regain physical, social, and spiritual balance. Prayer is the most common traditional method for treating illness (Spector, 1985).

Caribbean immigrants. Traditional beliefs as to the causes of illness among Caribbean (Jamaican, Haitian, and Bahamian) immigrants are most common among low income people. Mitchell (1983) identified six explanations for the causes of illness: cold, gas and wind, heat, bile, blood imbalances, and germs. Traditional medicines act by their qualities of bitterness, cutting, cooling, scraping and building, scratching, purging or washing out, and drawing out. Jamaican traditional medicine prescribes treatments based on symptoms. This can lead to problems in the Western health care system because the traditional medicines all have specific qualities. Caribbean people need to experience some traditionally defined effect from their medication. They especially want to know that the disease is being removed from the body. Western medicines may be perceived as useless because they don't meet expectations. Mitchell (1983) concluded that the most important actions Western care givers can take are to teach their clients about how the prescribed drugs work and help fit them into the traditional beliefs. Lack of information and misuse of over-the-counter drugs can be major barriers to compliance with Western treatments.

In summary, there are two important points to remember about these health beliefs and treatments: (1) they are completely foreign to many Blacks, and (2) they are shared by low-income Whites from the same geographical areas.

Health Status in the United States

Life expectancy for Blacks has been lower than for Whites ever since this data was first recorded. However, every year in the 1900s has shown improvement for both groups until 1984–1986 when the life expectancy of Blacks decreased. Health experts say the reasons are due to early deaths of male Blacks from murder, violence related to drugs, AIDS, pneumonia (which may be related to AIDS), infectious diseases, and social factors (homelessness, poor nutrition, and cuts in Medicare) (Halpert, 1988). Black men are becoming a population at risk, because of overrepresentation in jail, discrimination in the legal system, poor education, unemployment, and poor or no health care (White and Parham, 1990). The consequences are early death from homicide, drug abuse, suicide, and accidents.

A person's chances of being murdered depend on who that person is (Table 2-5). Debro (1988) indicated that the high rate of homicide among African Americans was the result of few economic opportunities with little money and capital, lack of skills, segregated schools with inadequate education, class differences, and alcohol abuse. The problem of high mortality can be expected to get worse because health care is becoming even less available, cigarette smoking is high among Black males (Table 2-6) who have the highest rate of lung cancer in the U.S. (Table 2-5), heavy consumption of alcohol along with refusal to be treated if treatment is even available, and an educational system that is not effective for Black males (White and Parham, 1990).

Compared to Whites, Blacks have excessive deaths from homicides, accidents, infant mortality, strokes, cirrhosis, cancer, and diabetes. Comparison of mortality from 1973–74 to 1985 shows a 27 percent decrease in deaths from coronary heart disease and a 58 percent decrease in stroke deaths for Blacks. These decreases were accompanied by an overall decrease in hypertension probably because more people were being treated, but not by a decrease in obesity as might be expected. Also, during this time there was no decrease in the prevalence of cigarette smoking; however, heavy smoking did decrease among Black men (Folsom, et al., 1987). Hypertension is twice as prevalent among Blacks as Whites; it starts at an earlier age and is more severe (Spector, 1985). Nationally, Blacks make up 12 percent of the population but are 34 percent of the people with end stage renal disease, a consequence of hypertension (Gaston, et al., 1993).

Kong (1984) speculated that increased risk of hypertension among minorities is related to their social devaluation. He suggested that the internalized feelings of anger, anxiety, and rejection result in strategies which overcompensate in an attempt to gain some power. The six strategies themselves can result in poor health: (1) Battlers take on anyone anytime; (2) Escapists are isolated from society; they rely on welfare programs and are found in jails; (3) Imitators try to copy the behaviors of the dominant group; (4) Consumers purchase material goods; (5) Deviators are dropouts; they abuse drugs, gamble, and steal; and (6) Pleasure seekers search for short term pleasures. According to Kong (1984), because all these strategies fail, they result in increased stress. Thus, stress from the original social devaluation and from the compensating strategies causes physiological reactions leading to hypertension. Without stating his sources, Kong reported that in all "out-groups of society—the poor, the uneducated, the weak, the ugly, the obese, the old, the handicapped, the under-employed and the unemployed—a greater predisposition to hypertension apparently exists" (p. 34–35). He explained that hypertension does occur among in-group members because some people do not perceive themselves as successful. The ideal person in American society is intelligent, has money and status, and is physically attractive; the farther a person is from the ideal, the greater their stress (Kong, 1984).

Research tends to support Kong's thesis. A group of medical doctors (Klag, et al., 1991) reported research findings in which they proposed that if hypertension in Blacks is genetic, as some believe, blood pressure would vary depending on skin color. That is, Blacks with the darkest skin color would have the highest percentage of African ancestry and the most hypertension. These researchers found no association between skin color and hypertension among their Black subjects. However, when they analyzed their data for socioeconomic status and education, they found that among Blacks of low socioeconomic status with no high school education there was a positive association between skin color and hypertension. In persons of higher socioeconomic status with high school degrees, there was no relation between skin color and blood pressure. In discussing their results, the authors speculated that "persons of lower socioeconomic status presumably would be more susceptible to the stress created by limited access to economic and social resources associated with having darker skin color" (p. 602). Richardson (1990) also concluded that socioeconomic status may have more effect on health than race. Other researchers have speculated that hypertension among Blacks is related to preferential survival of hypertensive individuals who retained salt and water. Water retention might have favored survival during the long ocean voyage from Africa to the U.S. and under the severe work conditions of slavery. This theory has not been confirmed (Fackelmann, 1991).

The incidence of diabetes mellitus among African Americans is high, especially among women who have an accompanying high rate of obesity (Lieberman, 1988). The complications of diabetes are severe among Blacks. Compared to White diabetics, Blacks have 40 percent more eye disease (retinopathy), 4 times more kidney disease, 2 times more amputations of lower extremities, and other increased complications (Lieberman, 1988; Diabetes in Minorities, 1989).

Sicklecell anemia is a genetic disorder in which the red blood cells "clump" in the veins, resulting in severe pain. In children, growth is slow and there may be jaundice and protruding abdomens caused by enlarged livers and spleens. In the U.S., sicklecell anemia occurs primarily in Blacks with about 8 percent having the disorder. Blacks may refer to sicklecell anemia as bad blood. Adults who have the problem can be counseled on the risk of bearing children with the disorder (Wright and Phillips, 1988).

Infant mortality in the first year of life is at least twice as high for African Americans as for Whites. In their study of infants born to college educated parents, Schoendorf, et al. (1992) concluded that Black and White infants of normal birth weight had similar mortality rates, and Black infants had excessive deaths only because of greater numbers of low birth weight infants. Kempe, et al. (1992) studied the cause of premature births among Black women and concluded that there were many medical causes of premature delivery in African American women and that effective preventative measures would have to address all possible causes. Attempts to decrease infant mortality have been based on assumptions that the behaviors of African American women are the cause of low birth weight. Yet, public health programs intended to improve the problem have not helped. Many people believe that the underlying social causes must be addressed and that blaming the victim is not a viable approach (Gates-Williams, et al., 1992).

Studies show that Black youths do not drink as much alcohol as White youths. However, heavy drinking among Black males begins after the age of 30 (Herd, 1986). During slavery, alcohol was consumed by Blacks as a means of escape as well as a form of recreation. Drinking on weekends and holidays was encouraged by the White slave owners. This pattern of drinking continues today. Blacks are more likely than Whites to drink in groups and at parties (Harper, 1989). Alcohol contributes to problems related to crime, automobile accidents, family crises, and unemployment. Blacks who drink heavily may deny alcoholism and resist treatment (Harper, 1989; Brisbane and Wells, 1989).

Some Blacks believe that alcoholism is the result of behavioral problems and alcohol can be consumed in large amounts as long as the person decides to act properly. Others believe that alcoholism is caused by racism, poverty, and other social problems; once these conditions are corrected the need to abuse alcohol will disappear. Others think drinking alcohol is sinful, and they pray to help stop the sinning. Men are likely to accept alcohol abuse as normal behavior. Because there is a lack of understanding about alcoholism, there is little support for treatment, and there are few treatment or preventative programs available (Brisbane and Wells 1989).

Esophageal cancer and cirrhosis are related to heavy alcohol consumption. The rate of cirrhosis among Blacks is twice that of Whites (Table 2-5), and esophageal cancer is 10 times higher among Black males ages 35-44 than White males. It was estimated that Blacks (12 percent of the population) account for as much as 25 percent of the alcohol consumed. Even though fewer Blacks drink alcohol than Whites, those who do drink, drink more. Black women are more likely to abstain than White women (Black community ties . . ., 1989).

Although African Americans are about 12 percent of the population, they suffer from 30 percent of all AIDS cases. This increasingly high rate of infection is primarily due to intravenous drug use among males, who transmit the disease sexually to females (Bowser, 1992).

This all adds up to a probability of dying for U.S. Blacks that is higher than in some of the world's poorest nations (Gambia, India, and El Salvador) (Murry, 1990). Many poor inner city Blacks obtain all their health care from hospital emergency rooms. For them, preventative care is not an option (Willis, 1992). In Harlem, an inner city of New York City which is populated 96 percent with low income African Americans, statistics spell out some of the problems of inner city health.

Based on the 1980 census, the median family income in Harlem was $6,497, compared to $12,674 for all U.S. Blacks and $21,023 for the U.S. total population. For 40.8 percent of Harlem families, incomes were below the poverty level. Health needs in Harlem are high and health services low compared to the per capita averages in New York City. McCord and Freeman (1990) reported that during 1980 in Harlem the emergency room hospital use was 73 percent higher per capita, outpatient services were used 134 percent more per capita, and the number of physicians per 1000 people was 74 percent lower than in other parts of New York City. For men over 40 years old, death rates in Harlem were higher than in Bangladesh, one of the poorest countries in the world. In Harlem, a substantial portion (35 percent) of the excess deaths for persons under 65 years of age were caused by violence and drug abuse, but the other major causes of all deaths were cardiovascular disease (23.5 percent), and cancer (12.6 percent). Since excessive chronic disease rates are related to lifestyle factors, including tobacco use, diet, alcohol and other drugs, health education could improve health status in Harlem and other inner cities (McCord and Freeman, 1990).

One factor that puts Blacks at greater health risk is lack of health education and underrepresentation in the health professions. Airhihenbuwa (1989) cited 1977 statistics that show 6.6 percent of students who enter medical school are Blacks and 2.6 percent of physicians are Blacks, compared to about 12 percent representation in the total population. When ill, Blacks prefer to be seen by Black health care professionals. Because of cost, Blacks have less access to health care and the quality of care that is received is lower compared to White care (Airhihenbuwa, 1989).

Food and Nutrition in the United States

No single dietary pattern exists for Blacks. Southern Black cooking developed in the period of slavery. Black slaves either worked in the fields or were house workers. Those who worked in the fields prepared foods in quantity either with minimum cooking or by leaving the pot boiling all day. Stews of dried beans, peas, and greens were used commonly. Hoecake, a cornbread baked on the back of a hot hoe or on hot rocks, was eaten frequently. Cuts of meat not eaten by Whites were given to the slaves (pig's tail, feet, chitterlings or fried small intestine, and ears). Blacks who worked in the homes of the masters ate the same foods as Whites: fried chicken, fried pies, potato salad, hot biscuits, and rolls. Pork was the main meat (Lowenberg and Lucas, 1976).

Soul food reflects the feeling of kinship which originated from the necessity to survive by eating leftovers and scraps from the slave-owner's kitchen. Soul food is a cultural blend of influences from American Indians, Europeans (French, English, and Spanish), and Africans. It is simple, economical, and delicious; it is symbolic of Black hospitality.

Two basic methods of cooking are Southern (Black) boiling and frying. Traditionally there are two or three *boiling* days and about three *frying* days each week. Boiled foods are served at dinner and fried foods at breakfast and dinner. The main *heavy* foods served at dinner are meat, dry beans and peas, and greens. A light meal does not contain these foods. *Heavy* foods can be boiled or fried and they "stick with you." *Light* foods "don't stick with you" and are served for breakfast, lunch, and snacks (Jerome, 1975).

Contemporary meal patterns of Blacks are similar to those of Whites from the same geographical area and with similar socioeconomic status. It is worth noting that low income could be a factor in food selection. Another factor important in food selection is lactose intolerance. Many Blacks are unable to consume milk for this reason (Cassidy, 1982). Some Blacks are Muslims and practice dietary restrictions (see Chapter 5); Muslims avoid pork, alcohol, and soul foods which may be prepared with lard (Spector, 1985).

In the North, Blacks consume more beef, potatoes, citrus fruit, and milk, and less pork, chicken, lard, cornmeal, sugar, greens, and legumes than in the South (Jerome, 1980). The U.S. military has studied food preferences of military personnel for many years. Grilled steak was found to be the most preferred food for both Black and White men, while tossed green salad was the preferred food for Black and White women. In a study controlled for the geographical origin of respondents, Blacks were more likely to consume soul food items and popular Southern foods than Whites from the same area. Thus, some foods consumed by Blacks were not acceptable to Whites (boiled pig's feet, collard greens, and grits). The most striking food difference was a long list of fruit-flavored drinks consumed by Blacks but not Whites. Researchers have found that the use of soda pop and artificial, fruit-flavored drinks is high among Blacks.

In the military studies, food preferences of Blacks were: fruit and vegetable juices, fruit drinks, iced tea, hot breads, doughnuts, breakfast cereals and pancakes, fish and seafood, and canned fruits. Rated among the top 20 foods preferred significantly more by Blacks than by Whites were barbecued spare ribs, fried chicken, corn bread, sweet potato pie, and collard greens (Wyant and Meiselman, 1984).

Pica, the practice of ingesting non-food items such as clay, dirt, ice, laundry starch, has been reported among children and adults of all races, most frequently among low-income people and especially among pregnant Black women. The most frequently consumed substance is laundry starch (Argo). Mexican and White migrant workers also practice pica, with the most frequently used substance being dirt (Brun and Pangborn, 1971). Causes of pica are not known. It has been suggested that it is related to nutritional deficiencies of iron or other minerals or vitamins; however, not all researchers agree. Pica may be based on cultural practices and tradition passed down for generations (Grivetti and Paquette, 1978).

Blacks have been found to be more malnourished than Hispanics or Whites (Ten State Nutrition Study, 1972). In reporting on a review by Jerome, Sanjur (1982) indicated that calcium and vitamin C were the two nutrients most likely to be deficient in Black diets. Since Blacks do eat a variety of vegetables and drink fruit juices, it must be assumed that either the selection of foods is particularly low in vitamin C or the long cooking practices destroy the vitamin. The lack of calcium is apparently due to low intake of milk related to dislike and lactose intolerance. Despite the low intake of calcium, it is common knowledge that Blacks are less subject to osteoporosis than Whites (Groziak and Diemond (1989). Armstrong and Larsen (1990) confirmed a low calcium intake among urban Black men of high socioeconomic status. They also found high intakes of meat, fish, poultry, and fast foods.

Implications for Health Care

Communication among people of different cultures may be enhanced by observing guidelines of common courtesy. Such as using titles (Mr., Mrs., Ms., or Miss) unless already on a first-name basis (Willis, 1992). Blacks should be treated the same as anyone else, as individuals with unique needs.

Older Blacks may be subservient, while young people may be hostile. As always, it is important to develop trust. The importance of direct eye contact may vary from person to person, but it may insult a Black person to abruptly break off eye contact (cut-eye).

Patronizing or condescending behavior should be avoided; this includes attempts to impress clients by discussing other Black friends (Bloch, 1983). Acknowledge differences related to race rather than ignore them.

A patient's cultural beliefs and understandings of illness should be acknowledged and discussed in the clinical setting. Self-treatment among African Americans is common, so the health professional should inquire about use of these treatments (Greathouse and Miller, 1981). Self-treatment and traditional medicines must be accepted. Any humiliating comment will increase the client's perception of racism (Spector, 1991). If remedies being used are harmless, they should not be forbidden. Every effort should be made to incorporate the patient's health and illness beliefs into the treatment plan. Family members should be included in treatment plans (Bloch, 1983).

Effective educational methods include an oral/visual approach with encouragement of family involvement. Client feedback should be oral (Willis, 1992). Messages regarding health promotion need to be transmitted through Black communities by trusted people who live there and are well-known.

As discussed in Chapter 5, some Blacks are Muslims who follow dietary restrictions. In addition to dietary restrictions, Muslims may refuse to use insulin manufactured from the pancreases of pigs (Spector, 1991).

Blacks may be suspicious of clinical tests. They may fear that they are being used as experimental subjects (Greathouse and Miller, 1981). This fear could stem from the Tuskegee syphilis experiment conducted by the U.S. Public Health Service from 1932 to 1972. In this study, the health of 400 illiterate Black men was observed by a medical team for 40 years or until the subjects died, at which time autopsies were performed. The purpose was to learn about the effects of syphilis on the body. These men were never informed about why they were being studied or even that they had syphilis. They submitted to the study because they were promised burial expenses. When penicillin was discovered in 1946, the men were not treated and the experiment was not stopped. When this situation finally was exposed, the doctors claimed the men had been told they had *bad blood* and the failure to stop the experiment after the discovery of penicillin was typical protocol for the time (Jones, 1993). Many Blacks are familiar with this experiment and may not trust health providers as a result.

Elderly Blacks are more likely than Whites to occupy useful family roles and less likely to be institutionalized (Holmes, 1983). Home care is often preferred to nursing home placement. The illness of family members is viewed as a family illness, and members will likely be involved in care giving (e.g., family and friends will come and "sit up" with the patient in the hospital).

Health care providers need to be sensitive to the historical perspective and the values, beliefs, and culture of African Americans in the United States. It is important to use all available social support systems including church, kin, coworkers, and social service agencies (Wilson and Stith, 1991; Todisco and Salomone, 1991). In addition, White health care providers need to consider their own values and be aware of how these might influence interactions with African Americans. It is helpful to have some idea of what it is like to be Black. Remember that each person is unique and that generalizations should not be made (Todisco and Salomone, 1991).

References Cited

Airhihenbuwa, C. 1989. Health education for African Americans: a neglected task. *Health Education* 20(5):9-14.

Armstrong, J. and B. Larson. 1990. Dietary practices and concerns of adult urban black men of high socioeconomic status. *Journal of The American Dietetic Association* 90(12):1716-1717.

Benjamin, L. 1991. *The Black elite: facing the color line in the twilight of the twentieth century.* Chicago: Nelson-Hall, Publishing.

Black community ties to alcohol and tobacco. 1989. *The San José (CA) Mercury News*, Aug. 14.

Black men's college enrollment registers a dramatic decline. 1989. *San Jose (CA) Mercury News*, Feb. 5, p. 18A.

Bloch, B. 1983. Nursing care of black patients, Chapter 3 in *Ethnic nursing care: a multicultural approach*, edited by M. Orque, B. Bloch, and L. Monrroy. St. Louis: C. V. Mosby.

Brisbane, F. and R. Wells. 1989. Treatment and prevention of alcoholism among Blacks, in *Alcoholism in minority populations*, edited by T. Watts and R. Wright, Jr. Springfield, IL: Charles C. Thomas Publisher.

Bowser, D. 1992. Cross-cultural medicine, a decade later. African American culture and AIDS prevention, from barrier to ally. *The Western Journal of Medicine* 157(3):286-289.

Brun, C. and R. Pangborn. 1971. Reported incidence of pica among migrant families. *Journal of The American Dietetic Association* 58(5):417-420.

Cassidy, C. 1982. Subcultural prenatal diets of Americans, in *Alternative dietary practices and nutritional abuses in pregnancy*; Proceedings of a workshop. Food and Nutrition Board, Commission on Life Sciences, Committee on Nutrition of the Mother and Preschool Child, National Research Council. Washington, D.C.: National Academy of Sciences.

Cohn, A. 1990. Young Black male: odds are 1 in 3 will go to jail. *San José (CA) Mercury News*, Nov. 2, p. 1D.

Cole, J. 1970. Culture: Negro, black, and nigger. The black scholar, cited by L. Llorens in Black culture and child development. *The American Journal of Occupational Therapy*, Vol. xxv (3):144-148.

Coner-Edwards, A. and J. Spurlock, editors. 1988. *Black families in crisis: the middle class*. New York: Brunner/Mazel Publishers.

Debro, J. 1988. Homicide in Black communities: A public health perspective, in *Ethnicity and health* edited by W. Van Horne. The University of Wisconsin System, WI: Institute of Race and Ethnicity.

Diabetes in minorities. 1989. National Institutes of Health, Dept. of Health and Human Services, Public Health Service. *Diabetes Dateline* 10(1):1-2.

Fackelman, K. 1991. The African gene? *Science News* 140(Oct. 19):254-5.

Freebairn, J. and K. Gwinup. 1979. *Cultural diversity and nursing practice: instructors manual, #2 Folk health practices - illness, #7 Overcoming language barriers, #8 Beyond language*. Irvine, CA: Concept Media, Inc.

Folsom, A., O. Gomez-Marin, J. Sprafica, R. Princas, S. Edlavitch, and R. Gillum. 1987. Trends in cardiovascular risk factors in an urban Black population, 1973-74 to 1985: The Minnesota Heart Study. *American Heart Journal* 114:1199.

Gardner, J. and D. Herz. 1992. Working and poor in 1990. *Monthly Labor Review* 115(12):20-28.

Gaston, R., I. Ayres, L. Dooley, and A. Diethelm. 1993. Racial equity in renal transplantation. *Journal of the American Medical Association* 270(11):1352-1356.

Gates-Williams, J., M. Jackson, V. Jenkins-Monroe, and L. Williams. 1992. Cross-cultural medicine, a decade later; the business of preventing African-American infant mortality. *The Western Journal of Medicine* 157(3):350-356.

Gelman, D. 1988. Blacks and Whites in America. *Newsweek* March 7, p. 18-23.

Greathouse, B. and V. Miller. 1981. The Black American, Chapter 4 in *Culture and child rearing* by Anne Clark. Philadelphia: F. A. Davis Co.

Green, J. 1982. *Cultural awareness in the human services*. Englewood Cliffs, NJ: Prentice-Hall, Inc.

Grivetti, L. and M. Paquette. 1978. Culture, diet, and nutrition: selected themes and topics. *Bioscience* 28(3):109-112.

Groziak, S. and L. Diemond. 1989. Diet and nutrition related diseases of ethnic minorities. *School Food Service Journal* 43(6):82.

Halpert, D. 1988. Life expectancy of U.S. Blacks falls while Whites gain. *San José (CA) Mercury News*, Dec. 14, P. 1A.

Harper, F. 1989. Alcoholism and Blacks: an overview, in *Alcoholism in minority populations*, edited by T. Watts and R. Wright, Jr. Springfield, IL.: Charles Thomas Publisher.

Heckler, M. 1985. *Report of the Secretary's Task Force on black and minority health, Volume 1, Executive summary*. Washington, D.C.: U.S. Department of Health and Human Services.

Herd, D. 1986. *A review of drinking patterns and alcohol problems among U.S. Blacks*. Department of Health and Human Services. Washington, D.C.: U.S. Government Printing Office.

Herskovits, M., Editor. 1966. *The new world Negro, selected papers in Afroamerican studies*, edited by F. Herskovits. Bloomington: Indiana University Press.

Holmes, L. 1983. Other cultures, elder years, Chapter 8 in *Minority aged in America*. Minneapolis, MN: Burgess Pub. Co,

Incomes decline for Black Americans while conditions improve for Whites. 1988. *Spartan Daily (San José State University, San José, (CA)*, Sept. 2.

Jackson, J. 1991. *Life in Black America*. Newberry Park, CA: SAGE Pub. Inc.

Jackson, J. 1981. Urban Black Americans, in *Ethnicity and medical care*, edited by A. Harwood. Cambridge: Harvard University Press.

Jerome, N. 1980. Diet and acculturation: the case of Black American immigrants, in *Nutritional anthropology, contemporary approaches to diet and culture*. Pleasantville, New York: Redgrave Publishing.

Jerome, N. 1975. Flavor preferences and food patterns of selected U.S. and Caribbean Blacks. *Food Technology* 29(6):46-51.

Jones, J. 1993. *Bad blood: the Tuskegee syphilis experiment*. New York: The Free Press.

Kempe, A., P. Wise, S. Barkan, W. Sappenfield, B. Suchs, S. Gortmaker, A. Sobel, L. First, D. Pursley, H. Rinehart, M. Kotelchuck, F. Cole, N. Gunter, and J. Stockbauer. 1992. Clinical determinants of the racial disparity in very low birth weight. *The New England Journal of Medicine* 327(14):969-973.

Klag, M., P. Whelton, J. Coresh, C. Grim, and L. Kueller. 1991. The association of skin color with blood pressure in U.S. Blacks with low socioeconomic status. *Journal of the American Medical Association* 265(5):599-602.

Kochman, T. 1981. *Black and white styles in conflict*. Chicago: The University of Chicago Press.

Kong, B. W. 1984. Dominant group values and the increased risk of hypertension in minorities. *Urban Health*, May:33-35.

Lieberman, L. 1988. Diabetes and obesity in elderly Black Americans, in *The Black American elderly*, edited by J. Jackson. New York: Springer Pub. Co.

Llorens, L. 1971. Black culture and child development. *The American Journal of Occupational Therapy*, Vol. xxv(3):144-148.

Lowenberg, M. and B. Lucas. 1976. Feeding families and children. *Journal of The American Dietetic Association* 68(3):207-215.

Martin, E. and J. Martin. 1986. The Black woman: perspectives on her role in the family, in *Ethnicity and women*, edited by W. VanHorne. University of Wisconsin System, American Ethnic Studies Coordinating Committee.

McCord, C. and H. Freeman. 1990. Excess mortality in Harlem. *The New England Journal of Medicine* 322(3):173-177.

Mitchell, M. 1983. Popular medical concepts in Jamaica and their impact on drug use. *The Western Journal of Medicine* 139:841-847.

Murry, J. 1990. Mortality among Black men. Correspondence section. *The New England Journal of Medicine* 322:205.

Richardson, J. 1990. *Aging and health: Black American elders*. Working Paper Series No. 4, Ethnographic Reviews. Stanford, CA: Stanford Geriatric Education Center.

Sanjur, D. 1982. *Social and cultural perspectives in nutrition*. Englewood Cliffs, NJ: Prentice-Hall, Inc.

Schoendorf, K., C. Hogue, J. Kleinman, and D. Rowley. 1992. Mortality among infants of Black as compared with White college-educated parents. *The New England Journal of Medicine* 326(23):1522-1526.

Snow, L. 1983. Traditional health beliefs and practices among lower class Black Americans. The Western Journal of Medicine 139:820-828.

Snow, L. 1974. Folk medical beliefs and their implications for care of patients: a review based on studies among Black Americans. *Annals of Internal Medicine* 81:82-96.

Spector, R. 1991. *Cultural diversity in health and illness*, 3rd edition. Norwalk, CT: Appleton and Lange.

Spector, R. 1985. *Cultural diversity in health and illness*, 2nd edition. Norwalk, CT: Appleton-Century-Crofts.

Staples, R. 1989. Changes in Black family structure: the conflict between family ideology and structural conditions, in *Gender in intimate relationships: a microstructural approach*, by B. Risman and P. Schwab. Belmont, CA: Wadsworth Pub. Co.

Taylor, A. 1986. Contours of black reconstruction. *The World and I*, Vol. 1 (6):204-215.

Ten State Nutrition Study (Highlights from the). 1972. *Nutrition Today* 7(4):4-11.

Todisco, M. and P. Salomone. 1991. Facilitating effective cross-cultural relationships: the White counselor and the Black client. *Journal of Multicultural Counseling and Development* 19(4):146-157.

U.S. Bureau of the Census. 1992. *Statistical abstract of the United States*, 112th edition. Washington, D.C.: Government Printing Office, Table 69, p. 55.

White, J. and T. Parham. 1990. *The psychology of Blacks: an African American perspective*, 2nd edition. Englewood Cliffs, NJ: Prentice-Hall.

Willis, W. 1992. Families with African American roots, Chapter 6 in *Developing cross-cultural competence, a guide for working with young children and their families*, edited by E. Lynch and M. Hanson. Baltimore: Paul Brookes Publishing Co.

Wilson, L. and S. Stith. 1991. Culturally sensitive therapy with Black clients. *Journal of Multicultural Counseling and Development* 19(1):32-43.

Wright, H. and L. Phillips. 1988. Psychosocial issues in sickle cell disease, Chapter 16 in *Black families in crisis: the middle class*, edited by A. Coner-Edwards and J. Spurlock. New York: Brunner/Mazel Inc.

Wyant, K. and H. Meiselman. 1984. Sex and race differences in food preferences of military personnel. *Journal of The American Dietetic Association* 84(2):169-175.

Chapter 11

CHINESE AMERICANS

The earliest Asian immigrants to the United States were the Chinese who came to California as early as 1785. In 1849 many Chinese came to work in the gold mines. Most Asian immigrants from 1849 through the 1940s were male. In 1890 there were 2,678 Chinese men for every Chinese woman (Parrillo, 1985). This shortage of women was not balanced until after World War II. The first groups of male workers came to the United States without women and families because most intended to return to their homelands after earning their fortunes. The practice of leaving families in China was encouraged by the Chinese government to assure that money was sent home to support elderly parents (Wong, 1988). Though hard-working, the Chinese men were typically paid low wages and worked long hours under harsh conditions. In addition to working in the gold mines, some were laborers on the railroads and others were farm laborers, fishermen, domestic servants, and unskilled factory workers. Many employers preferred Chinese to White workers because they worked harder for lower wages.

Because of the shortage of women, Asian communities attracted prostitution, leading to negative racial stereotypes. Some Asian men sought the company of White women which resulted in further racial tensions and the passage of legislation in 14 states outlawing marriages between Whites and non-Whites (miscegenation laws). These early Asian immigrants encountered discrimination and hostility. Whites established taxes which were specifically levied against Chinese workers. Laws were written prohibiting Chinese from many activities; for example, they couldn't testify against a White person in court, public agencies were not allowed to hire them, and they could not become U.S. citizens. Eventually, the resentment against Chinese grew into violence, and several incidents occurred in which Asians were killed. The federal government supported discrimination by passing the Chinese Exclusion Act of 1882 which, with additional restrictions, effectively stopped Chinese immigration (see Chapter 6).

Hostility and racial discrimination continued. Asians moved to their own communities (Chinatowns) where they opened small businesses (laundries, grocery stores, and restaurants) and worked as cooks and dishwashers. Recent immigrants and refugees are received with less hostility and racial prejudice than earlier immigrants. Since 1968, when the 1965 immigration laws took effect, the number of Asian immigrants has increased rapidly. During 1969-1973, 27.4 percent of all immigrants were Asian compared to 7.6 percent from 1961-1965 (Momeni, 1984). In 1990, 2.9 percent of the U.S. population was Asian and Pacific Islander (Table 11-1).

Asians in the United States have diverse backgrounds and countries of origin. Today, in the United States, the largest number of Asian immigrants comes from China. Of the total Asians and Pacific Islanders in the United States in 1990, 23 percent were Chinese, 19 percent Pilipino, 12 percent Japanese, 11 percent Asian Indian, and 11 percent Korean. Fifty-three percent were living in the Pacific states of Washington, Oregon, California, Alaska, and Hawaii. Asians made up 61.8 percent of the Hawaiian population and 10 percent of the California population (U.S. Bureau of the Census, 1992B). Most Chinese in the United States live in the West and Northeast, particularly in the metropolitan areas of San Francisco/Oakland, Los Angeles, and New York City (Chan, 1992). Chinese immigration is

Table 11–1.
Asian-Pacific Islander population characteristics.

Ethnic group	1990 % of U.S. population[1]	1979 Median family income dollars[2]	% Families below poverty, 1980[2]	% With 4 or more years college, 1980[2]
Total, Asian Pacific Islander	2.9	22,713	10.7	32.9
East Asian:				
Chinese	0.7	22,559	10.5	36.6
Japanese	0.3	27,354	4.2	26.4
Korean	0.3	20,459	13.1	33.7
Southeast Asian:				
Vietnamese	0.2	12,840	35.1	12.9
Pilipino and Pacific Islander:				
Pilipino	0.6	23,687	6.2	37.0
Hawaiian	0.1	19,196	14.3	9.6
Samoan	<0.05	14,242	27.5	7.3
Guamanian	<0.05	18,218	11.6	8.3
South Asia:				
Asian Indian	0.3	24,993	7.4	51.9
Total U.S. Population[2]	100.03	19,917	9.6	16.2

[1] U.S. Bureau of the Census, 1992. *Statistical Abstract of the United States, 112th ed.*, Washington, D.C.: U.S. Government printing office, *Table 16*.
[2] *Ibid.*, 1991. 111th ed., *Table 44*.
[3] Since Whites are 80.3% of the population, these values closely reflect the values for White Americans.

expected to remain high throughout the 1990s, partly because of the agreement between Great Britain and China converting Hong Kong to a Special Administrative Region with Chinese sovereignty beginning on July 1, 1997. Large numbers of Hong Kong residents are leaving because of fear of a repressive communist government.

Chinese Americans carry the burden of many stereotypes. They are perceived as mysterious and exotic. Men are typically seen as devious and sinister; women are viewed as sex objects. When Chinese appear in movies and television their roles are usually subservient. News reports often focus on unusual aspects of the culture such as acupuncture or martial arts (Chen-Louie, 1983). However, the health care professional who serves Chinese Americans must recognize these views as stereotypes and move on to a balanced understanding of attitudes and beliefs regarding health and illness.

In the United States, Asians are overrepresented at the highest levels of income and at the lowest levels. Many hold professional and skilled positions and have incomes higher than White Americans (Table 11-1). In 1991 the median family income of Asians in the United States was $42,245 compared to the median incomes for Whites of $36,915 and Blacks of $21,423 (U.S. Bureau of the Census, 1992A). Measures that use median income values, however, mask the number of Asians and Pacific Islanders who live in poverty and have low educational levels. Incomes vary considerably for the different Asian groups and within each group. Overall, Japanese in the U.S. have the highest incomes and Vietnamese the lowest. Many aged immigrant males live on very low incomes within ethnic communities (especially Chinatowns). In addition, recent refugees are crowded into ethnic communities which are troubled with poor living conditions, sweatshops, low income levels, youth gangs, and high rates of tuberculosis (Parrillo, 1985).

World View

Traditional Chinese values and behaviors are rooted in the teachings of Confucianism, Taoism, and Buddhism. Chinese medicine is based on the philosophy of Taoism, which means the "way of all nature." Tao is the law that regulates all heavenly and earthly matters. To live this philosophy, a person must let things take their natural course in order to maintain harmony (Hoang and Erickson, 1982). No one thing can exist in the universe without the others. Everything is in harmonious balance. According to Hoang and Erickson (1982), Buddhism teaches that there are "Four Noble Truths . . .: (1) life is suffering, (2) suffering is caused by desire, (3) suffering can be extinguished by eliminating desire, and (4) to eliminate desire one follows the eightfold path of right understanding, right purpose, right speech, right conduct, right vocation, right effort, right thinking, and right meditation" (p. 714). Confucianism teaches that people are destined by heaven (*t'ien*) to fulfill a specific mission on earth, fate guides a person's life (Chen-Louie, 1983), and social hierarchy stresses the worship of ancestors, king, teachers, and family (Hoang and Erickson, 1982). Confucius also taught that a person's body is a gift from parents and ancestors, and that at the end of life the body should be returned whole and sound (Spector, (1985). The collective teachings of Confucianism, Taoism, and Buddhism may be practiced including the belief in many gods that coexist. Buddhism mandates that people be responsible for their own behavior, but does not require the belief in any god (Chan, 1992).

Philosophical principles. One concept important to traditional health practices is the belief that each organism is affected by others in the universe and that the energy for regulating the universe is made up of two opposite forces, *yin* and *yang*. Everything is made up of these two opposing forces, and when they are not balanced, disease and disaster occur (Campbell and Chang, 1981).

The concepts of *yin* and *yang* and the five elements (*wu hsing*), which were developed from observations of nature, are the oldest of the philosophical principles. *Yin* (earth, moon, dark, cold, water, feminine, internal, negative, small, soft) and *yang* (heaven, sun, bright, warm, fire, masculine, positive, external, big, hard) represent the opposing forces of the universe which must remain balanced in order to maintain harmony and health. The five elements are earth, wood, fire, metal, and water. In addition to a relation with body organs, the five elements are associated with the planets, colors, tastes, emotions, and directions. Further classification of organs and diseases as *yin* or *yang* constitute a foundation for Chinese medicine and demonstrate the relations of people with nature. Based on Taoist teachings, there must be an harmonious relationship between people and nature. In addition, people need to understand the workings of nature and the ways in which humans become part of harmony in the cosmos (Pang, 1991; Ebrey, 1981; Matsumoto and Birch, 1983).

Social rules. The social rules govern everyday life and have been followed for many generations. They are an integral part of Chinese culture. Most rules for social interactions are rooted in Confucian teachings. Filial piety (*xiao*) demands unquestioning obedience to one's elders and superiors. Reciprocity (*pao*) is the Chinese equivalent to the Christian golden rule: "Do unto others as you would have them do unto you." These traditions are responsible for the strong emphasis on authoritarianism and obedience to one's elders including the expectation to care for parents in old age. Respect for oneself is demonstrated by exhibiting self-restraint and self-reliance. These practices promote social harmony in conjunction with benevolence and righteousness. Benevolence (*jen*) encourages sensitivity to others and includes treating them with goodness and kindness. Righteousness (*yi*) involves behaving in an appropriate and morally correct manner. These values in turn promote honor, or face (*mien*). It is important to maintain a favorable image in the eyes of others. Goodwill toward others is expressed through words or gifts, and is known as social reciprocity (*jen-ching*). It is expected that a favor will be returned through gifts or another favor. Traditional Chinese honor and respect their ancestors. They may believe that the spirits of ancestors hover around and watch over them (Char, 1981; Chen-Louie, 1983; Chan, 1992).

Family Structure and Interactional Styles

Many characteristics of Chinese American families reflect their traditional world view. Solidarity, harmony, and upholding the name of the family are valued. Elders are respected and cared for by their offspring, especially by sons. Educational and occupational achievements are highly valued, as they bring honor to the family (Chan, 1992). Conflict may arise in Chinese American families as a result of the contrast between the Chinese values of authoritarianism, filial piety, and self-control and the traditional American values of assertiveness, self-expression, and individualism (Chen-Louie, 1983).

Asians traditionally live in patrilineal, extended family groups. However, in the United Sates, extended family members may not live together (Chang, 1981). When women marry, they usually transfer their loyalties to their husband's family. The family is the primary social unit and psychological support system, and family interests are more important than those of the individual. Family members feel obliged to consider the effects of their actions on the family. Any feelings and behaviors that might disrupt family harmony are suppressed. To do otherwise could embarrass the individual and bring shame and loss of face to the entire family. Children are continuously reminded of their family obligations with discipline administered through the use of guilt and shame (Sue, 1981). Strong family values affect behaviors of U.S. Asians; less than 13 percent of Asian/Pacific Islander households are headed by women; this is lower than the percentage for White families (Table 2-3). Filial piety is an obligation in Asian families. Children are required to respect their elders and to care for their parents in old age. With some changing values and lifestyle pressures in the United States, the obligations of filial piety may not be fulfilled and elderly parents not cared for as they expected. On the other hand, the adult children of an aged parent may feel extreme guilt if it becomes necessary to place the parent in a long-term care facility (Orque, 1983).

Since the traditional Chinese family is patriarchal, decisions are usually made by the father; nevertheless, the mother's opinion is important. The husband is expected to earn and spend money, while the wife is expected to be thrifty and raise as many sons as possible. Sons are valued in the traditional family: since daughters move into the families of their spouses, they are not valued. Thus, the parents depend on sons to provide for them in old age. Children are taught self-control, and everyone in the family is expected to work for the family honor. The extended family consists of husband, wife, their unmarried children, grandparents, and married sons with their wives and children. However, in the United States, the early immigrants had few family members and if they were able to form families at all, the families tended to be nuclear.

After the 1965 immigration law took effect in 1968, Chinese women entered the United States in greater numbers. Some single men returned to China to participate in arranged marriages; many returned to the United States with their wives and lived in ghetto conditions in West coast Chinatowns (Wong, 1988). Today, many first-generation Chinese live in Chinatowns where the traditional culture is preserved. Major problems are found within Chinatowns including a limited job market and consequent under-employment, limited health and social services (especially for the young and elderly), social isolation of the elderly, crowding, inadequate housing, large numbers of elderly persons, low educational levels, long working hours at low wages, youth gangs, limited English language training, no monitoring of cultural healers, and inadequate health services (Chen-Louie, 1983).

Four types of Chinese households in the United States were identified by Gould-Martin and Ngin (1983):

- The sojourner is a young male who entered the U.S. to earn money. His usual employment is in restaurants and laundries in Chinatown. He speaks almost no English and lives alone with little hope of being joined by family.
- The old immigrant couple who were both able to enter the United States and raise their children in the U.S. In some cases the man came with the couple's children and left his wife in China to care for his parents until they died. These families have had problems with the generational differences of their children, who prefer American culture to Chinese. Even then, many parents managed to send their children to college and they now live in completely separate cultures. If the wife came to the U.S. years after the husband and children, she was not able to adapt to the changes and the cultural differences within the family, and many problems resulted. The "old immigrant couple" families usually live in poverty.
- The new immigrant family is based on a young male who has come to the U.S. to work; he hopes to bring his wife who will also work in a low-paying job. The new immigrants are underemployed, poor, and in dead-end jobs. They have large families to support including family members in China; and
- The acculturated, suburban family. If the father was born in China, he is a white collar worker or a professional; he may be American-born and educated. Both parents usually have college educations and their combined incomes are higher than the median U.S. family income. This family is highly acculturated, but retains some characteristics of traditional families such as filial piety (Gould-Martin and Ngin 1983; Wong, 1988).

Generational difficulties occur when the first-generation parents attempt to strictly control their children, who are determined to behave like their peers. The children do not want to be restricted by the values of their parents, and they sometimes rebel against strict authority (Heckler, 1985). Many Chinese families have become acculturated and, for them, the generational gap is no longer a problem.

The worship of ancestors also influences family members in determining appropriate behavior. Asians may believe that the actions of individuals will influence the lives of their descendants. Shame ("loss of face") is brought to the family when an individual does not behave in the expected way. An example of this is the expectation for children to excel in school. Asians value education, and despite the large number of recent immigrants and refugees, education and income levels exceed those for Whites (Table 11-1). Compared to other Americans, traditional Asians appear to be more conforming, obedient, introspective, dependent, and inhibited.

Communication

The traditional Chinese behaviors of self-control, self-discipline, social reciprocity, acceptance, and submission may be interpreted by the health care worker as modest and passive. When communicating with Chinese American patients, it is important to be sensitive to these values and encourage self-expression and participation in decision making (if the patient so desires). Elderly patients will sometimes refrain from asking questions, out of deference toward authority or to "save face" (Chen-Louie, 1983). However, many Chinese are highly acculturated and their interactions with others do not reflect strong traditional values.

Health Beliefs and Practices

For many Asians, Chinese medicine has a strong influence on health beliefs and practices. Asian Americans are more likely to use traditional Chinese health practices if they are recent arrivals or are residents of ethnic communities such as Chinatowns. Traditional Chinese medicine is a complex system in which each of the five elements corresponds to two organs or bodily systems, one of which is *yin* and the other *yang* (Mann, 1972). In a healthy person, *yin* and *yang* are in balance. Each of nature's elements is associated with human organs and diseases of those organs. The *yin* organs and their corresponding elements are: liver/wood, heart/fire, spleen/earth, lung/metal, and kidney/water. The *yang* organs and their corresponding elements are: gall bladder/wood, small intestine/fire, stomach/earth, large intestine/metal, and bladder/water. Each element corresponds to a season: wood to spring, fire to summer, earth to late summer, metal to fall, and water to winter. Winter and spring diseases are *yin*, and summer and fall diseases are *yang*. All of these relations are used in diagnosing and treating illness.

Chinese medicine also identifies two vital forces in the body that support life, *ch'i* and blood. *Ch'i* is described as an energy force derived from three sources: one's parents, the air of breath, and food and water. *Ch'i* flows through the body via pathways called meridians. Blood flows through the blood vessels and at certain locations there is believed to be an interaction between ch'i and blood. Like *yin* and *yang*, *ch'i* is present in all things. Imbalance, blockage, or deficiency of blood or *ch'i* will result in illness. Also, aging and fatigue are associated with a deficiency of *ch'i* or blood. Some Chinese may believe that having blood drawn will weaken the body, and they may be reluctant to do so because they do not understand that blood will be replenished. Hospitalization and surgery are also feared (Chen-Louie, 1983; Gould-Martin and Ngin, 1981).

The concepts of "hot" (*yang*) and "cold" (*yin*) are also used in reference to illness. A "hot" state may be caused by excessive intake of "hot" foods (examples: fried foods, spices, red foods, broccoli, wine, liver, and peanuts), and may be characterized by dry mouth and constipation. Digestive problems and exhaustion may also precipitate the "hot" condition. Conversely, overconsumption of "cold" foods (such as watercress, water, bamboo shoots, fruits, vegetables, and milk) or exposure to cold weather, wind, or rain may bring on the "cold" condition. Symptoms include dizziness, blurred vision, and respiratory problems. The elderly and women are believed to be especially susceptible to "cold." Harmony and balance between hot/cold and *yin/yang* must be maintained to prevent illness. Therefore, moderation is a key component of Chinese health beliefs (Chen-Louie, 1983; Gould-Martin and Ngin, 1981).

In addition to imbalance, wind and poison may also cause illness. Wind (*feng*) is believed to enter the body and cause symptoms such as bloating and flatulence. Arthritis and digestive disorders may be caused by wind. Children and postpartum women are especially susceptible to cold and wind. Poison (*tu*) may originate from outside the body (i.e., from food), or from within. Allergies and infections may be caused by poisons (Chen-Louie, 1983).

Magic and religion also enter into Asian folk medical beliefs. These concepts include "fright", an illness which occurs in children. Its symptoms are lack of appetite, mild fever, crying, and listlessness. Fright is caused by loss (or scattering) of the soul (Gould-Martin and Ngin, 1981). Many Asians believe that the soul resides in the head and that patting a child on the head may startle the soul and cause it to run away.

In Chinese medicine, diseases are diagnosed by physical appearance, listening to the body, asking the patient, and feeling (especially the pulses). Six pulses in each wrist are diagnosed by Chinese doctors and are believed to be controlled by *yin* and *yang*. Each pulse is related to specific organs. This very complex system associates a color with each organ. In a healthy body, the colors are fresh and shining (Yanchi, 1988).

Chinese medicine, as practiced in Chinatowns, is not pure traditional Chinese medicine, but is partly folk medicine based on religion and magic (Gould-Martin and Ngin, 1981). Chinese medicine does not distinguish between mental and physical illness (Chan 1992). An emotional imbalance disturbs organ function and an organ imbalance disturbs the emotions (Lin, 1983). Mental illness may be attributed to possession by spirits. No matter what the cause, mental illness brings shame to an Asian family and is generally hidden as long as possible (Muecke, 1983).

Treatment methods. In the United States, Asians may treat common medical problems at home with herbs, food, and patent medicines. More serious ailments may be taken to a cultural doctor or a Western health practitioner. It is a common practice for alternative medical treatments to be used at the same time as Western medicine. Prescriptions for herbal remedies, which are obtained from a variety of sources including friends, newspapers, and even contacts in China, are made up by Asian Herbalists. Other self-treatments and treatments used by cultural healers include acupuncture, coin-rubbing, cupping, moxibustion, dietary changes, massage, exercises, steam baths, and setting of bones. In addition, recommendations may be made about sleep, diet, work, and relaxation. Gould-Martin and Ngin (1981) found no evidence that the use of Chinese medicine prevented or delayed the use of Western medicine. These authors reported that Chinese were likely to continue Western treatment if traditional care was acknowledged rather than discounted by the Western practitioner. The major reason that Chinese Americans do not use Western medicine is the cost and their inability to pay. Additional barriers include language problems and lack of familiarity with Western medicine. Chinese women are traditionally modest and if they do use Western medicine, they prefer female physicians (Gould-Martin and Ngin, 1981).

Typically, Western medicine is seen as more effective for acute illnesses, whereas cultural healers are preferred for chronic conditions. Acupuncture (needle pressure) and acupressure (finger pressure) are methods designed to open the flow of *ch'i* in the meridians in order to restore the balance of *yin* and *yang*. Moxibustion is a treatment that uses burning wood held over certain meridian points in the treatment of *yin* diseases (Spector, 1991). Cultural healers include herbalists, acupuncturists, and bone setters. Many herbs, plants, and foods may be used as medication to restore balance to the body or prevent illness. In China, patent medicines are sold over-the-counter. They include a wide range of substances from antacids to wonder drugs. Some are dangerous, especially if used in conjunction with Western medications. Although there are many testimonials concerning the effectiveness of Chinese medicine, it has not been adequately studied in controlled research (Bonica, 1974).

Mental illness. Traditional Chinese medical theory also explains mental health behavior. Psychologic and physiologic functions are believed related. Each of five primary emotions corresponds to an internal organ. An emotional imbalance disturbs the functions of these organs, and, conversely, organ function affects emotions. As a result, moderation and emotional suppression are encouraged. If emotional or psychologic imbalance occurs, treatment focuses on physiologic methods; consequently, mental illness may be expressed through physical symptoms (somatization). This practice protects the patient and family against the shame and stigma associated with mental illness by providing an acceptable physical explanation for the problem (Lin, 1983).

Chinese families were observed to follow a typical coping pattern in dealing with severe mental illness. First, family members tried diligently to correct the problem within the family unit. Then, elders or friends were asked for help, followed by outside resources such as herbalists or religious healers. Finally, physicians were consulted. When the patient was labeled as mentally ill by a trusted physician or agency, treatment was usually accepted on an outpatient or inpatient basis. If hope for recovery faded, the mentally ill family member was sometimes rejected. The family accepted its fate and the patient was often institutionalized (Lin, 1983).

Health Status in the United States

Asian/Pacific Islanders are the healthiest group in the United States. Compared to Whites, they have no overall excessive deaths. However, there are problems within subgroups (Heckler, 1985). Recent immigrants and refugees are more likely than the general population to have tuberculosis, infectious diseases, and intestinal parasites. Some of these health problems go untreated because health care in the United States is not readily accessible. One doctor found 68 percent of the Chinese women he studied had no knowledge of the Pap test (Johnson, 1990). Many children do not receive inoculations to prevent communicable diseases. In California in the winter of 1989–90 an outbreak of measles was particularly severe for Asians.

Lifestyles of some Chinese Americans contribute to their health problems. Untreated mental illness is believed related to a high suicide rate. Crowded, unsanitary conditions in Chinatowns contribute to a high incidence of tuberculosis. Unfortunately, national health statistics do not break Asians into subgroups, so there is little information on the specific health problems of the Chinese.

In general, alcohol consumption is moderate, is usually acceptable, and is mostly consumed by males. Many, but not all, Asians have a physiological reaction to alcohol consumption called "flushing syndrome." When alcohol is consumed, the skin feels hot; other symptoms may include increased rate of breathing, increased heart rate, breaking out in hives, and headaches. It is believed that when alcohol is consumed its metabolism results in the build-up of a byproduct compound, acetaldehyde, related to the absence of an active enzyme which breaks it down (Suddendorf, 1989). The extent to which the lower alcohol abuse rate is due to the discomfort of the flushing syndrome is not known. Lin (1983) reported that "Alcoholism has never been a social or a medical problem in Chinese society anywhere in its long history . . ." (p.60). Chinese culture stresses moderate use of alcohol and emphasizes its consumption with food (Kitano, 1989). Intolerance of public drunkenness and the cultural pressure to avoid alcohol abuse are major reasons for moderation. In the United States there is some alcohol abuse within Asian communities, but few Asians participate in U.S. alcohol treatment programs. It is believed that families protect (hide) heavy drinking and, as a result, health care is not received (Kitano, 1989).

Food and Nutrition in the United States

Chinese cuisine is universally recognized for its rich variety of foods and regional differences. Chinese Americans consume a variety of foods from the four basic food groups with the exception of the milk group. Asians are usually lactose intolerant. Small amounts of milk can be consumed, but the tolerable amount depends on the individual. In addition, dairy foods are generally not available in Asian countries, and most people never learn to like the taste of milk and milk products. It isn't surprising, then, to realize that milk is not usually consumed by Asians even in the United States. If dairy foods are consumed, ice cream and flavored milks seem to be preferred. Many Asian immigrants do not like cheese. Calcium sources in Chinese diets include tofu and soy milk, but both must be fortified with calcium as soybeans are not a natural source. Fish and shellfish are eaten frequently. In the United States, many Chinese vegetables are only available in specialty stores. The usual cooking method is to stir-fry vegetables with small amounts of vegetable oil and small portions of meat in a wok. This is a rapid procedure in which few nutrients are lost. Chinese cooking methods are fast and use little fuel. Baking in ovens is not a traditional method of food preparation; however, in the United States, Chinese Americans may consume bakery goods. Rice is the staple food for most Chinese, but persons from northern China, where the weather is dry, consume wheat noodles and steamed wheat buns. Chinese balance their meals in portions of *fan* (rice and other grains and starchy staples) and *ts'ai* (meats and vegetables which are chopped and cooked). *Fan* is the primary food and is needed for satiety; *ts'ai* is secondary food which adds variety and flavor (Sanjur, 1982). Traditional Chinese meals usually do not include desserts. First generation Chinese in this country increase their intake of breakfast cereals, bread, and milk. They continue to eat rice, soy sauce, and a variety of fruits and vegetables (Chau, et al., 1990).

Many Chinese condiments such as monosodium glutamate and soy sauce are high in sodium. These are difficult for hypertensive patients to eliminate from their diets. Gradual reduction in the use of high sodium condiments is advised rather than sudden deprivation. Studies confirm that Chinese continue to eat traditional foods in the United States. Nutritional deficiencies of calcium, iron, and zinc have been reported (Sanjur, 1981).

Implications for Health Care

Refer to Chapter 13, Korean Americans.

References Cited

Bonica, J. 1974. Therapeutic acupuncture in the People's Republic of China. *Journal of the American Medical Association* 228(12):1544-1551.

Campbell, T. and B. Chang. 1981. Health care of the Chinese in America, Ch 11 in *Transcultural health care*, edited by G. Henderson and M. Primeaux. Menlo Park, CA: Addison-Wesley.

Chan, S. 1992. Families with Asian roots, Chapter 8 in *Developing cross-cultural competence: a guide for working with young children and their families*, edited by E. Lynch and M. Hanson. Baltimore: Paul H. Brookes Pub. Co.

Chang, B. 1981. Asian American patient care, Chapter 17 in *Transcultural health care*, edited by G. Henderson and M. Primeaux. Menlo Park, CA: Addison-Wesley Publishing Company, Inc.

Char, E. 1981. The Chinese American, Chapter 6 in *Culture and child rearing*, edited by Ann Clark. Philadelphia: F. A. Davis, Co.

Chau, P., H-S. Lee, R. Tseng, and N. J. Downes. 1990. Dietary habits, nutrition beliefs, and food practices of elderly Chinese women. *Journal of The American Dietetic Association* 90(4):579.

Chen-Louie, T-Y. 1983. Nursing care of Chinese American patients, Chapter 6 in *Ethnic nursing care: a multicultural approach*, edited by M. Orque, B. Bloch, and L. Monrroy. St. Louis: C. V. Mosby.

Ebrey, P., editor. 1981. *Chinese civilization and society, a sourcebook*; pp. 36-37, 404-406. New York: The Free Press.

Gould-Martin, K. and C. Ngin. 1981. Chinese Americans, Chapter 2 in *Ethnicity and medical care*, edited by A. Harwood. Cambridge, MA: Harvard University Press.

Heckler, M. 1985. *Report of the Secretary's Task Force on black and minority health, Volume 1, Executive Summary*. Washington, D.C.: U.S. Department of Health and Human Services.

Hoang, G. and R. Erickson. 1982. Guidelines for providing medical care to Southeast Asian refugees. *Journal of the American Medical Association* 248(6):710-714.

Johnson, S. 1990. Health care eludes Asians, panel says. *San José (CA) Mercury News*, April 21, p. 1A.

Kitano, H. 1989. Alcohol and the Asian American, in *Alcoholism in minority populations*, edited by T. Watts and R. Wright, Jr. Springfield, IL: Charles C. Thomas Publisher.

Lin, T. 1983. Psychiatry and Chinese culture. *The Western Journal of Medicine* 139(6), 862-867.

Mann, F. 1972. *Acupuncture: cure of many diseases*. London: William Heinemann Medical Books.

Matsumato, K. and S. Birch. 1983. *Five elements and ten stems*. Brookline, MA: Paradigm Publications.

Momeni, J. 1984. *Demography of racial and ethnic minorities in the United States*. Westport, CT: Greenwood Press.

Muecke, M. 1983. In search of healers: Southeast Asian refugees in the American health care system. *The Western Journal of Medicine* 139(6):835-840.

Orque, M. 1983. Nursing care of South Vietnamese patients, Chapter 8 in *Ethnic nursing care: a multicultural approach*, edited by M. Orque, B. Bloch, and L. Monrroy. St. Louis: C. V. Mosby.

Pang, K.-Y. 1991. *Korean elderly women in America*. New York: AMS Press.

Parrillo, V. 1985. *Stranger to these shores: race and ethnic relations in the United States*, 2nd edition, Chapter 8: The Asian immigrants. New York: John Wiley and Sons.

Sanjur, D. 1982. *Social and cultural perspectives in nutrition*. Englewood Cliffs, NJ: Prentice-Hall, Inc.

Spector, R. 1991. *Cultural diversity in health and illness*, 3rd edition. Norwalk, CT: Appleton and Lange.

Spector, R. 1985. *Cultural diversity in health and illness*, 2nd edition. Norwalk, CT: Appleton-Century-Croft.

Suddendorf, R. 1989. Research on alcohol metabolism among Asians and its implications for understanding causes of alcoholism. *Public Health Reports* 104(6):615-620.

Sue, D. 1981. *Counseling the culturally different*, Chapter 6, Cultural and historical perspectives in counseling Asian Americans. New York: John Wiley and Sons.

U.S. Bureau of the Census. 1992A. *Statistical abstract of the United States*, 112th edition. Washington, D.C.: Government Printing Office, Tables 41 and 42.

U.S. Bureau of the Census. 1992B. *Statistical abstract of the United States*, 112th edition. Washington, D.C.: Government Printing Office, Table 26.

Wong, M. 1988. The Chinese American family, in *Ethnic families in America*, 3rd edition, edited by C. Mindel, R. Habenstein, and R. Wright, Jr. New York: Elsevier.

Yanchi, L. 1988. *The essential book of traditional Chinese medicine, Vol. 1: Theory*. Translated by F. Tingyu and C. Laidi. New York: Columbia University Press.

Chapter 12

JAPANESE AMERICANS

Japanese in the U.S. are identified by their generational group, each with its own characteristic features. The *Issei* (first generation) immigrated to the United States between 1890 and 1924; most were young, single males. They worked as laborers on farms, railroads, and in lumber mills and canneries. Some started small family businesses such as grocery stores, hotels, barber shops, and gardening services. Victims of racial discrimination, the *Issei* established self-sufficient communities (Japantowns) and through hard work were able to collect modest savings. Laws were enacted to restrict the activities of Japanese in the United States (see Chapter 6), and they were not allowed to marry Whites or to own land. Through arranged marriages and "picture book" brides from Japan, many of the single men did marry.

Issei had great expectations for their children who were American citizens. They especially valued education as a way of improving their status. *Issei* family life was strengthened by the support of the organizations they developed in Japantowns. They had little interaction with people of the dominant culture (Kitano, 1988). Of the original *Issei* generation, most are now retired elderly or are deceased.

Many *Nisei* (second generation) were born in the U.S. during the pre-World War II period. In most cases, the Nisei are now the oldest of all family members. Although they achieved higher levels of education and greater fluency in English than their parents, they also retained many characteristics of Japanese culture. They experienced racism, and many remained close to Japanese communities (Hashizume and Takano, 1983). *Nisei* developed social groups and participated in Japanese community activities. They also adopted many American lifestyle practices and this caused conflict with their traditional *Issei* parents (Kitano, 1988).

In 1942, as a reaction to the bombing of Pearl Harbor, the United States government moved all Japanese Americans who lived in the states of Washington, Oregon, and California into detention camps. Presumed to be disloyal to the U.S. simply because of their race, these Japanese were imprisoned for seven months to three years under deplorable conditions. Life in the camps was organized according to American culture rather than Japanese culture, and this created further conflicts between parents and children. Men were no longer breadwinners and women became more independent. Children understood American culture better than their parents, and some children became the family protectors (Sobetani-Shibata, 1981). The older *Issei* maintained a fatalistic outlook, as expressed by the saying *shikata ga nai* ("It can't be helped"). However, the *Nisei* (who were American citizens by birthright) were emotionally scarred in addition to being financially devastated. Only a few of the Japanese living in Hawaii were taken into custody and held in detention camps despite their more sensitive location. Japanese represented 39 percent of the Hawaiian population; without them, Hawaii could not have functioned.

Many young *Nisei* males were allowed to leave the camps by volunteering in the United States Army during World War II. These men were physically small; their average height was 5'4" and weight in combat gear was 125 pounds. The famous 442nd regimental combat team of the 100th Battalion was made up of Japanese Americans and was the most decorated unit in the U.S. Army (Zich and Yamashita, 1986). After the war many *Nisei* attended colleges and were able to expand their employment opportunities. Nisei lifestyles are extremely variable depending on their degree of acculturation.

Many years later, in 1980, Congress established a commission to investigate the order of President Franklin Roosevelt to intern West Coast Japanese. The commission concluded that the order was a "grave injustice" and not justified by military necessity. The commission recommended that the victims be compensated for their losses. The U.S. government passed legislation to provide monetary compensation for these people, many of whom will be dead of old age and will never receive their money (House approves payments . . . , 1989).

Sansei (third generation) immigrants were born after World War II. For the most part this group is well-educated and affluent. They, and the *Yonsei* (fourth generation), are moving away from the traditional Japanese communities of their parents for education and employment (Hashizume and Takano, 1983). By 1981, 88 percent of *Sansei* children were attending college, and in California (where one-third of Japanese Americans live), Japanese family incomes were 15 percent higher than the state average (Zich and Yamashita, 1986).

Recent immigrants who arrived after 1965 are known as the *Shin-Issei* generation. These people will not be as acculturated as the *Sansei* and *Yonsei* generations. However, their knowledge of Western culture is much greater than that of the original *Issei* immigrants.

World View

The Japan of the *Issei* was a feudal land in which a rigid class system existed. Individuals were very conscious of their social position. Many of the cultural values of this society continue to influence Japanese Americans.

One highly valued characteristic among the Japanese is *gaman*, or self-control. This may appear to Westerners as perseverance or restraint. Suppression of emotions as well as self-sufficiency are encouraged. As a result, a patient may not complain even in the face of severe pain. Rather than seeking outside assistance or resources, the family may attempt to deal with its problems alone. *Damatte* means to avoid a verbal confrontation. A related concept is *enryo*, which is often observed as a quiet reserve. *Enryo* includes aspects of politeness, hesitation, and humility. It is the opposite of the assertiveness which is encouraged in American society. Thus, the unquestioning, undemanding Japanese American patient may be misunderstood or inadvertently ignored (Hashizume and Takano, 1983) which could lead to *shikata ga nai* (fatalism).

Behavior is also influenced by *haji* (shame). People must always behave according to society's rules of acceptability so as not to bring shame on themselves or their families. The importance of familial responsibilities is also embodied in the practice of filial piety (*koko*). In return for the responsibilities that parents have for their children, it is expected that parents will be respected and cared for in their old age by their children.

The world view and experiences of Japanese Americans have caused them to value time as a precious resource which is to be used wisely. Thus, they tend to be very punctual regarding appointments and treatment schedules (Hashizume and Takano, 1983). Time is M-time, but many other aspects of Japanese culture are polychronic. For example, in business, the Japanese take a long time to make decisions. Japanese men in Japan take their evenings to socialize with clients and associates. They are formal in business and do not use first names (Hall and Hall, 1987).

Japanese value education. In Japan, 99 percent of the population is literate. The group (be it family, work, or nation) is a very strong network where individuals strive to benefit the group, not themselves. The work force in Japan is very disciplined and employees are considered family. Japanese try to avoid conflicts, so Japan has few lawyers. Japanese Americans are thrifty; they save and invest much higher percentages of their incomes than other Americans. They believe in working hard and playing hard. Age and seniority are respected and in business are the major factors in determining promotion. However, merit promotions are increasing in Japan (Harris and Moran, 1987).

Family Structure and Interactional Styles

As in most Asian cultures, the traditional priorities of the extended family group take precedence over those of the individual. The high value placed on the group results in devaluation of the individual. Japanese believe in their saying, "the nail that sticks up is hit." They do not want to be singled out for praise or for blame. This is almost opposite to dominant-culture group behavior, where people are praised or blamed as individuals. Even when acculturated Americans work in groups, the group is viewed as a collection of individuals. In Japanese culture, the individual is subordinate to the group; if the group is successful then the individual is also successful. If someone does something wrong, then the group is responsible (Cathcart and Cathcart, 1988).

The strong group affiliation of the Japanese leads them to be dependent on the group, which is opposite to American cultural values of individual independence. Japanese are indebted to the group; ceremonies and holidays tend to celebrate the group and not the individual. For example, individual birthdays are not celebrated, but there is a boy's day and a girl's day (Samovar and Porter, 1988). Group relationships last a lifetime. For employees, time not spent at work, including vacations, is expected to be spent with fellow workers. This is very difficult for families because it causes the fathers and husbands to spend little time at home (Cathcart and Cathcart, 1988). When a Japanese man is employed by a company it is as if he were adopted into the company; this lifelong affiliation applies almost entirely to men. Not many Japanese women work (Hall and Hall, 1987). Younger women have lower paying jobs and are not accepted into the group in the same way as men (Cathcart and Cathcart, 1988).

The extended family continues from the past into the future. It may be made up of blood relatives and of individuals who join the family by "adoption." Family members assist one another in overcoming problems before attempting to seek outside help. The individual is dedicated to maintaining the good reputation of the family and to obeying and respecting the parents (Kitano, 1988). Japanese children are very close to their mothers. The girls are taught to be good wives and mothers. In Japan, there is tremendous pressure on the children to be accepted into the best universities; competition is so great that many become ill, some even commit suicide. For the women, there is little to look forward to when the children leave home because the husband spends much of his time socializing with clients and associates when not at work (Hall and Hall, 1987). The traditional family is patriarchal, but this is also changing because the father/husband is not home enough to maintain his role as the family decision maker.

In the United States, Japanese extended family members probably do not live together. Grandparents usually maintain separate houses. Most of today's Japanese families are parented by *Sansei* couples. Sixty percent have selected their own spouses and even to have married non-Japanese (Kitano, 1988). *Sansei* are more open and verbal than their parents and grandparents; although they are probably more reserved than most Whites and less likely to show affection in public. Education is highly valued and the children expect to work to get good grades. They usually retain some of their cultural concerns for others and do not want to "stand out," but the culture of most *Sansei* families is more American than Japanese (Kitano, 1988). Generally, children are willing to care for their parents in old age. Only when the situation becomes unmanageable will they consider placement in long term care facilities. Children usually express feelings of guilt if they are not able to care for their parents; the elderly expect to be cared for by younger family members. (Hashizume and Takano, 1983).

Communication

Communication patterns may vary among generations of Japanese Americans. The *Shin-Issei* often have difficulty communicating orally in English. They may prefer to have a Japanese-speaking health care provider or have an interpreter present. The Japanese language is very difficult to learn; and, for a Japanese person, English is difficult. Word selection in the Japanese language depends on the context and the rank, sex, and relationship of the receiving person (Ramsey and Birk, 1983).

Respect is shown for age or status through rules of communication. For example, *Shin-Issei* should not be called by their first names, because only children are addressed in this way in the traditional culture. Close friends or parents may call others by their first names if the suffix *-chan* (child) or *-san* (adult) is added. In the United States, many *Nisei* and most *Sansei* and *Yonsei* do not adhere to these rules.

Nonverbal (body) language is an important part of Japanese communication (Ramsey and Birk, 1983). This is evidenced in child rearing by gestures and facial expressions and by role modeling rather than by dispensing verbal orders and physical punishment (Hashizume and Takano, 1983).

Health Beliefs and Practices

The major belief systems of the Japanese include the concept that health is derived from a balance between the individual and society. Physiological imbalance can result from poor diet, lack of sleep, lack of exercise, or unhappiness. Some Japanese believe that eating certain combinations of food will cause illness. Japanese health beliefs have been shaped by several influences.

Shinto religion. In the Shinto religion, humans are considered inherently good. Evil, therefore, is brought about by spirits as punishment for incorrect behavior. Likewise, disease is caused by bodily contact with substances such as blood, corpses, or skin diseases. Purification rites are part of the Shinto religion, and this has led to the Japanese emphasis on cleanliness. Examples of this include the bathing ritual and use of herbal cathartics or laxatives (Hashizume and Takano, 1983).

Chinese medicine. Chinese medicine has also influenced the health beliefs of the Japanese. The concept that harmony and balance (particularly between oneself and society) lead to good health is shared throughout most of Asia and has influenced traditional health beliefs in the Western world as well. Conversely, disharmony or improper care of the body causes illness. Asian medicine treats the individual in relation to the environment; the goal is to restore equilibrium. Treatments are generally mild in comparison to Western medical practice. Natural herbs, acupuncture, and massage are among the therapies used.

Western medicine. Western medicine (including the germ theory of disease) has also influenced Japanese health beliefs and practices. Many Japanese Americans use both Western and traditional practitioners, depending on the situation and their past experiences (Hashizume and Takano, 1983).

Health Status in the United States

The Japanese emphasis on the group (family and society as a whole) may influence the health of the Japanese, including Japanese Americans. It has been suggested that family and community ties protect against illness by providing the individual with a sense of "coherence" which reduces the stress of adapting to an unfamiliar culture (Lock, 1983).

Although the traditional power of the group and the accompanying respect for authority are not usually openly challenged by the individual, they may be resisted indirectly. This phenomenon has been called "ritualistic resistance." It refers to the inward maintenance of nonconformist values while outwardly conforming with traditional behaviors (Lock, 1983). As a result of inward resistance, the Japanese personality has been described as multilayered, fostering psychological suppression. This in turn may be responsible for the observed tendency toward somatization (the expression of psychological distress by physical symptoms). Physical complaints may be the patient's way of communicating stress or feelings of oppression. Traditional Japanese health practices view physical and mental health as one. Japanese may believe that if physical balance is restored, emotional balance will follow (Lock, 1983).

Japanese Americans have a lower probability of death than Whites, and the rates of death for most identified causes are also lower than for Whites. However, as Japanese (in Japan and in the United States) become more westernized and eat diets more like American diets, their death rates increase and the causes of death become more like those of U.S. Whites (Marmot and Syme, 1976). Health problems that are more common among Japanese than Whites include hypertension and stress-related diseases such as ulcers, colitis, and depression (Hashizume and Takano, 1983). Alcohol is consumed primarily by males. However, in a Los Angeles study, Japanese American females were found to have the heaviest alcohol consumption of all Asian females. In the United States, Japanese Americans who drink alcohol are more educated, younger, and more likely to go to nightclubs. Males born in Japan were more likely to drink alcohol than males born in the United States (Kitano, 1989). In Japan, alcohol consumption among males is increasing partly due to the practice of conducting business in nightclubs after business hours.

Non-insulin dependent diabetes mellitus (NIDDM) is prevalent among Asians in the United States. For example, in Japan the Japanese have a 3 to 4 percent rate of NIDDM, but in Los Angeles Japanese Americans have a 20 to 22 percent rate. In Hawaii, Asians have three to four times more NIDDM than non-Asians. Researchers believe that Asians have a predisposition to diabetes which surfaces because of American diets. Development of diabetes among Asian Americans occurs even without weight gain (Lipson and Kato-Palmer, 1988).

Food and Nutrition in the United States

The traditional Japanese diet is generally low in fat, cholesterol, animal protein, and sugar, and high in complex carbohydrates and sodium. The high sodium intake is due to the extensive use of soy sauces, monosodium glutamate, and pickled foods. Complete elimination of these foods from the diet of the hypertensive patient may be unrealistic; instead, a gradual reduction in salt and use of reduced sodium products and substitutes may be appropriate.

Dairy products are used in small quantities; lactose intolerance is common (as in others of Asian descent). Soy products (including tofu and soy milk when fortified with calcium), sesame seeds, small fish with bones, and calcium-containing vegetables provide some calcium in the diet. Use of milk as a beverage is increasing among the young and those in urban areas.

Many varieties of fish (fresh or processed including smoked, dried, and canned) are consumed; fish may be served broiled, baked, or boiled and is often used in soups. Fish is consumed raw on occasion. Often the main course in a meal is a combination of meat (beef, pork, or poultry) and vegetables seasoned with soy sauce. Other protein sources include eggs and dried beans and peas. Vegetables are consumed in abundance. Fruits are often used as dessert or snacks between meals. Tea is the most popular beverage (Hashizume and Takano, 1983).

The elderly as well as new immigrants may hold beliefs regarding the beneficial or harmful effects of food combinations. For example, eel and pickled plums and cherries and milk are thought to result in illness if eaten together. Pickled plums and hot tea are used to promote regular bowel habits; pickled plums and rice gruel are served to those recovering from illness (Hashizume and Takano, 1983).

Implications for Health Care.

Refer to Chapter 13, Korean Americans.

References Cited

Cathcart, D. and R. Cathcart. 1988. Japanese social experience and concept of groups, in *Intercultural communication: a reader*, 5th edition, edited by L. Samovar and R. Porter. Belmont, CA: Wadsworth Pub. Co.

Hall, E. T. and M. Hall. 1987. *Hidden differences: doing business with the Japanese*. Garden City, NY: Anchor Press.

Harris, P. and R. Moran. 1987. *Managing cultural differences*, 2nd edition. Houston: Gulf Publishing Co.

Hashizume, S. and Takano, J. 1983. Nursing care of Japanese American patients, Chapter 7 in *Ethnic nursing care: a multicultural approach*, edited by M. Orque, B. Bloch, and L. Monrroy. St. Louis: C. V. Mosby.

House approves payments for Japanese Americans. 1989. *San José (CA) Mercury News*, Oct. 27, p. 1A.

Kitano, H. 1988. The Japanese American family, in *Ethnic families in America*, 3rd edition, edited by C. Mindel, R. Habenstein, and R. Wright, Jr. New York: Elsevier.

Lipson, L. and S. Kato-Palmer. 1988. Diabetes, an equal opportunity disease: Asian Americans. American Diabetes Association; *Diabetes Forecast*.

Lock, M. 1983. Japanese responses to social change—making the strange familiar. The *Western Journal of Medicine* 139(6), 829-834.

Marmot, M. and S. Syme. 1976. Acculturation and coronary heart disease in Japanese Americans. *American Journal of Epidemiology* 104:225.

Ramsey, S. and J. Birk. 1983. Preparation of North Americans for interaction with Japanese: consideration of language and communication style, in *Handbook of intercultural training, vol. III, Area studies in international training*, edited by D. Landis and R. Brislin. New York: Pergamon Press.

Samovar, L. and R. Porter. 1988. *Intercultural communication: a reader*, 5th edition, edited by L. Samovar and R. Porter. Belmont, CA: Wadsworth Pub. Co.

Sobetani-Shibata, A. 1981. The Japanese American, Chapter 5 in *Culture and child rearing*, edited by Ann Clark. Philadelphia: F. A. Davis Co.

Zich, A. and M. Yamashita. 1986. Japanese Americans—home at last. *National Geographic Magazine*, April, p. 512.

Chapter 13

KOREAN AMERICANS

Because of its geographical location, Korea has been dominated by the influence of outside forces for many years. Korea purposely isolated itself from the world for 300 years during which time China was the main outside influence. Japan gained influence beginning in 1876 through a trade agreement with Korea, and then invaded Korea leading to the Sino-Japanese war in 1895. Japan's victory over China resulted in increased control of Korea by Japan. Russia attempted to expand into Korea in 1905 but was defeated by the Japanese. At this point, Korea was a protectorate of Japan. From 1905 until the end of World War II in 1945, Japan dominated and attempted to change Korean culture. At the end of World War II, Japan was disarmed and Korea was divided at the 38th parallel into North Korea, occupied by Soviet communist troops, and South Korea, occupied by United Nations (United States) troops. In 1950, troops from the communist north and troops from the People's Republic of Korea (South Korea) skirmished at the 38th parallel, initiating the Korean war (1950 to 1953). The Korean people endured complete devastation and hardship during the war; millions of civilians were killed. Since the Korean war, South Korea has been rebuilt and is now an economic leader in the world. However, the threat from the north continues.

With the exception of a few early immigrants (students, political refugees, diplomats, and ginseng merchants) to the mainland United States, the first Korean immigrants to enter U.S. territory were 7,226 people (mostly men) who immigrated to Hawaii between 1903 and 1905. They had been recruited, with the help of American Christian missionaries in Korea, to work on the sugar plantations. About 800 Korean picture brides immigrated to Hawaii between 1910 and 1924 (Jung, 1991). Picture brides were so named because the single Korean men in Hawaii sent their pictures home to Korea, and women elected to marry them based on the pictures. This differs from the usual picture bride situation in which women would send their pictures to single men and the men would select brides. In Hawaii, many of the pictures sent by the Korean men were of themselves at much younger ages, so when the women arrived they found the men to be older and less attractive than expected. Some of the disappointed women returned to Korea without marrying. Those who did marry, encouraged their husbands to leave farm labor and seek improved employment. Many of the Koreans in Hawaii moved to California for more opportunities. They worked on farms and in railroad construction and mining. In cities they were employed as waiters, kitchen workers, janitors, and house cleaners. Some started their own businesses, including grocery stores, laundry shops, and vegetable markets (Jung, 1991).

In 1905 the Japanese prohibited emigration from Korea, and by 1924 all immigration into the United States from Asia had been stopped. After the Korean war, some Koreans entered the United States; these immigrants were the wives and children of American servicemen or were refugees. Immigration of Koreans opened up in 1968 when the 1965 immigration laws became effective. Since 1975 about 30,000 Koreans a year have immigrated. The continued presence of U.S. troops in South Korea has resulted in some intermarriages and subsequent immigration of family members (Kim, 1980; Parrillo, 1985; Locke, 1992).

In 1990 there were 799,000 Koreans (0.3 percent of the U.S. population) in the United States. This is only slightly less than the 1990 populations of Asian Indians (815 thousand) and Japanese (848 thousand) (U.S. Bureau of the Census, 1992B). This is remarkable growth, considering that most Koreans in the United States entered after 1970. Emigration from Korea is caused by a rapid population increase in Korea which has resulted in overcrowding with many restrictions on freedoms as well as extreme competition for good jobs and educational opportunities. Also, many immigrants wish to avoid the political conflicts between North and South Korea.

Most recent Korean immigrants to the United States come from middle class families and are from urban areas of Korea. They enter the U.S. as family members of someone already here (Jung, 1991). They have high educational levels (Table 11-1) and many have immigrated because of better educational opportunities for their children in the United States (Min, 1988). Seventy percent of Koreans in the United States are Christians (Marden, Meyer, and Engel, 1992). The Korean Christian churches in the United States are mostly Methodist, Episcopal, and Presbyterian. They were established as centers for maintaining language, values, culture, and politics. Since second- and third- generation Koreans have different expectations of their churches, conflicts within the congregations have caused new churches to be formed.

One-third of Koreans in the United States live in California. Los Angeles has the largest Korean community; outside Los Angeles, Koreans are scattered in urban areas throughout the United States (Min, 1988).

Korean families in the U.S. have grouped together to form family associations that are not necessarily made up of related people. These associations provide financial support and have been credited for the apparent ease with which Koreans have opened small businesses (grocery and liquor stores, dry cleaners, fast food restaurants, etc.). Their businesses are frequently located in inner city Latino and Black neighborhoods, which has resulted in racial conflicts. In Los Angeles, disputes between Black residents and Korean business owners have led to boycotts, murder, and arson. Blacks contend that the Korean merchants are prejudiced, they hire only Koreans without providing jobs for Blacks, and they don't contribute money to the community. Blacks believe that their communities are being drained of resources (Bonachich, 1989) and that the Koreans feel superior to them (Yu, 1983). Most Koreans live in the suburbs, not in the inner city locations of their businesses. Blacks do not look favorably on the Koreans' methods of financing (family associations) because they do not see this as an option for themselves (Min, 1988; Marden, Meyer, and Engel, 1992).

In addition to racial problems with Blacks, Korean grocers have experienced price discrimination by Jewish wholesalers. To counter this problem, Koreans have formed trade organizations to deal directly with suppliers and protect their interests (Min, 1988).

There is a high percentage of college graduates and professionals among Korean Americans (Table 11-1), but many are not able to practice their professions because of discrimination and licensing requirements. Thus, a large number hold blue-collar jobs resulting in lower incomes than would be expected. Many Koreans who immigrate to the United States are not prepared for the cultural differences they find. They have a difficult time learning English and face discrimination.

World View

Ancient religious practices involved the worship of spirits. Shamans were intermediaries between spirits and people. Among their skills, shamans were believed able to prevent, diagnose, and cure illnesses. Older rural people may continue to believe in shamanism and the division of the universe into the heavenly world, the earthly world, and the underworld. The influence of Chinese religions (Taoism, Buddhism, and especially Confucianism) provides the major ideology and value systems for Koreans.

Family Structure and Interactional Styles

Korean values are similar to those of other Asians. They emphasize the family over the individual, have formal relationships rather than informal, and males are dominant (Locke, 1992). Korean (and other Asian) family relations are influenced by Confucius, who taught a social order between parents (strict and loving) and children (reverent and respectful), between old (wise and gentle) and young (respectful), between husband (good and understanding) and wife (submissive), between friends (trustworthy), and between ruler (righteous and benevolent) and subject (loyal) (Locke, 1992). In Korea, marriage is almost an obligation (Pares, 1985). The purpose, of course, is to carry on the family name. Elderly family members are honored and respected.

Throughout their lives in Korea, women are ruled by men: first by the father, then the husband, and, in old age, by the son. After marriage, a woman joins the household of her husband's family and learns from her mother-in-law. Gradually, as the mother-in-law ages, the daughter-in-law takes over the family responsibilities. At age 60, a woman is rewarded with leisure time in which she can enjoy her grandchildren (Pang, 1991).

There are few family surnames in Korea. Locke (1992) reported that over 53 percent of the population has one of five surnames. As with some other Asian cultures, the family name is stated first, a middle name identifies the generation, and the third name is the given name.

Korean American women outnumber Korean men in the United States. Much of the excess immigration of females is related to the number of women who entered the U.S. as wives of servicemen and later divorced. Marriage prospects for women are further diminished because some Korean men consider acculturated women too aggressive and disobedient; so, many men return to Korea to select brides. Once families become established and obtain citizenship, they usually arrange to have family members in Korea immigrate to the United States. Currently, most Korean immigrants enter as family members of U.S. citizens (Kim, 1987). Many extended families in Korea are broken by emigration (Jung, 1991).

Korean American females over 16 years of age are much more likely to be employed (56 percent) than married women in Korea (19 percent). Min (1988) explained that the wife must work for the family's economic survival in the United States. In addition, Korean women earn more money in the U.S. than in Korea, so are encouraged to work. Also, there is no stigma associated with female employment in the United States as in Korea. The work roles of Korean women have not resulted in a decrease in their household tasks. Because of the high number of working women, male dominance is decreased in the United States, and women no longer accept the superiority of males. These conflicts lead to the breakdown of families and a high divorce rate (Yu, 1983).

Korean Americans have fewer children than the general U.S. population and than their counterparts in Korea. This is somewhat surprising since most immigrant populations have high fertility rates when they first arrive. However, most Korean immigrants have higher socioeconomic and educational levels than many other immigrants; these characteristics are associated with lower fertility. Also, the rapid change in employment of married women from Korea to the United States has resulted in family adjustments and pressures on Korean American women that discourage them from having large families (Min, 1988). Korean children assimilate readily and tend to ignore their parents' authority. In some families, the children speak English and very little Korean; the language skills of parents are reversed; which creates poor communication and adds to serious generational conflicts (Jung, 1991).

The large number of Korean American women in the work force has been associated with the number of small businesses owned by their families. Family members must work in the business if it is going to be successful. Money received by the business is family income; women do not receive separate incomes, which has been a source of criticism from outsiders who believe this practice is a form of exploitation (Bonacich, 1989).

Communication

Korean language (*Han'gul*) is spoken with four levels of formality (honorific to familiar). The speaker selects the level depending on the relationship with the listener. *Han'gul* contains many Chinese words and has some grammatical similarities to Japanese. Chan (1992) described the social flexibility of the Korean language. Similar to Japanese language, the verb is placed at the end of the sentence. The speaker introduces a topic with the sentence subject and object while watching the listener's reactions. Then, the verb can be adjusted to suit the perceived reaction of the listener and harmony can be preserved. If necessary, a negative ending can be added to completely change the meaning.

Health Beliefs and Practices

Koreans may have a pluralistic view of medicine using treatments from traditional shamans, herbalists, Confucian beliefs, Chinese medicine, and Western medicine. In some cases, Western medicine may be the first treatment choice. Supernatural beings may be blamed for illness (Chin, 1992). Shamanism in Korea is based on the belief that spirits bring illness and also cure people. A *mudang* (shaman) is a mediator between people and the spirits. According to Pang (1991), in Korea the *mudang* are usually female and are consulted almost entirely by women.

Traditional Korean health clinics (*hanbang*) and health practitioners (*hanui*) do business in the United States. In Korea, the practitioners of traditional (*hanyak*) or Chinese medicine are licensed professionals. The concepts of harmony between *yin (um)* and *yang* and the five elements are the basis of Korean medicine. An excess or deficiency of the vital force, *ch'i* (or *ki* in Korean), causes imbalance in *um* and *yang* and the person becomes ill. Many traditional methods of diagnosis and treatment are similar to those of Chinese medicine including acupuncture (*ch'im*), herbs (*hanyuk*), moxibustion (*d'um*), and cupping (*buh wang*). Other traditional treatments include steam baths, ginseng, and deer horns. New immigrants and older Koreans seem to prefer using *hanbang* (traditional clinics) to Western medicine. For them, the advantages include convenient hours, no need for an appointment, client input in treatment methods, and usually a low cost. However, some *hanyak* treatments are expensive because they involve the importation of unusual ingredients. Although Western practitioners and *hanui* do not cooperate, their clients continue to use both types of medicine (Pang, 1989).

Food and Nutrition in the United States

Traditional Korean staple foods are rice, noodles, soup, and *kim ch'i* (a spicy-hot, fermented pickled vegetable combination). Small amounts of meat and fish are consumed. Pregnant women may avoid eating blemished fruit in the belief this could cause undesirable physical effects in the baby (Ludman, Kang, and Lynn, 1992).

Implications for Health Care of Chinese, Japanese, and Korean Americans

Traditional values such as extended families, harmony, filial piety (respect for parents), self-control of feelings, humility, and praise of others affect communication between health professionals and Asian clients. Asians attempt to avoid social conflict and establish harmony. Communication may be indirect in uncomfortable situations. For example, rather than offend the professional, Asian clients may say "yes" when they really mean "no," or they may seem evasive in order to avoid direct confrontation. A "yes" response to a negative question could mean agreement with the negative statement ("Yes, I didn't take my pill"). A "yes" response could also mean, "I hear you." If possible, questions should be phrased so that the meaning of "yes" is clear.

Out of respect for authority, the client may avoid questioning health care professionals or looking directly in their eyes, especially if the health professional is of the opposite sex. Generally, eye contact with Asians is acceptable, but should not be prolonged. Arm and body motions should be minimized; the practitioner is cautioned to be restrained, formal, and polite. Although practitioners should avoid asking personal questions immediately, they should be prepared for an Asian client to ask them personal questions.

Hostility toward an authority figure (the health professional) may be hidden, giving a false appearance of acceptance (Nguyen, 1985). Because Asians tend to avoid confrontation, the health professional may discover that the use of confrontation as a counseling technique causes the client to become withdrawn and silent.

Because it is important to Asians to control their feelings, the expression of feelings such as pain and anger may be subdued. This doesn't mean that Asians lack emotions or feel less pain. When people are less expressive, there is a tendency to judge them as cold and possibly even as hiding something. For health professionals this could mean difficulty in assessing the severity of a health problem.

Japanese do not like to have physical barriers (table, chair) between them when conversing. Thus, in counseling situations, the health care provider should be especially careful of the room arrangement. Everyone in the room should receive equal treatment. Japanese may avoid use of the number four because the word means death, so health care providers should avoid it in the care of Japanese clients (Ethnic diversity, ND).

Many Asians, especially recent arrivals, fear some aspects of Western medicine, particularly the drawing of blood, hospitalization, and surgery. Some believe that blood is present in a fixed amount and is very difficult or impossible for the body to replace. Blood loss is considered a serious health problem and a reason to avoid Western medical treatment. These fears, combined with the problems of cost, language, and unfamiliar food, are all reasons to avoid the Western medical system (Gould-Martin and Ngin, 1981).

Health care providers need to inquire about the use of alternative treatments. All degrees of acculturation are represented among Asians, and it is important to learn about the health practices of each individual.

References Cited

Bonacich, E. 1989. Viewpoint. The role of the petite bourgeoisie within capitalism: a response to Pyong Gap Min. *Amerasia Journal* 15(2):195-203.

Chan, S. 1992. Families with Asian roots, Chapter 8 in *Developing cross-cultural competence: a guide for working with young children and their families*, edited by E. Lynch and M. Hanson. Baltimore: Paul H. Brookes Pub. Co.

Chin, S. 1992. Multicultural medicine, a decade later. This, that and the other: managing illness in a first generation Korean American family. *The Western Journal of Medicine* 157(3):305-309.

Ethnic diversity and the care of the terminally ill in Santa Clara County: a handbook. ND. San José, CA: Hospice of the Valley.

Gould-Martin, K. and C. Ngin. 1981. Chinese Americans, Chapter 2 in *Ethnicity and medical care*, edited by A. Harwood. Cambridge, MA: Harvard University Press.

Jung, J-D. 1991. *A study of Korean immigrants in America, 1872-present*. Unpublished master's thesis, San Jose State University, San José, CA.

Kim, H-C. 1980. Koreans, pp. 601-606 in *Harvard encyclopedia of American ethnic groups*, edited by S. Thermstrom, A. Orlov, and O. Handlin. Cambridge, MA: Harvard University Press.

Kim, I. 1987. Korea and East Asia, Chapter 14 in *Pacific bridges: the new immigration from Asia and the Pacific Islands*, edited by J. Fawcett and B. Carino. New York: Center for Migration Studies.

Locke, D. 1992. *Increasing multicultural understanding*, Chapter 8 Korean Americans. Newbury Park, CA: SAGE Pub.

Ludman, E., K. Kang, and L. Lynn. 1992. Food beliefs and diets of pregnant Korean American women. *Journal of The American Dietetic Association* 92(12):1519-1520.

Marden, C., G. Meyer, and M. Engel. 1992. *Minorities in American society*, 6th edition. New York: Harper Collins Pub. Inc., pp. 375-380.

Min, P. G. 1988. The Korean American family, Chapter 9 in *Ethnic families in America*, 3rd edition, edited by C. Mindel, R. Habenstein, and R. Wright, Jr. New York: Elsevier.

Nguyen, D. 1985. Culture shock: a review of Vietnamese culture and its concepts of health and disease. *The Western Journal of Medicine* 142:409.

Pang, K-Y. 1991. *Korean elderly women in America*. New York: AMS Press.

Pang, K-Y. 1989. The practice of traditional Korean medicine in Washington, D.C.. *Social Science Medicine* 28(8):875-884.

Pares, S. 1985. *Korean Western culture in conflict: crosscurrents*. Seoul, Korea: Seoul International Pub. Co.

Parrillo, V. 1985. *Stranger to these shores: race and ethnic relations in the United States*, 2nd edition, Chapter 8 The Asian immigrants. New York: John Wiley and Sons.

Yu, E. 1983. Korean communities in America: past, present, and future. *Amerasia Journal* 10(2):23-51.

Chapter 14

SOUTHEAST ASIANS

The three largest groups of Southeast Asian immigrants and refugees in the United States are from Vietnam, Cambodia (Kampuchea), and Laos. Except for a period of Japanese occupation during World War II, all three countries were French colonies from 1883–93 to 1953–54. When the French left in 1954, Cambodia became a monarchy, Laos was governed by the Royal Lao, and Vietnam had been divided after eight years of war into North Vietnam and South Vietnam. The Vietnam war was between the Communist north (supported by China and the Soviet Union) and South Vietnam (supported by the United States). In 1973 a cease-fire agreement was signed and the United States consented to withdraw all troops. After most U.S. troops were removed in 1975, the Khmer Rouge (Communists) military took over South Vietnam (Chan, 1992). The governments of Laos and Cambodia also fell into the hands of Communists (Pathet Lao and Khmer Rouge) who then killed many of the tribespeople or forced them to flee into dense jungle or to Thailand. Widespread destruction, genocide, starvation, and persecutions followed. In Cambodia, nearly all the professional and educated people were killed.

In 1979 Vietnam set up a puppet government in Cambodia and with a little more freedom of movement many additional Cambodians (Khmer) were able to escape over land and water to Thailand and other countries (Richardson, 1990). Gradually the power of the Khmer Rouge in Cambodia has been reduced and in 1993 a return of the monarchy was supported by the United Nations. However, the stability of the returned monarchy is in question.

The first major influx of Southeast Asians to the United States began with the Vietnamese and lowland Lao who came in 1975 after the withdrawal of U.S. troops and the fall of Saigon (Ho Chi Minh City). This first group of refugees included almost equal percentages of men and women who were generally young (43 percent were 17 years old or under). Most were well educated, and arrived with extended family groups. Almost one-third were Catholic. Many spoke English because of their close ties to the American military (Muecke, 1983; Chan, 1992).

Mass exodus of refugees from Vietnam, Cambodia, and Laos began in 1979, resulting in a second group of Southeast Asian refugees sometimes referred to as "boat people." The boat people had less formal education than the first group of refugees. Many of the people in the second group came from the rural and mountain areas of Cambodia, Vietnam, and Laos (Hmong and Mien) and were farmers; others were fishermen and soldiers. Few had been exposed to Western culture. In the second group, a high proportion of single men came alone. Life for this group has been exceptionally harsh. Their experiences in escaping persecution in their native lands were especially difficult and required a dangerous trek or boat trip into a neighboring country. Many of them, their friends, and family members were robbed of their few possessions; women were raped. Up to 50 percent died because of the dangers inherent in their escape or because they were murdered (Gilman, et al., 1992; Chan, 1992; Muecke, 1983). The hill people of Laos (Hmong and Mien) had been trained as guerrilla soldiers by the United States military in an attempt to stop the movement of Communist troops and supplies from the north on the Ho Chi Minh trail. Many of these men were killed. The survivors of all this devastation left their familiar world behind and entered into refugee holding camps in host countries where life was placed on "hold" for years. Families were often separated in the confusion of relocation to camps. However, eventually over many years, families have been relocated to other countries where they have been accepted on a permanent basis. Everything about their new homes is different (Santopietro and Lynch, 1980; Muecke, 1983).

Some of these refugees have been met by hostility and contempt in the United States (Chan, 1992). Many Americans are not aware of the involvement of the U.S. Central Intelligence Agency in the secret war in Laos. Americans do not always realize that many Southeast Asian refugees are here because they had no choice. Many (if not most) of those who had any connection with the United States had to leave their homelands or be killed by the Communists. The United States government did not even help them escape. Now, if given a choice, most of the Southeast Asian refugees would much prefer to be in their homelands (of course, under prewar conditions). In the United States many of the refugees are isolated from the dominant society because of racism, poor English language skills, and no job training; other minorities resent their presence as they are perceived to be using limited resources (welfare money) that would otherwise go to other groups.

Most Southeast Asians in the United States are refugees, not immigrants. Most live in the Western states (40 percent are in California). An estimated 47 percent of the Southeast Asians in California reside in Los Angeles, Orange, and San Diego counties. The San Francisco bay area is home to about 23 percent of the California population (Christensen, 1987). Southeast Asians will continue to enter the U.S. as refugees and immigrants who join family members. Their numbers are predicted to grow from 1.1 million in 1990 to 5 million in 1995 as the result of immigration and high birthrates (Chan, 1992). In the United States, Southeast Asian women have a fertility rate that is three times higher than for the average U.S. woman (Kulig, 1990).

World View

The major cultural factor influencing health and illness beliefs of Southeast Asians is their world view of a Universal Order. This represents the influence of several philosophies and religions. In Vietnam, for example, the religions include: the native animistic religion (belief in the existence of good and bad spirits), Confucianism, Taoism, Buddhism, Christianity, and Islam (Tran, 1988). The predominant belief is that the universe, an harmonious and orderly system, determines each person's fate. Life's experiences are predestined by nature's forces, especially the powers of eternal gods and spirits. A central belief is that each person reflects the same forces (*yin* and *yang*) that govern the cosmos.

Behavior is influenced by the worship of one's ancestors and the belief that their spirits live among their descendants and confer protection. The Hmong view time as repeating itself, which adds to their respect for the past (Meyers, 1992). Some Southeast Asians believe in reincarnation (Hoang and Erickson, 1982). Children are taught to honor and obey their parents (filial piety) (Nguyen, 1985). A related concept is *am duc*, the belief that people's actions will influence their own and their descendants' lives to come. *Am duc* represents the total of all the good deeds performed by one's ancestors. The emphasis on harmony within the universe extends to social interactions; thus, any benefit for the individual is subordinate to that of society. Hospitality and politeness are highly valued (Orque, 1983; Chan, 1992).

Family Structure and Interactional Styles

The extended family is the major influence and source of support for Southeast Asians. However, because of war and relocation, extended families were separated. In addition, the U.S. government purposely separated some extended families in an attempt to settle refugees in small groups throughout the country to force acculturation (Santopietro and Lynch, 1980). Subsequently, some Southeast Asians resettled themselves so that they could be together. Because of the many family separations, a higher number of families are headed by women (14.2 percent) than in other Asian groups (Tran, 1988).

The extended family of the Vietnamese includes all family members, living and dead. Traditionally, the family head is the oldest male who, in Vietnam, had absolute power over the family. He was also legally responsible for the actions of family members and could be punished if they committed a crime. Under certain conditions it was permissible for a man to leave his wife, but a woman could never leave her husband. Children had to obey and honor their parents, and siblings protected each other. Children had a great responsibility to the family; they were expected to work hard and be successful. Marriages were usually arranged by the parents; after marriage the Vietnamese couple would live with the husband's parents until they had a house of their own. In Cambodia and Laos the young couple usually would live with the bride's family. When they did move out on their own, it would be the first time that either the husband or wife was permitted to live away from their parents. In rural areas, women were expected to marry someone from their own village because of the strong kinship ties (Richardson 1990; Tran, 1988). Age was respected, with older persons having more power than younger persons. American values of assertiveness and aggression differ from Southeast Asian values of individual dependence on the family (Green, 1982).

Although the father has traditionally been the decision-maker, this is changing in the United States. The strong traditional value of filial piety is a problem in the United States, where the children and wives prefer more freedom and question absolute obedience to the father/husband (Ethnic diversity . . . , ND). Out of economic necessity, many Vietnamese women have entered the work force, creating conflicts with the men who traditionally provide for the family. The money that women earn gives them more power in the family (Tran, 1988; Gold, 1992; Dinh, Ganesan, and Waxler-Morrison, 1990). Family tension is also created by the influence of American society on the children, who want to be independent and behave like their peers. Young people in the United States have a number of freedoms, including dating and going out at night. Southeast Asian children are acculturated through schools, television, and by their playmates. Since both parents are usually employed, they have less cultural influence on their children than in the past. Contrary to tradition, many young people are employed and move away from their families before marriage (Tran, 1988). Vietnamese parents feel that their authority and the family's solidarity are threatened in the United States (Nguyen, 1985). Since the father no longer has absolute power, discipline of children is more difficult (Tran, 1988). One recurring theme in the literature about Vietnamese families is the concern for the youth and their lack of Vietnamese values. Health care practitioners may have contact with adults who spent their childhoods in relocation camps. The culture of the camp is the only culture they knew before coming to the United States. Tran (1988) indicated that the children are learning American ways, but without American values of school, work, and productivity.

In 1980, 35 percent of Vietnamese families lived below the poverty line compared to 26 percent of Blacks, 21 percent of Hispanics, and 7 percent of Whites (Tran, 1988). A major contributor to low income among Southeast Asians is the inability to speak English. Compared to other Asians, unemployment levels are high. Vietnamese believe that the family should care for itself. They do not understand the U.S. welfare system and may have trouble accepting outside help (Ethnic diversity . . . , ND).

Health care is seen as the family's responsibility, and outside assistance is often requested only as a last resort. Health care decisions are made by the oldest person in a family (Hoang and Erickson, 1985). Family members will seek active participation in the patient's care, both in the hospital and at home. Placement of elders in long-term care facilities is not readily accepted (Orque, 1983).

The Vietnamese and Cambodian systems of names present the family name first, followed by the middle name(s) and finally the first name. There are relatively few Vietnamese family names. Usually, Southeast Asian individuals prefer to be called by their given names. Most Vietnamese change the order of their names in the United States, but some retain their cultural name order. Southeast Asian women usually retain their own names after marriage (Nhu, 1987; Richardson, 1990).

Communication

In addition to the obvious differences in spoken language, there are other cultural differences in communication patterns between Southeast Asians and the dominant U.S. society. For example, the American sense of time urgency is absent in some Asian cultures. Social obligations receive priority in order to preserve social harmony. Therefore, personal interactions are not rushed to conform to rigid Western schedules (Nguyen, 1985).

Signs of disrespect may include raising one's voice, pointing at or beckoning another person with one's finger, pointing a foot at someone, and displaying the bottom of the foot/shoe. Touching a person's head is believed to cause loss of spirits (Nguyen, 1985). Because a "yes" response can mean "no," Asians learn to read the nonverbal behaviors of others. It is not considered devious or dishonest to respond affirmatively; some take pride in their ability to accurately assess the meaning of nonverbal behaviors which have more importance in high context cultures than in the United States. Men and women avoid touching in public, but members of the same sex commonly hold hands in public (Chan, 1992).

In a Vietnamese home, hospitality may be shown by offering food or drink; to refuse is impolite. Etiquette also differs in the manner of expressing thanks. Vietnamese may give gifts rather than send a "thank you" note. They may believe that if they accept someone's help, they are then indebted to that person. So, if they think they can't repay the debt, they won't accept help (Ethnic diversity . . . , ND; Richardson, 1990). Vietnamese are shy and modest. They rarely display emotions in public; to do so would be a sign of weakness and lack of self-control.

Health Beliefs and Practices

Health beliefs and practices of Southeast Asians reflect a combination of the traditional culture (Chinese and folk medicine), a variation of French medicine, and Western medicine. Western medicine was introduced to Southeast Asians by the French. It was practiced in cities, but was too expensive for most people, so a variation of French-Western medicine developed as an alternative to Western medicine (Hoang and Erickson, 1982).

Health beliefs. The Vietnamese may believe that everything in the cosmos influences an individual and that spirits and deities control the universe. Illness may be the result of destiny or disharmony caused by the wandering spirits of the dead. For Laotian hill people (Hmong and Mien), illness may be considered the result of the wrath of gods, but good spirits provide protection. In addition to supernatural causes, illness may be caused by natural phenomena such as wind. The physical and social environments determine whether a person is in harmony or disharmony with nature and, thus, healthy or ill (Muecke, 1983). Many health beliefs center on the belief in balancing hot and cold. Conditions which cause the body to be cold and subject to illness include blood loss, childbirth, and fever. Illness may occur because of destiny. To foresee destiny, practices such as astrology, fortune-telling, physiognomy (the practice of judging character and mental qualities by observation of bodily features), and divination (divine instruction or prophesy) are used (Orque, 1983).

Health practices. Medical pluralism, the use of more than one system at a time, is common among Southeast Asians in the United States. Minor health problems are usually taken to a traditional healer or doctor of Eastern medicine, and more severe problems to a Western doctor. Factors other than the perceived seriousness of an illness also determine which system is used or whether medical pluralism occurs; these factors include the client's age, education, and socioeconomic status (Schultz, 1982). In contrast to the supernatural medical beliefs (animism) of the Mien and Hmong, the major traditional system among most Southeast Asians is called "natural medicine." In situations where heat is lost from the body, every effort is made to keep the body warm, and cold foods (many of the fruits and vegetables) are avoided. In a health care setting, Southeast Asians may be reluctant to give blood samples. Not only will blood loss upset the balance of hot and cold, but, like many other Asians, they fear that blood cannot be replaced (Muecke, 1983).

Cultural health practices include the extensive use of home remedies (Rairdan and Higgs, 1992). In Vietnam, drugs can be purchased without a prescription. Family and friends are relied on for medical assistance before outside help is sought. Cultural healers, who may be thought to have supernatural powers, may also be consulted. Their healing methods include the use of magic, prayers, talismans, bloodletting, pinching skin, roots and herbs, coin-rubbing (*cao gio*), cupping (*giac hoi*), herbal steam inhalation, and balms (Hoang and Erickson, 1985). Herbal medicines may be used or a shaman may be called in (Meyers, 1992). The concept of balance is important in health matters. In regrettable incident reported in 1976, a Vietnamese father took his three-year-old son to an American hospital for treatment of influenza. Because of marks on the boy's back from coin rubbing, the father was suspected of child abuse and jailed. Subsequently, the father committed suicide (Nong, 1976). Many Southeast Asians are now aware of this problem and no longer use treatments which leave marks on children (Gilman, 1992).

Diet modifications are derived from the "hot" and "cold" (*yin/yang*) theory. Because foods and diseases are characterized as either "hot" or "cold," certain foods will be prescribed or restricted in order to regain balance in the body. Most Western medications are considered hot and very potent; they are expected to act quickly. If they are not obviously effective or if they are perceived to upset the hot/cold balance, Western methods may be discontinued (Muecke, 1983). It may be difficult to convince a Southeast Asian patient to continue long-term treatment, especially when there are no symptoms such as in diabetes and hypertension (Dinh, Ginesan, and Waxler-Morrison, 1990).

Health Status in the United States

In the United States, the health problems of Southeast Asian refugees include high rates of intestinal parasites, tuberculosis, hepatitis, and other infectious diseases. Additionally, Uba (1992) reported malnutrition, conjunctivitis, trichinosis, anemia, and leprosy. Once the infectious diseases are controlled, a stress-related syndrome becomes evident (Sutherland, et al., 1983). The long relocation periods and subsequent traumas have affected the emotional and physical health of Southeast Asian refugees. Many suffer from depression and other mental problems. Mental illness carries a stigma among most Southeast Asians, who may believe the afflicted person (as well as the entire family) is being punished by evil spirits. Cultural taboos often prevent patients from revealing their emotional problems. Instead, psychological concerns may be expressed as physical symptoms. Refugees from Southeast Asia, who have been subjected to the trauma of fleeing their homelands followed by culture shock in the United States, are highly susceptible to mental problems. Depression, grief, and a passive fatalistic outlook are components of the "survivor syndrome," which commonly affects refugees even years after arrival in the U.S. (Santopietro and Lynch, 1980; Gold, 1992). Treatment of mental illness is more acceptable if accompanied by a physical exam and medical treatment (Dinh, Ganesan, and Waxler-Morrison, 1990).

In Santa Clara County (California), Cambodian refugees suffer mental problems six times more frequently than the general population.

Three-quarters of the Cambodian refugees are in need of counseling with 18 percent in serious need compared to one-third of the general population in need of counseling and 3 percent in serious need. Of all Southeast Asians, Cambodians had the worst experiences in relocating to the United States. They suffered more deaths among family and friends, more assaults and rapes, more imprisonments, and worse food shortages in refugee camps. Low incomes among the refugees in the United States contribute to their problems, with 19 percent of the Vietnamese, 25 percent of the Cambodians, and 38 percent of Chinese refugee families earning less than $6,000 per year. In contrast, over 50 percent of Chinese immigrants (compared to refugees) had household incomes greater than $35,000/year (Asian refugees can't . . ., 1984). Uba (1992) reported a number of barriers to Western medicine. Of course, cost is a major deterrent. Other barriers include (1) beliefs in the inevitability of illness and the predetermination of death, (2) cultural explanations regarding the causes of illness which are not compatible with Western medicine, (3) perception that death is a consequence of using Western medicine, (4) failure to understand Western medicine, (5) lack of understanding of Asian cultures among Western practitioners, (6) differences in communication and values, (7) lack of bilingual staff members, (8) failure of Western treatments to fit traditional systems, (9) lack of knowledge about Western clinics, and (10) inaccessibility of clinics because of hours of business and lack of transportation.

The Hmong do not usually seek Western medicine and can be expected to be in advanced stages of disease when first seen in a clinic. Compliance with prescriptions is poor. They frequently will refuse surgery or any invasive procedure because they want the body to be whole when they die to avoid being reincarnated with a deformity (Meyers, 1992). In addition, a Southeast Asian may believe that the soul will escape during surgery leading to death. The fear of hospitalization is increased by the view that the hospitals in their native countries were places to die. Death away from home is considered tragic (Dinh, Ganesan, and Waxler-Morrison, 1990). The beliefs in the supernatural have implications for practitioners. An example of this influence on health care occurred in Fresno County, California (Judge orders surgery . . ., 1990). A Superior Court judge ordered corrective surgery for a six-year-old boy who could not walk because of deformed clubfeet, after his parents refused to allow the operation. Previously a shaman had warned the family that the child should "stay as he is." An earlier operation in a Southeast Asian refugee camp was not successful. Subsequent to that operation, two children were born with cleft lips and the warning of the shaman seemed to be true. Thus, the parents objected to the operation. The press report indicated that many Hmong who have been in this country for a while had learned to trust doctors and did support surgery for the boy.

Food and Nutrition in the United States

Food patterns of Southeast Asians vary according to their country of origin. Southeast Asia is a humid, tropical area. It is an agricultural region where people outside of cities grow their own food. For the rural and hill people, hunting and gathering are also food sources. Sixty percent of the calories eaten come from rice which is mostly white, not enriched (Chang, 1977), usually eaten at every meal. In addition to rice, wheat bread and noodles are eaten. In the United States, cereal is consumed, but mostly by children. The traditional Southeast Asian diet is low in fat and virtually free of "junk food." However, in the United States the refugees may consume excessive calories from fat and sugar and have little concept of the relationships between diet and health (Harwood, 1987).

Pork is the preferred meat. Unfortunately, many Southeast Asians eat raw or rare pork which may infect them with "trichinae," a nematode parasite that lives in the muscle tissue of pork (and bear) and will live in human muscle tissue if consumed alive. Although Southeast Asians may deny eating raw pork (Harwood, 1987), they have a disproportionate incidence of trichinosis (Uba, 1992). There is no cure, so this infection must be prevented by eating only well-cooked pork.

Chicken and fish are also favorite meats. Fish may be fresh, dried, salted, or fermented. Traditional meats consumed less frequently include beef, deer, buffalo, and rabbit. Other protein foods are eggs, peanuts, soybeans, and other legumes. Many types of fruits and vegetables are consumed. Vegetable preferences include bamboo shoots, beans, bok choy, broccoli, cabbage, carrots, cauliflower, corn, cucumbers, egg plant, greens, mushrooms, squash, tomatoes, potatoes, radishes, and sweet potatoes. Fruit preferences include bananas, grapefruit, grapes, lemons, lychee, mangoes, oranges, papaya, peach, pineapple, pomegranate, strawberries, tamarinds, tangerines, and watermelons. Food spices vary. Vietnamese foods tend to be hotter than Chinese foods. Some Laotian foods are hot and most Cambodian foods are not hot. Processed foods (canned and frozen) are only available in cities. Without electricity and refrigeration many foods (milk, for example) are not used (Krause and Mahan, 1984; Dairy Council . . . , 1981).

The Vietnamese diet includes fish, *nuoc-mam* (fish sauce), fruits and vegetables, noodle soups, spices, and dessert sweets made of rice gluten with coconut. Usually several foods are combined in one dish. The years of French influence brought French bread to Southeast Asia. Dairy foods are seldom used, with the exception of canned, sweetened (condensed) milk. Lactose intolerance is common (Anh, Thuc, and Welsh, 1977). Some researchers in the United States have questioned the adequacy of dietary vitamin D and calcium. Calcium sources in the traditional Vietnamese diet include tofu (calcium-fortified soybean curd), fish sauces, and small dried fish with bones. A calcium source in the diets of Southeast Asian immigrants was described by Rosanoff and Calloway (1982). Leftover bones of chicken and pork are soaked in vinegar. The acid releases the calcium from the bones into the liquid which is then added to stock for cooking soups, vegetables, rice, and stews. The heat of cooking volatilizes the acid and leaves the calcium. One tablespoon of the vinegar extract was found to contain 100 mg. or more of calcium, which is equivalent to the calcium in one-third cup of milk (Kim et al., 1984). This practice is believed not to be common in the United States. The routine addition of small amounts of vinegar to soup stock has little effect on the calcium content of the soup (Hadfield, Beard, and Leonard-Green, 1989). High sodium foods commonly used include soy/fish/oyster sauces, monosodium glutamate (MSG), fermented beans, pickles, and salted fish. These may be significant factors in the hypertensive, sodium-sensitive person (Orque, 1983).

Because of the years involved in resettling, many Southeast Asians enter the U.S. with poor nutritional status. A cultural practice of restricting food during the last trimester of pregnancy, to produce a small baby and ease childbirth, contributes to increased risk for the infant and mother. The diets of Vietnamese immigrants have been observed to change in the United States. More dairy products, eggs, poultry, and red meat, and fewer vegetables and fish are consumed. Children often seem to prefer "American" food to traditional Vietnamese fare (Orque, 1983). However, adults consider the American diet bland. Vietnamese traditional food preparation methods are stir-frying and broiling over charcoal.

Among those immigrants from rural and agricultural backgrounds (for instance, the Hmong of Laos), adaptation to American foods has been especially difficult. They are used to growing their own foods, but few have access to land in the U.S. cities where they live. They have been known to harvest wild plants from public lands, which are subject to dangerous pollutants (Christensen, 1987). On arrival in the U.S. they do not understand the use of household appliances, plumbing, and chemicals. Modern supermarkets are confusing to them since they have only seen food in its unprocessed, unpackaged state. Even chemicals commonly used in the American kitchen (such as soap and cleansing agents) are foreign.

Hmong living in central California have intakes of less than 80 percent of the Recommended Dietary Allowances (RDA) for riboflavin, calcium, iron, magnesium, and zinc. Pregnant women had low intakes of these and vitamin B-6 and folacin. Pregnant women did not take nutrient supplements for fear the baby would be too large for natural childbirth. Caesarean births are not acceptable because of the fear of surgery. Hmong women do not usually breastfeed their infants in the United States. Many of the Hmong consume only two meals a day, but nutrient intake is not improved among those who consume three meals (Ikeda, et al., 1991). The Hmong and Laotians differ from the Vietnamese somewhat in food selection. Hmong do not usually consume tea or coffee; soup broth and water are the most common traditional beverages. In addition, the Hmong use forks and spoons for eating utensils, not chopsticks. Like the Vietnamese, Hmong adults prefer traditional foods in the U.S. but the children are shifting to American foods (Story and Harris, 1989).

Implications for Health Care

Gaining trust is an important first step in increasing acceptance of Western medicine (Chan, 1992; Green, 1982). Respected persons and organizations within the Asian community should be cultivated by health care professionals (Chan, 1992). It is important to learn about the client's refugee experiences and degree of acculturation in order to evaluate the impact of these influences on current health and health care practices (Gold, 1992). Barriers to health care should be discussed and acted on (Uba, 1992).

Southeast Asians expect to develop a personal (polite) but formal relationship with health professionals (Richardson, 1990). This takes time because it delays discussion about health matters. To start with, Southeast Asian clients may arrive early or late for an appointment if they haven't acculturated to M-time. Introductions should address the oldest male family member first. The professional will be expected to provide advice and give direct recommendations. Respect for the client can be shown by handing papers or other items with both hands. Using the left hand only is considered dirty.

Health professionals need to be cautious about touching a Southeast Asian on the head; always ask first. The head is sacred and some may believe that if it is touched the soul can be lost. The feet are the lowest part of the body, and the bottom of the foot should not be pointed towards a Southeast Asian. If there seems to be a hesitancy to keep eye contact it could be because they do not look into the eyes of someone is of higher status. A patient may not ask questions or complain, but may be very passive. To give the health provider an answer of "no" could be perceived as disrupting harmony; a "yes" answer could mean that they hear you, rather than agree with you. In other words, a "yes" answer may be given to avoid a "no" answer. If Southeast Asian clients smile a lot it could be that they are trying to cover up nonverbal behaviors and feelings. Self-treatments, folk medicine, and Chinese medicine may all be used before seeing a Western practitioner (Hoang and Erickson, 1985).

Although Southeast Asians don't want invasive treatments, they do expect some treatment, possibly in the form of pills (Indochinese refugees and the clinical encounter, 1983; Richardson, 1990).

References Cited

Anh, N., T. Thuc, and J. Welsh. 1977. Lactose malabsorption in adult Vietnamese. *The American Journal of Clinical Nutrition* 30:468.

Asian food guide for teachers. 1981. Oakland: Dairy Council of California.

Asian refugees can't escape their past. 1984. *San José (CA) Mercury News*, Dec. 12, p. 1A.

Chan, S. 1992. Families with Asian roots, Chapter 8 in *Developing cross-cultural competence: a guide for working with young children and their families*, edited by E. Lynch and M. Hanson. Baltimore: Paul H. Brookes Pub. Co.

Chang, K. C. 1977. *Food in Chinese culture.* New Haven: Yale University Press.

Christensen, C. 1987. Presentation to California Nutrition Council. Sacramento, CA, Sept. 25.

Dinh, D.-K., S. Ganesan, and N. Waxler-Morrison. 1990. The Vietnamese, Chapter 8 in *Cross cultural caring*, edited by N. Waxler-Morrison, J. Anderson, and E. Richardson. Vancouver, BC: University of Columbia Press.

Ethnic diversity and the care of the terminally ill in Santa Clara County (CA): a handbook, ND. San José, CA: Hospice of the Valley.

Gilman, S., J. Justice, K. Saepharn, and G. Charles. 1992. Cross-cultural medicine a decade later. Use of traditional and modern health services by Laotian refugees. *Western Journal of Medicine* 157(3):310-315.

Gold, S. 1992. Cross-cultural medicine, a decade later. Mental health and illness in Vietnamese refugees. *Western Journal of Medicine* 157(3):290-294.

Green, J. 1982. *Cultural awareness in the human services*. Englewood Cliffs, NJ: Prentice-Hall, Inc.

Hadfield, L., L. Beard, and T. Leonard-Green. 1989. Calcium content of soup stocks with added vinegar. *Journal of The American Dietetic Association* 89(12):1810-1811.

Harwood, J. 1987. Presentation to California Nutrition Council. Sacramento, CA, Sept. 25.

Hoang, G. and R. Erickson. 1985. Cultural barriers to effective medical care among Indochinese patients. *Annual Review of Medicine* 36:229-39.

Hoang, G. and E. Erickson. 1982. Guidelines for providing medical care to Southeast Asian refugees. *Journal of the American Medical Association* 248(6):710-714.

Ikeda, J., D. Ceja, R. Glass, J. Harwood, K. Lucke, and J. Sutherlin. 1991. Food habits of the Hmong living in central California. *Journal of Nutrition Education* 23:168-175.

Indochinese refugees and the clinical encounter. 1983. Family planning paper; Refugee Health Services Program. Santa Clara County (CA), Health Department.

Judge orders surgery for Fresno boy over objections of parents. 1990. *San José (CA) Mercury News*, Feb. 23, p. 1A.

Kim, K., M. Kohrs, R. Twork, and M. Grier. 1984. Dietary calcium intakes of elderly Korean Americans. *Journal of The American Dietetic Association* 84(2):164-169.

Krause, M. and K. Mahan. 1984. *Food, nutrition, and diet therapy*. Philadelphia: W.B. Saunders and Co., Tables 16-6, 16-7, and 16-8.

Kulig, Judith. 1990. A review of the health status of Southeast Asian refugee women. *Health Care for Women International* 11(1):49-63.

Meyers, C. 1992. Hmong children and their families: consideration of cultural influences in assessment. *American Journal of Occupational Therapy* 46(8):737-744.

Muecke, M. 1983. In search of healers: Southeast Asian refugees in the American health care system. *The Western Journal of Medicine* 139:835.

Nguyen, D. 1985. Culture shock: a review of Vietnamese culture and its concepts of health and disease. *The Western Journal of Medicine* 142:409.

Nhu, T. 1987, Dec. 27. What's in a name? *San José (CA) Mercury News*, p. C 7.

Nong, T. A. 1976. "Pseudo-battered child" syndrome. *Journal of the American Medical Association* 623:2288.

Orque, M. 1983. Nursing care of South Vietnamese patients, Chapter 8 in *Ethnic nursing care: a multicultural approach*, edited by M. Orque, B. Bloch, and L. Monrroy. St. Louis: C. V. Mosby.

Rairdon, B. and Z. Higgs. 1992. When your patient is a Hmong refugee. *American Journal of Nursing* 92(3):52-55.

Richardson, E. 1990. The Cambodians and Laotians, Chapter 2 in *Cross cultural counseling*, edited by N. Waxler-Morrison, J. Anderson, and E. Richardson. Vancouver, BC: University of British Columbia Press.

Rosanoff, A. and D. Calloway. 1982. Calcium source in Indochinese immigrants. *New England Journal of Medicine* 306(4):239.

Santopietro, M. and B. Lynch. 1980. What's behind the "inscrutable" mask? *RN* 43(10):55-61.

Schultz, S. 1982. How Southeast Asian refugees in California adapt to unfamiliar health care practices. *Health and Social Work* 7:148-156.

Story. M. and L. Harris. 1989. Food habits and dietary changes of Southeast Asian refugee families living in the United States. *Journal of The American Dietetic Association* 89:800.

Sutherland, J., R. Avant, W. Franz III, C. Monzon, and N. Stark. 1983. Indochinese refugee health assessment and treatment. *The Journal of Family Practice* 16(1):61-67.

Tran, T. Van. 1988. The Vietnamese family, in *Ethnic families in America*, 3rd edition, edited by C. Mindel, R. Habenstein, and R. Wright, Jr. New York: Elsevier.

Uba, L. 1992. Cultural barriers to health care for Southeast Asian refugees. *Public Health Reports* 107(5):544-555.

Chapter 15

PILIPINOS AND PACIFIC ISLANDERS

PILIPINO AMERICANS

Pilipinos are racial mixtures of people from many countries, including China, Spain, Malaya, United States, Japan, and India. As a result of Spanish domination from 1521 to 1898, the Philippines is the only Christian country in Asia. With the exception of a five-year period of domination by Japan during World War II, the United States controlled the Philippines from 1898 until independence was granted in 1946 (Aquino, 1981). Pilipinos have immigrated to the United States in three distinct time periods. The first Pilipinos arrived in small numbers over the span of many years from the mid-1700's to the mid-1930's. Early immigrants included laborers from Spanish merchant ships who escaped and eventually settled in Louisiana, Pilipino students, and men who worked on Hawaiian sugar plantations. Others came to the Western U.S. and worked on farms, in canneries, and as servants. This first group of Pilipino Americans was primarily composed of young, single men with rural backgrounds and little education. Victims of discrimination, they stayed together in close-knit communities (Orque, 1983). In 1903, a few students were carefully selected and sent to the United States to obtain educations. They all returned to the Philippines where they became leaders in many professions (Aquino, 1981). In 1934, legislation reclassified Pilipinos as aliens and limited their immigration to 50 people a year (Chan, 1992).

The second group of immigrants consisted of those who entered the U.S. between 1946 and 1964. Many in this group had been promised United States citizenship if they served in the U.S. Armed Forces during World War II. The promise wasn't fulfilled until December 1991 during ceremonies to observe the 50th anniversary of the bombing of Pearl Harbor. This second group has generally not achieved the higher educational and socioeconomic status of other "second group" immigrants in the United States (Orque, 1983; Chan, 1992).

The most recent group has immigrated since 1965 when immigration quotas were significantly liberalized. In contrast to the first two groups, the third group of immigrants consists predominantly of young professionals who enter the U.S. with families; they are from urban areas, are well educated, and speak English. Most are Catholics. Many have experienced difficulty obtaining positions commensurate with their professional skills (Parrillo, 1985). Discrimination has interfered with social and economic advancement. Pilipino men in California received 64 percent of the pay of White men in 1980 even though they had equivalent work experience and education. Pay for Pilipino women in 1980 was 45 percent of the pay of White men, which was only slightly lower than for White women who had 51 percent of the pay of White men. The lower pay for Pilipino women compared to White women reflects fewer years of work experience and a younger age (Cabezos, Shinagawa, and Kawaguchi, 1986-87). For some professions, training received in the Philippines is not accepted in the United States, adding to underemployment.

Pilipino World View

Bahala na is the belief that the universe is controlled by God's will and other supernatural forces. A person who lives a good life on earth will be rewarded by eternal life after death, while a sinful life brings about misfortune and illness as punishment. Chan (1992) argues that *bahala na* does not lead to a fatalistic outlook on life but can be "viewed more positively as determination in the face of uncertainty" (p. 276). The world is believed to be controlled by external forces and humans should be willing to accept what life brings. This concept influences the Pilipino view of time. Punctuality, especially for social events, is not a priority because unavoidable delays are expected and accepted. In the business setting, however, Pilipino Americans usually adapt to the Western sense of time urgency (Orque, 1983).

The world is seen as hostile and unpredictable. To counter this, friends and family provide security and comfort. Proper social conduct and smooth interpersonal relations are highly valued. One aspect of social acceptance is the avoidance of shame (*hiya*). *Hiya* is related to "face" and the opinion of other people. It is important to maintain "face" through proper behavior. Similarly, self-esteem (*amor propio*) is highly valued in Pilipino society (Chan, 1992).

Also included in society's expectations for proper behavior is the fulfillment of *utang na loob* or reciprocity. This is an obligation to repay others for their favors. In other words, favors must be repaid by gifts or a reciprocal favor. Since it is important to maintain group cohesiveness and smooth relations, it is customary in Pilipino society "to go along with" (*pakikisama*) the suggestions of others (Chan, 1992). In the clinical setting, Pilipino American patients may be reluctant to disagree with others because of the importance of *pakikisama*. Studies of Pilipino traits and values have identified "family orientation, joy and humor, flexibility, adaptability and creativity, hard work and industry, faith and religiosity, and ability to survive" as characteristics of Pilipinos (Chan, 1992, p. 275).

Family Structure and Interactional Styles

The family is highly valued in Pilipino culture. Members are seen as mutually dependent, and an individual's behavior reflects on the entire family. As in other Asian cultures, the interests of the group are given priority over those of its members. The relation of husband and wife can be described as egalitarian. Decisions are based on concessions and are made by both husband and wife (Aquino, 1981). Women hold high status in families and in society (Chan, 1992). Children of both sexes are highly valued (Aquino, 1981). They learn to value interdependence, obedience, modesty, and respect for elders and authority figures (Anderson, 1983). The household frequently includes many extended family members from both sides of the family. Pilipino American families are often large and may be further extended by the *compadre* (godparent) system. In the Catholic church, a coparent (godparent) is designated at baptism; this person is responsible for the child's religious education and provides financial support in times of need. The relationship is lifelong (Orque, 1983).

During illness, the family is the primary source of psychological support for the patient. Frequently, family members remain at the patient's side throughout hospitalization, and participate in hospital care. Health-care decisions are also greatly influenced by members of the family.

Communication

Communication patterns of Pilipinos reflect the cultural emphasis on smooth social relations. For example, direct disagreement or conflict is often avoided. This tendency may be misinterpreted by mainstream Americans as evasive or devious. Personal feelings may also be expressed indirectly, if at all. When disagreements do occur, the use of "go-betweens" is common. These mediators act to solve the problems between two people and avoid unpleasant face-to-face conflict. In this way dignity (face) is maintained.

Language may be another barrier in delivery of effective health care. Members of the Pilipino community may speak any one of a large number of languages and dialects. The elderly, especially, may have limited knowledge and comprehension of English. Use of interpreters and/or visual aids is helpful in this event.

Health Beliefs and Practices

Individuals vary in the degree to which they adhere to cultural practices depending on their background and the situation. Many Pilipino Americans use both their traditional healing system and Western medicine. According to traditional Pilipino medicine, illness may have many different causes. These causes fall into two general categories; natural and supernatural. Natural causes generally involve imbalance or irregularity in some aspect of one's life. For example, overwork, exposure to cold, heat, imbalance of hot/cold, rain, wind, overeating, worry, anxiety, and lack of sleep or food may lead to illness (Montepio, 1986-7). Good health is the result of a balanced life and personal cleanliness.

The entry of cold air (wind) is believed to be harmful to the system. Even sudden changes in the weather are potential causes of illness (Anderson, 1983). A woman's body is considered "open" to illness, especially following childbirth. For this reason, many new mothers may avoid bathing for up to one month after delivery (Orque, 1983).

Supernatural forces are also believed to cause illness. Spirits, souls of the dead, ghosts, witches, sorcerers, and evil people may curse an individual. Illness may also be punishment from God for sins. Often, illnesses that do not respond to Western medical treatment are attributed to supernatural causes. These are believed to be better treated by cultural healers (Orque, 1983; Montepio, 1986-87).

Cultural healers include several types of practitioners. Some specialize; for example, the lay midwife uses massage therapy and is consulted before, during, and after childbirth. A "chief" cultural healer is one who is gifted with supernatural powers. He may use techniques such as offerings to the spirits, chanting rituals, or curing herbs, medicines, and beverages (Orque, 1983). Many Pilipinos first seek help from cultural healers because of a personal relationship; the healer may be a relative, friend, or neighbor. Trust, which is important in Pilipino relationships, is easily established with a cultural healer. In addition, costs are generally low and communication is less a problem. Healing is considered a gift of God and to charge a fee is not acceptable; however, voluntary contributions are acceptable (Montepio, 1986–87). Western health practitioners must be aware that patients will frequently receive treatment from both a cultural healer and a Western practitioner simultaneously. Self-medication with powerful medicinal herbs is common (Anderson, 1983). Medical practitioners are expected to heal their clients immediately, and if results are too slow the patient will change doctors and even healing systems (Montepio, 1986–87).

In a study conducted among Los Angeles Pilipinos, Montepio (1986-87) found that people from rural areas in the Philippines had more knowledge of traditional healing methods, and people from urban areas used more over-the-counter medicines. Despite college degrees, most of the respondents blamed disease on food (too much food, wrong food combinations, etc.), pollution, viruses, abuse of the body, and punishment for sins. These Los Angeles Pilipinos believed that supernatural causes of illness did not occur in the United States, possibly because the supernatural forces couldn't cross the ocean or survive in a noisy urban location (Montepio, 1986–87).

In responding to illness, the Pilipino patient frequently exhibits the *bahala na* attitude (acceptance of one's fate). Patience and endurance teach Pilipinos to tolerate pain and illness with little complaint. Religion and family support are primary means of comfort and strength to the patient. Unfortunately, medical care may not be sought until the condition is quite advanced (Orque, 1983).

Mental illness carries a strong social stigma; many cases are kept hidden by the family. Psychological distress is often suppressed in an effort to maintain a proper front and smooth social relations (Anderson, 1983).

Traditional healing practices of the Pilipino culture include flushing, heating, and protection. Flushing is intended to release impurities and debris from the body. Various flushing methods are used to purge the body by stimulating perspiration, vomiting, flatus, or menstrual bleeding. Heating is practiced in order to balance the hot and cold elements in the body for optimal health. Protection refers to methods of guarding against illness, such as the wearing of religious medals and other articles to repel evil forces. Some practices are also based on the theory of imitative magic. According to this belief, traits of objects or people may be transferred to an individual. For example, pregnant women are encouraged to look at beautiful objects or at happy, intelligent people so that their babies will be born with these characteristics (Orque, 1983).

Health Status in the United States

Although national statistics do not provide separate data for Pilipinos (see Chapter 2), smaller studies show that the incidence of some types of cancers are lower among Pilipinos than Whites and Japanese. Pilipinos are more likely than Whites to have gout, thalassemia (a genetic anemia), hypertension, diabetes mellitus, cancer of the liver, and tuberculosis (Orque, 1983). With acculturation and dietary changes the incidence of coronary heart disease increases. Alcohol is consumed almost entirely by males, some of whom are heavy drinkers. Males with high incomes and attendance in Catholic church were the most likely to drink heavily (Kitano, 1989).

Food and Nutrition in the United States

Pilipino cuisine reflects the many cultural influences in the Philippines, including Malayan, Chinese, Spanish, and American. In addition, there are many regional differences in Pilipino dietary practices. Traditional staple foods include fish, rice, and vegetables. Common Pilipino American specialties are *adobo* (pork, beef, or chicken which is simmered after being marinated in vinegar, garlic, and other seasonings), *pancit* (a noodle dish including chicken, ham, shrimp, beef, and/or pork which is sauteed in soy sauce and garlic), and *lumpia* (an egg roll stuffed with vegetables) (Orque, 1983).

Pilipino immigrants have been observed to change their diets from that consumed in the Philippines. Although fish and rice remain dietary staples in the United States, a wider variety of vegetables and fruits is consumed, and more meat is eaten. It has been suggested that this higher meat intake may be related to the increased incidence of gout among Pilipino Americans. Many Pilipinos are also lactose intolerant and don't drink milk (Orque, 1983).

A number of condiments used in the Pilipino diet are high in sodium. These include *patis* (boiled, salted shrimp), *bagoong* (anchovy or shrimp paste), *dilis* (small salted and cured fish), and soy sauce. The hypertensive Pilipino patient may be encouraged to experiment with alternative seasonings, such as lemon juice, and other herbs and spices.

Dietary practices are also influenced by the concepts of "hot" and "cold" and imitative magic. Balance is achieved by combining "hot" and "cold" foods in cooking (for example, "hot" beans are prepared with "cold" green vegetables). Dark foods (for example, prunes) may not be eaten by a pregnant woman in the belief they will cause the baby to have a dark complexion (imitative magic). Since this reasoning is familiar, Pilipino American women are receptive to the idea that diet during pregnancy affects the baby's health. Many Pilipino Americans are devout

Catholics and may practice religious dietary restrictions, such as the avoidance of meat on Fridays and Ash Wednesday (Orque, 1983).

Implications for Health Care

The general rules which govern communication and etiquette also apply in the health care setting. The caregiver may be viewed as an authority figure causing the Pilipino patient to behave with formality and modesty and give the appearance of being shy or aloof (Orque, 1983).

Also, in keeping with the Pilipino tradition of respect for the elderly, health professionals should not call older patients by their first names. Gender as well as age differences may affect communication. For example, eye contact between elderly men and younger women indicates anger or seduction; so, the elderly male patient may seem somewhat distant to a younger female caregiver (Orque, 1983).

Reflecting the cultural emphasis on avoiding shame and maintaining self-esteem, certain topics are considered very personal and may be uncomfortable for the Pilipino patient to discuss openly. These subjects may include sex, socioeconomic status, and tuberculosis (this disease is still feared by many Pilipinos due to its continued prominence in the Philippines). Sensitive topics should be addressed subtly and indirectly; the patient's privacy must be respected. Pilipino patients may be uncomfortable expressing personal feelings in group settings, so a one-on-one approach may be more effective. Men are especially reluctant to admit any emotional problems. Sexual topics are best discussed with men and women separately (Orque, 1983).

PACIFIC ISLANDERS

The Pacific Islands are home to many cultural groups. Throughout history, the peoples of the Pacific have migrated and mixed to produce many diverse populations. Significant numbers immigrate to the United States in hopes of finding better employment, education, and health care. Pacific Islanders in the U.S. are primarily Natives of Hawaii or of American Samoa, Guam, or the Trust Territories of the Pacific Islands (Northern Marianas, Palau, the Marshalls, and the Federated States of Micronesia). Samoa was divided into two countries in 1900; American Samoa is a territory of the United States. Western Samoa in now independent, but was administered for many years by Germany and New Zealand (Fitzpatrick-Nietschmann, 1983).

The first settlers of Hawaii were Polynesians from the Marquesas Islands around 200 B.C. to A.D. 900 and from Tahiti and surrounding islands from A.D. 900 to 1300. Captain James Cook landed in Hawaii in 1778 and introduced the island people to Western culture. In the years from 1778 to 1823 there was a rapid decline in the Native Hawaiian population because of high infant mortality, decreasing fertility, diseases brought by foreign ships and emigration. Venereal diseases were introduced by Cook's crew and are believed responsible for the decreased fertility; diseases introduced by foreign visitors are believed responsible for the increased infant mortality. Between 1804 and 1853 epidemics of cholera, influenza, mumps, whooping cough, measles, and smallpox killed many Native Hawaiians. Other diseases, including leprosy, were introduced by Chinese crew members. Through all of these disasters, the Hawaiian people were very reluctant to use foreign doctors. The resulting deaths reduced the pure Hawaiian population from 276,000 in 1779 to 11,294 in 1960. People who are now counted as Hawaiian by the U.S. Bureau of the Census are mixtures of many races with Native Hawaiian blood as little as one-sixteenth of their heritage (Nordyke, 1989). Native Hawaiians make up almost one-fifth of Hawaii's population. Their socioeconomic status and life expectancy are among the lowest in the state (Fitzpatrick-Nietschmann, 1983).

Other than Hawaiians, the majority of Pacific Islanders living on "mainland" U.S. came from Samoa and are concentrated in San Diego, Los Angeles, and San Francisco (Daly City).

Centered on 27 churches, the Daly City community is noted for its structured and close-knit political/social framework. American Samoans are U.S. nationals and Guamanians are U.S. citizens. Both groups have free entry into the U.S. (Xenos, et al., 1987). In 1980 the per capita income of Samoans was only 49 percent of the general U.S. population. Guamanians per capita incomes were 76 percent of the general population. Twenty-eight percent of Samoan families, 12 percent of Guamanian families and 10 percent of the general population were below the poverty line in 1980 (Xenos, et al., 1987).

World View

It is believed that each human is made up of a body and a spirit/soul. Many people who are native to this geographical area believe that the soul is visible; that is, it can be seen in shadows and in water reflections. It is also believed that the soul may leave the body during sleep, in illness, and at death. Beliefs in what happens to the soul at death vary. Some think that the soul becomes a ghost. Ghosts (of human souls) differ from spirits, which do not originate from humans; spirits may be strong enough to become deities and demons. Magic is practiced among some Natives of the Pacific Islands to control events and is believed effective because of its effects on spirits. Prayers, offerings, sacrifices, and worship are also used to effect the actions of spirits (Oliver, 1989). Samoans may believe that lives are controlled by supernatural powers and that individuals have little control over their own lives. Missionaries in the 1830s converted many Pacific Islanders to Christianity.

Many Hawaiians retain a belief in spiritual relationships among their ancestors, their family members, and nature. Ancestors may be represented in animals or other products of nature. However, Hawaiians have little remaining of their original culture (Nordyke, 1989).

Family Structure and Interactional Styles

As in some other cultures, the family group is more important than any one family member; cooperation is preferred to competition. Samoans structure their lives around the family, which may be extended to include an entire village. Religion is very important in Samoan family life. Samoans are less affected than Hawaiians by the influence of Western culture (Mokuau and Touili'ili, 1992). Care of young Samoan children is the responsibility of older siblings. Hawaiian children are valued highly and provided with considerable attention. Many family members are involved in the care of Hawaiian children (Mokuau and Touili'ili, 1992).

Health Beliefs and Practices

The traditional Hawaiian medicine man (*Kahuna lapa au*) used prayers, massage, plants and herbs, and chants to treat illnesses (Mokuau and Touili'ili, 1992). Illness was believed caused by imbalance of spiritual strength (Nordyke, 1989). Traditional Samoans have considerable faith in herbal remedies and traditional doctors who use massage as a treatment (Mokuau and Touili'ili, 1992).

Health Status

Western medical services have been provided on many Pacific islands at various times during the exploration, settlement, and military defense of the Pacific. Although immunization and sanitation practices were initiated by outsiders, these services were usually discontinued when the providing nation withdrew from the area. As a result, there is limited access to medical care on many islands in the Pacific. However, U.S.

funding does support the establishment of regional medical centers with the goal of improving health care services (Fitzpatrick-Nietschmann, 1983). Prior to the arrival of Captain Cook, Native Hawaiians had good health. Their diets were low in fat and they were personally very clean.

Immigrants from the Pacific Islands do not suffer from tropical infectious diseases. Instead, the chronic diseases of civilization (hypertension, cardiovascular disease, and diabetes mellitus) are of major concern. Drastic lifestyle changes—from rural, agricultural settings to sedentary, urban Western city life—have resulted in health risks. Most notable of these is obesity, which is very prevalent among many Pacific Island populations. Samoans traditionally considered high body weight to be beautiful, but this value is decreasing among migrants. Unfortunately, values regarding obesity have not changed in time to reduce health risks for first- and second-generation American Samoans. The consumption of processed, high-fat foods and the sedentary lifestyles have contributed to obesity. McGarvey (1991) speculated that the apparent genetic predisposition to obesity could be related to the survival of overweight individuals during long ocean voyages in which food was limited.

The stress of migration to the mainland United States may also be a health risk. Due to cultural differences, the Pacific Islander may not share the Western view of individual responsibility for health care. Additionally, the new immigrant is likely to be of low socioeconomic status due to language barriers and lack of marketable skills. Thus, social and economic pressures create stress which increases the likelihood of illness (Fitzpatrick-Nietschmann, 1983).

Compared to Whites in Hawaii, Native Hawaiians in Hawaii have excess deaths from heart disease, cancer (especially stomach and lung), diabetes, infant mortality, and accidents (Heckler, 1985). Curb, et al. (1991) reported many risk factors for heart disease among Native Hawaiians. These authors found over 60 percent of their subjects were overweight, 42 percent of the males smoked, 36 percent of those from ages 40 to 59 had hypertension, and 23 percent of those from ages 50 to 59 had diabetes which was mostly not treated.

Food and Nutrition

In their homelands, traditional Pacific Islanders plant many tree-fruit crops. Coconut palms provide coconut meat and water; sometimes the meat is pressed to express its milk (oils). The pulp of the trunks of Sago palms is pulverized to obtain a starch used in cooking pancakes and soups. Breadfruit is a starchy fruit that is eaten fresh or fermented and is a major source of nutrients including protein, calcium, iron, vitamin C, and the B vitamins. Coconuts supply dietary fat, and fish are a good source of protein. Cultured crops are taro root, yam, sweet potatoes, arrowroot and many other plants depending on the geographical location and growing conditions. Chickens are eaten, but usually eggs are not. Pigs are kept by some groups and used for food, but seldom does a family eat its own pig. They obtain pork from others by bartering. Pork is not a regular food (Oliver, 1989). Traditional beverages include fresh water, coconut milk, and kava, a narcotic made from water and pulverized roots of a plant. In Micronesia, the fresh sap of certain palm trees is consumed regularly as a beverage (toddy), in some places fermented into an alcoholic drink.

Most households have their own food gardens. The men do the heavy work of clearing the land and are usually responsible for harvesting fruit from tall trees. Garden work is done by almost everyone except in some Polynesian societies, where upper class people are supplied with food by their servants (Oliver, 1989).

Many of the traditional cultures have taboos on certain foods which cannot be eaten because "of age, gender, marital status, pregnancy, illness, and bereavement" (Oliver, 1989, p. 295). Some traditional diets do not contain enough protein for growing children and there is evidence that malnutrition existed when people ate traditional diets.

Implications for Health Care

Many members of this group are highly acculturated, and no special precautions are needed. Among those with more traditional beliefs it is important to be considerate of any beliefs in spiritualism and not to impose Western values and beliefs. Because Pacific Islanders may have low income, they might benefit from referral services and efforts to remove barriers to health care. Health education in this population should focus on obesity, diet, and exercise (Fitzpatrick-Nietschmann, 1983).

References Cited

Anderson, J. 1983. Health and illness in Pilipino immigrants. *The Western Journal of Medicine*, 139(6),811.

Aquino, C. 1981. The Filipino in America, Chapter 7 in *Culture and child rearing*, by Ann Clark. Philadelphia: F. A. Davis Co.

Cabezos, A., L. Shinagawa, and G. Kawaguchi. 1986-7. New inquiries into the socioeconomic status of Pilipino Americans in California. *Amerasia Journal* 13(1):1-21.

Chan, S. 1992. Families with Pilipino roots, Chapter 9 in *Developing cross-cultural competence*, edited by E. Lynch and M. Hanson. Baltimore: Paul H. Brookes Pub. Co.

Curb, J., N. Alali, J. Kautz, H. Petrovitch, S. Knutsen, R. Knutsen, H. O'Conner, and W. O'Conner. 1991. Cardiovascular risk factors in ethnic Hawaiians. *American Journal of Public Health* 81(2):164-167.

Fitzpatrick-Nietschmann, J. 1983. Pacific Islanders: migration and health. *The Western Journal of Medicine* 139(6):848-853.

Heckler, M. 1985. *Report of the Secretary's Task Force on black and minority health, Volume 1, Executive Summary*. Washington, D.C.: U.S. Department of Health and Human Services.

Kitano, H. 1989. Alcohol and the Asian American, in *Alcoholism in minority populations*, edited by T. Watts and R. Wright, Jr. Springfield, IL: Charles C. Thomas Publisher.

McGarvey, S. 1991. Obesity in Samoans and a perspective on its etiology in Polynesians. *American Journal of Clinical Nutrition* 53:1586S-1594S.

Mokuau, N. and P. Tauili'ili. 1992. Families with Native Hawaiian and Pacific Island roots, Chapter 10 in *Developing cross-cultural competence, a guide for working with young children and their families*, edited by E. Lynch and M. Hanson. Baltimore: Paul H. Brooke Pub. Co.

Montepio, S. 1986-7. Folk medicine in the Filipino American experience. *Amerasia Journal* 13(1):151-162.

Nordyke, E. 1989. *The peopling of Hawaii*, 2nd edition. Honolulu: University of Hawaii Press.

Oliver, Douglas. 1989. *Oceania, vol. I*. Honolulu: University of Hawaii Press.

Orque, M. 1983. Nursing care of Filipino American patients, Chapter 5 in *Ethnic nursing care: a multicultural approach*, edited by M. Orque, B. Bloch, and L. Monrroy. St. Louis: C. V. Mosby.

Parrillo, V. 1985. *Strangers to these shores*, 2nd edition. New York: John Wiley and Sons.

Xenos, P., R. Gardner, H. Barringer, and M. Levin. 1987. Asian Americans: growth and change in the 1970s, Chapter 11 in *Pacific Bridges: the new immigration from Asia and the Pacific Islands*, edited by J. Fawcett and B. Carino. New York: Center for Migration Studies.

Chapter 16

SOUTH ASIANS: ASIAN INDIANS

The largest group of South Asians is from India, and they are discussed here. Other South Asian countries include Pakistan, Bangladesh, Sri Lanka, Nepal, and Bhutan. Even though they are from Asia, many Asian Indians (also known as East Indians) are classified by anthropologists as Caucasian (Jensen, 1980). Prior to 1900 there were fewer than 800 immigrants from India in the United States; many of the first immigrants entered into Canada and then moved south to the United States. Early in the 1900s almost seven thousand Indian agricultural workers were admitted to the states of California, Oregon, and Washington where they worked in the lumber industry and for manufacturing companies; only a few were in railroad construction. In California, many worked in agriculture. These immigrants were mostly male with little education (Chandras, 1978). Because they were Asian, they faced considerable discrimination. Other workers resented them for the jobs they were taking and suspected they were being used by employers to lower wages. Like other immigrants of the time, their intentions were to save money and return home. Some of them did return to India, but the reason was more likely due to racial discrimination than to acquired wealth (Parrillo, 1985; Chandras, 1978).

A racial incident in 1907 in Bellingham, Washington forced 700 Asian Indians to flee into Canada. About the same time, a San Francisco organization was successful in getting immigration officials to reject the entry of over 1000 Asian Indians. However, the Western Pacific Railroad managed to gain entry for about 1500 workers from India between 1911 and 1920 (Jensen, 1980).

In 1923 the U.S. Supreme Court ruled that Asian Indians were nonwhites and were not eligible for citizenship. As a result of this decision, immigration from India essentially stopped. Those who were aliens in California became ineligible to own or lease land because of state laws against Asians. Many left the United States, and those who stayed had little choice but to become itinerant farm laborers. By 1946 there were fewer than 1,500 Asian Indian immigrants in the United States. They stayed together in communities, and many married Mexican women (Jensen, 1980; Chandras, 1978).

Legislation in 1946 allowed Asian Indian residents in the United States to become naturalized citizens. This same legislation set an immigration quota of 100 entries a year. Most Asian Indians who entered the United States between 1946 and 1965, when the quotas were changed, were admitted on student visas. The 1965 changes in immigration laws resulted in the second phase of Asian Indian immigration. The new law allowed admission to the United States based on two specific categories: (1) professionals and persons with skills needed in the United States, and (2) family members joining persons already admitted. In the five years from 1966 to 1970, almost 25,000 Asian Indians entered the United States. This was a dramatic increase in immigration. The maximum admissions from India were set at 20,000 per year (100,000 in five years). By 1985 there were over 400,000 Asian Indians in the United States (some estimates are higher). During this time many students decided to stay in the United States. In 1986 over half the Asian Indian immigrants admitted to permanent residence were already in the U.S. under temporary, non-immigrant visas (students). A large percentage of immigrants from India have been professionals and skilled workers who enter with their families. As more Indian immigrants become naturalized citizens, more highly educated young professionals will assist extended family members to enter the United States on the basis of relationship. Every year a higher proportion of women and children enter the U. S. from India. Most of the women are wives of men who entered earlier. Many of the recent immigrants are employed in service industries and in commerce and are not as highly educated as earlier immigrants. The greatest numbers have settled on the East and West Coasts of the United States, with the largest concentration in and around New York City. There are also large numbers of Asian Indians in California, most living in and around San Francisco and Los Angeles (Minocha, 1987; Jensen, 1980).

The overpopulation of India has contributed to the increase in immigrants to the United States and to other countries. India is second only to China in population density, with 15 percent of the world population and only 2.5 percent of the land. Literacy rate is low in India (32 percent) and there are serious problems with poverty and hunger. Unfortunately, the population of India continues to increase at a rapid rate and the economy is stagnant with little opportunity for employment of professionals. India has a low-cost educational system that provides more well-educated people than can be employed (Parrillo, 1985).

World View

The world view of Eastern cultures is very foreign to a person from the West. Much of the difference is based on religion. Western religions (Judaism, Christianity, and Islam) all come from the Middle East. Basically, Western religions adhere to the belief in one absolute God who started the universe, keeps it going, and eventually brings an end to all things. In other words, God determines things. Smart (1988) described all Western religions as starting with "God out there and everything else here" (p. 63). In Western religions, each human has only one lifetime in which to achieve everlasting life; people must obey God. Religion has structure in its churches and practices of worship.

Eastern religions (Hinduism, Buddhism, Jainism, and Sikhism) on the other hand, originated in India. Of the other major Eastern (or Asian) religions, Confucianism and Taoism originated in China and Shintoism in Japan. In the East, religion starts with humans and has to do with how humans relate to others and everything in the world including animals, rivers, mountains, etc. Eastern religions explain what happens within a person and among people. In fact, to a Western person, some Asian religions, especially Hinduism and Buddhism, sound more like psychology in their attempt to explain human behavior than like the Western concept of religion. The idea of god comes into the explanation when a person needs it. Unlike Western religion, god is not made in the image of man. Deities are believed to be in any form and in all locations. Life is an essence that is reincarnated in different forms and does not end. Eastern religions are oriented to life here and now (Smart, 1988; Jain, 1988).

Hinduism is the religion of 83 percent of the people in India, 11 percent of the population follows Islam, and the remaining 6 percent are Christians, Sikhs, Buddhists, Jains, and others (Ramakrishna and Weiss, 1992). Even though most Asian Indians are Hindus, a high proportion of the early immigrants to the United States were Sikhs (Chandras, 1978).

Hinduism is described to a Westerner as a method of knowing reality through a diverse system of traditions. The world is an illusion, nothing is permanent. Time is cyclical for all living things which continually undergo birth, death, and rebirth (reincarnation). To be saved is to escape the cycle and go into a state of eternal bliss (Nirvana). A code of conduct, Dharma, governs all personal and social aspects of life. There are many gods or no gods because Hinduism accommodates many views (Jain, 1988).

No one person founded Hinduism. It grew from many practices and beliefs. The caste system and the concept of purity are fundamental to Hinduism. Pure individuals must not have contact with impure persons. Brahmans (priests), the highest caste, must be pure to communicate with the gods. The untouchables are so low that they are below and outside the caste system. They are given the most polluting work. A person is born into a caste which also defines that individual's occupation (Chatterjee, 1983). Many efforts have been made to improve conditions for the untouchables, but any change threatens the positions of all people in the caste system and is strongly opposed. Some untouchables have changed their religious affiliation to Christianity, Buddhism, Islam, or other non-Hindu religion in an effort to escape. The caste system is so strong in India, however, that not much improvement is realized by the change, and many individuals are forced to retain their Hindu caste even in their new religion. Sikh communities are least influenced by the caste system (Chatterjee, 1983). One of the doctrines of Sikhism is the rejection of the caste system (Chandras, 1978).

One important rule of the caste system is that it prohibits anyone from accepting cooked food from a person of lower (less pure) caste. Milk is believed to be one of the most pure substances, and as a result the cow is protected throughout India (Jain, 1988; Chatterjee, 1983).

This brief description of religion and social structure in India is intended to demonstrate the very different (from Western) world view and the extreme heterogeneity of people who immigrate from India.

Family Structure and Interactional Styles

It is difficult to be specific about family structure in India because the many different family types include extended, nuclear, matrilineal, patrilineal, matriarchal, patriarchal, egalitarian, and so on. According to Chatterjee (1988), families in the north and west areas of India are likely to be male-dominated and in the south and northeast areas are more likely to be female-dominated. Extended families are more common than nuclear families in India, but migration to cities, increased educational levels of women, and Westernization of society contribute to the breakdown of large families (Chatterjee, 1988). Marriages may be arranged and involve the joining of two large family groups. However, marriage by self-selection is increasing in India.

A few of the early immigrants from Punjabi (Sikhs) followed their cultural tradition of extended families made up of brothers and their families. However, most Indian families in the U.S. are now urban and nuclear. Most are from urban areas in India and are young, married adults (30 to 40 years old) with small families. If they are single, they may return to India after several years for a prearranged marriage. Many hold master's degrees or higher (Saran, 1985). As a result, compared to other groups, Asian Indians are affluent (Table 11-1). They are making greater efforts to retain their cultural heritage than earlier immigrants. Contact with India is regular with trips to India and visits from Indian family and friends. Letters are exchanged and newspapers and magazines keep them informed. Many immigrants plan to move back to India, however, this desire is not being carried out (Jensen, 1980).

Asian Indians in the U.S. save money at a rate two to three times the national average. On the average, they save 20 percent of their incomes. Some of this money may be sent to relatives in India. Although they spend less money on material goods, they are willing to invest in their children's education and in houses. They also have heavy expenses in frequent travel to India and in hosting family and friends who visit from India (Saran, 1985).

Surveys of Asian Indians in the U.S. show that they face some discrimination, and the most difficult problem is discrimination in employment. Some are not able to find employment that reflects their professional qualifications or their previous professional experiences in India. In some cases (engineering, medicine, law), training in India is not directly acceptable and further education/training is necessary (Chandras, 1978; Ramakrishna and Weiss, 1992).

Adult immigrants, despite their acceptance of American life, usually retain their basic values, behaviors, and attitudes. This leads to conflicts with their children who participate in activities (school, sports, TV, etc.) outside the family influence. Many parents do not approve of dating, and are so concerned about U.S. sexual permissiveness, violence, and drugs that they often talk about returning to India when their children reach 14 or 15 years of age. Some parents plan to send their children to India for their college educations (Ramakrishna and Weiss, 1992). The children who are raised in the United States will undoubtedly have more liberal attitudes than their parents. Some authors fault the parents for failure to understand their children and predict some serious problems as the children grow older (Saran and Leonhard-Spark, 1980; Saran, 1985). According to Ramisetty-Mikler (1993), parents are less dominant in the United States than in India and do allow their children to have more freedoms.

Another value difference that Asian Indians find in the United States compared to India is the lack of respect for elders. Indians are critical of this. Also, in the United States, daughters cannot be as closely controlled by the family; some daughters decide to choose their own husbands and types of employment. In addition, sons do not feel as responsible for the family as traditional values require. Value differences are part of the reason for the strong efforts made by adults to maintain their culture and resist assimilation (Saran, 1985).

Today, most Asian Indians in the United States live as small families (not as single males) and maintain family contacts in the United States and in India. They belong to many Indian organizations, probably as a means of educating their children in Indian culture. At meetings and social functions the sexes tend to congregate separately. However, families in the United States are more egalitarian, with more sharing of responsibilities, duties, and decision-making than in India (Ramisetty-Mikler, 1993).

Communication

Many Asian Indians in the United States speak excellent English when they arrive. However, with the expected change in immigrants from highly educated professionals to family members who are not as well educated, English skills will diminish. For health professionals, it will be increasingly more important to evaluate the degree of acculturation among clients and their use of traditional healing methods. Less acculturated immigrants will be more dependent on family and less willing to act independently. There may be increased hesitation to discuss personal matters. It has been suggested (Ramisetty-Mikler, 1993) that individual care can best be approached through emphasis on family needs rather than individual problems. In counseling, sustained eye contact may be considered rude.

Health Beliefs and Practices

Asian Indians may not seek Western medicine at the first sign of illness. They report that they usually talk with a relative or friend first. Many practice Ayurvedic (traditional) medicine, a complete medical system with hospitals, textbooks, medical schools, and a pharmaceutical industry. It emphasizes a physical, mental, and spiritual balance with a positive view of health. Disease is believed caused by an imbalance of (1) five elements (earth, water, fire, air, and ether); (2) seven basic body substances (chyle, blood, flesh, fat, bone, marrow, and semen); and (3) three humors (wind, bile, and mucus). Some foods are classified hot or cold and are used to return balance and health. Health is maintained by a carefully planned daily routine in which diet, work, hygiene, and sleep are regulated. An upset will affect harmony and equilibrium and results in illness. Pregnancy is viewed as a normal condition, and many pregnant women do not seek health care (Assandand, et al., 1990; Rosengren, 1980; Ramakrishna and Weiss, 1992).

Western medicine is available in India and is preferred by many people, but it has not replaced Ayurvedic medicine. In general, Asian Indians respect and practice Western (allopathic) medicine. However, they avoid professional care for psychological/stress problems because of social stigma. Psychological problems are frequently expressed as physical disorders, and many Asian Indians are likely to believe that mental problems will be healed with time (Rosengren, 1980;

Ramakrishna and Weiss, 1992). Traditional medicine explains mental illness as due to possession by a spirit.

In India, when a person is hospitalized the relatives are expected (sometimes even required) to provide food and care throughout the stay of their relative (Ramakrishna and Weiss, 1992). In addition to Ayurvedic and Allopathic medical care, a variety of traditional (folk) healers also practice in India. The perception of effectiveness of medications or treatments depends on the form of administration. Injections are perceived as most effective with capsules less effective and tablets the least effective. Colorful medications are believed more effective than white ones. Injections are preferred and are so widely accepted that they are used by lay healers, traditional healers, and may even be self-administered. Most medications are available over-the-counter and do not require a prescription in order to be purchased (Ramakrishna and Weiss, 1992). Since the use of injectables is not controlled, even allopathic doctors may use inadequate sterilization procedures and contribute to the transmission of HIV, hepatitis B, venereal diseases, and poliomyelitis. The routine use of antibiotics contributes to the worldwide problem of resistant bacteria (Reeler, 1990). Physicians in India encourage the use of injections because of improved compliance and because fees for injections are high and the patient makes more frequent office visits. Also, physicians would lose patients if they didn't use injections. One study reported that general practitioners in India prescribed an average of 2.9 drugs per patient visit (Greenhalgh, 1987).

Health Status in the United States

Health problems include higher than average incidences of diabetes and hypertension in the United States. Also, there is an increased intake of calories and with little exercise weight gain may occur (Pitchumoni and Saran, 1980). Children have a typical U.S. pattern of morbidity. The communicable diseases (diphtheria, typhoid, whooping cough, and tuberculosis), common in India, do not occur in the United States (Gokulanathan and Gokulanathan, 1980).

Food and Nutrition in the United States

In India, women prepare the food and serve the men and children first. In the United States, women still have primary responsibility for food preparation even when men share in shopping and cleaning. However, the family usually eats together in the United States.

Hindus are not only concerned with the purity of a person, but also take great care in protecting food from polluting substances. Raw foods can be exchanged between people of different castes. However, cooked foods are subject to pollution and many rules apply. Foods that are deep fat-fried in clarified butter (*ghee*) are protected from impurities because the butter comes from cows, whose products are protected from pollution. Other food customs related to the caste system include designations regarding who prepares food, who eats with whom, how food is cooked, and who serves water, is a substance that is easily polluted (Kilare and Iya, 1992). Gupta (1976) reported that meat prohibition among Hindus is practiced in the highest castes in India. In addition, geographical location (as in central India) influences the people to be vegetarians. Many Asian Indians are not vegetarians. In her study, Gupta found that all non-vegetarian Hindus consumed beef within one year of arrival in the United States. However, vegetarian Hindus took up to seven years to eat beef, and some never ate beef. In India, beef is only consumed by Christians and Muslims. In the United States, children are more likely to eat American foods than adults, but children still have a preference for Indian foods. Breakfasts and lunches are most likely to follow the American food pattern: dinner is usually Indian (Ramakrishna and Weiss, 1992). Cereals (rice, wheat, barley) and legumes are the staple foods in Indian cuisine (Kilara and Iya, 1992). Traditional foods also include unleavened bread, vegetables, fruits, yogurts, and curries (Jensen, 1980).

Implications for Health Care

Many Asian Indians readily accept Western medicine. However, if they do not agree with the treatments offered, they may fail to object because they do not want to contradict the caregiver. They will deal with their objections by simply not returning to the same practitioner.

The popularity of injections may be partially related to the belief that anything that is ingested (including pills and liquid medicines but not injections) can upset the system. Adjustments in diet would then be necessary to balance the system. In the United States, health care providers should not be surprised to be asked for dietary recommendations to accompany any ingested treatments.

Although the caste system is not as important in the U.S. as in India, some beliefs in social status may exist. For example, a friendly smile from a health professional could be confusing to a client because smiles are exchanged only by people who are social equals in social situations (Ramakrishna and Weiss, 1992). Many people in India will avoid negative responses. As a result, a "yes" response may not be meaningful (Chatterjee, 1983).

Health care providers may have difficulty obtaining answers to personal questions because of modesty and preference to avoid being the center of attention. Ramsietty-Mikler (1993) recommended that, initially, discussions could relate to superficial topics.

Advice to Asian Indians should be authoritative (Assanand, et al., 1990). Many prefer to be given instructions or directions rather than be presented with several alternatives accompanied with predictions of the consequences of their actions. If the client's personal goals affect others in the family, any potential problems should be addressed in terms of the family needs.

Asian Indian women are likely to prefer female doctors. Relations between the client and the health professional are expected to be formal (Assanand, et al., 1990).

References Cited

Asssanand, S., M. Dias, E. Richardson, and N. Waxler-Morrison. 1990. The South Asians, Chapter 7 in *Cross cultural caring*, edited by N. Waxler-Morrison, J. Anderson, and E. Richardson. Vancouver, BC: University of British Columbia Press.

Chandras, K. 1978. *Racial discrimination against neither-White-nor-Black American minorities*. San Francisco: R and E Research Associates, pp. 80-96.

Chatterjee, B. 1983. Training and preparation for research in intercultural relations in the Indian subcontinent, in *Handbook of international training, Vol. III*, edited by D. Landis and R. Brislin. New York: Pergamon Press.

Gokulanathan, K. and I. Gokulanathan. 1980. Child health care of Asian Indians in the United States: conflicts and compromises, Chapter 16 in *The new ethnics, Asian Indians in the United States*, edited by P. Saran and E. Eames. New York: Praeger Publishers.

Greenhalgh, T. 1987. Drug prescription and self-medication in India: an exploratory survey. *Social Science Medicine* 25(3):307-318.

Gupta, S. 1976. Changes in the food habits of Asian Indians in the United States: a case study. *Sociology and Social Research* 60(1):87-99.

Jain, N. 1988. Some basic cultural patterns of India, in *Intercultural communication: a reader*, 5th edition, edited by L. Samover and R. Porter. Belmont, CA: Wadsworth Publishing Co.

Jensen, J. 1980. East Indians, in *Harvard encyclopedia of American ethnic groups*, edited by S. Thernstrom, A. Orlov, and O. Handlin. Cambridge, MA: Harvard University Press, pp. 296-301.

Kilara, A. and K. Iya. 1992. Food and dietary habits of the Hindu. *Food Technology* 46(10):94-104.

Minocha, U. 1987. South Asian Immigrants, Chapter 15 in *Pacific bridges*, edited by J. Fawcett and B. Carino. New York: The Center for Migration Studies.

Parrillo, V. 1985. *Strangers to these shores*, 2nd edition. New York: John Wiley and Sons.

Pitchumoni, C. and P. Saran. 1980. Health and medical care of Indian immigrants in the United States, Chapter 15 in *The new ethnics, Asian Indians in the United States*, edited by P. Saran and E. Eames. New York: Praeger Publishers.

Ramakrishna, J. and M. Weiss. 1992. Cross-cultural medicine, a decade later; health, illness and immigration: East Indians in the United States. *Western Journal of Medicine* 157:265-270.

Ramisetty-Mikler, S. 1993. Asian Indian immigrants in America and sociocultural issues in counseling. *Journal of Multicultural Counseling and Development* 21(1):36-49.

Reeler, A. 1990. Injections: a fatal attraction. *Social Science Medicine* 31(10):1119-1125.

Rosengren, W. 1980. *Sociology of medicine: diversity, conflict, and change*. New York: Harper and Row, Publishers.

Saran, P. and P. Leonard-Spark. 1980. Attitudinal and behavioral profile, Chapter 8 in *The new ethnics: Asian Indians in the United States*, edited by P. Saran and E. Eames. New York: Preager Publishers.

Saran, P. 1985. *The Asian Indian experience in the United States*. Cambridge, MA: Schenkman Publishing Company.

Smart, R. 1988. Religion-caused complications in intercultural communication, in *Intercultural communication: a reader*, 5th edition, edited by L. Samovar and R. Porter. Belmont, CA: Wadsworth Publishing Co.

Chapter 17

MIDDLE EASTERN AMERICANS

The Middle East is home for Arabs, Jews, Persians and many other groups. Countries in the Middle East include the Arab countries of Algeria, Bahrain, Egypt, Iraq, Jordan, Kuwait, Lebanon, Libya, Morocco, Oman, People's Republic of Yemen, Qatar, Saudi Arabia, Syria, Tunisia, United Arab Emirates, and Yemen Arabic Republic. The non-Arab countries are Iran, which is populated mostly by Persians, and Israel, which is populated mostly by Jews. People from the Arabic countries speak Arabic. Iranians are of central Asian origin and speak Farsi (Persian), Israelis speak Hebrew, and Turks speak Turkish. There are minority populations and languages in most Middle Eastern countries. For example, Kurds are located in Iraq, Syria, Turkey, and Israel; some French people live in Lebanon, Morocco, Syria, and Tunisia. Also, there are Arabs in Israel (Lipson and Meleis, 1983).

People in many of the Middle Eastern countries are poor and uneducated. The literacy rate among adults is about 50 percent or less in Algeria, Egypt, Iran, Libya, Saudi Arabia, Syria, and among the Arab population in Israel. Literacy is 70 percent or higher in Iraq, Jordan, Lebanon, and among the Jews in Israel (Spenser, 1986B).

Worldwide, infant mortality is a measure of hunger, poor nutrition, poor sanitation, and lack of health care. In the United States, infant mortality is 11.2 deaths per 1000 live births. The lowest infant mortality in the Middle East is in Israel at 14.1. In other countries the infant mortality ranges from 25 (Iraq) to 118 (Saudi Arabia) (Spenser, 1986B). The high infant mortality rates are partly responsible for the value placed on having many children.

ARABS AND PERSIANS

Early Arab (Syrian) immigrants (1880-1930) came to the U.S. for economic reasons. They had little education. A few became farmers in the southern and western states and others stayed on the East Coast in New York, New Jersey, Pennsylvania, and Massachusetts. (Elkholy, 1988). Many of the East Coast residents peddled jewelry, dry goods, and rugs door-to-door; some worked in factories. The Syrian peddlers were financially successful. Their work brought them into contact with Americans and, even though they originally planned to return to Syria, their rapid acculturation and financial success allowed them to settle in the United States. Most went into small businesses, especially into dry goods and grocery stores. There was little hostility towards the Syrians (Naff, 1980). However, a few generational problems developed between the immigrants and their American children who did not learn Arabic and had little interest in their ethnic heritage (Elkholy, 1988). Since the parents had accepted many aspects of American life, there were few assimilation problems (Naff, 1980).

The second wave of Arab/Persian immigrants started in 1950 and continues today. These immigrants are more highly educated and are scattered throughout the United States. The creation of Israel in 1948 resulted in the expulsion of 2 million Palestinians, some of whom came to the United States. Military revolutions in Egypt and other countries added to the immigration of professionals and intellectuals. The second group of immigrants has been estimated to be 78 percent Muslim. They plan to make the United

States their home and have adapted well to U.S. culture. Most have been single men. Many have received U.S. educations.

Of the second wave, 68 percent of the Muslim men married American women whom they met in college. Elkholy (1988) predicted that the wives would convert to Islam and become Muslims. Their children are raised as Americans and know little of their Arab cultures. However, the children value their parents and care for them in old age. Many second-wave Arabs are now bringing extended family members to the U.S. (Elkholy, 1988). The most recent Arab immigrants are interested in maintaining cultural traditions and have helped revive cultural interest among descendants of earlier immigrants (Syrians) who are now learning about their culture (Naff, 1980).

Arab Americans live in urban areas, many are professionals, and most are believed to be Christians. Statistical data reported in the literature are contradictory. For example, Naff (1980) reported there were slightly more than 1 million Arabs in the United States and 90 percent are Christians. Many of these would be descendants of the early Syrian immigrants. However, Lipson and Meleis (1983) stated that Arab consulates estimated 2 million to 3 million Arabs in the U.S., and Elkholy (1988) estimated that of the second wave of Arab immigrants (since World War II), 78 percent are Muslims. Naff (1980) estimated that from 1948 to 1976, there were 60 percent more Muslim Arabs than Christian Arabs entering the United States.

World View

Three major Western religions (Christianity, Judaism, and Islam) originated in the Middle East. Islam, built on a foundation of Christianity and Judaism, was founded by Muhammad (Mohammed) in the town of Mecca (now in Saudi Arabia). The teachings and revelations of Muhammad make up the religion of Islam and are written in the Holy Book of Islam, the Koran. People who practice the Islamic religion are called Muslims (Moslems). There are five basic requirements for Muslims: they must (1) testify that there is one God and Muhammad is His messenger; (2) pray five times a day facing the holy city of Mecca; (3) fast during the daylight hours in the holy month of Ramadan; not even a drop of water may be consumed (The Islamic calendar rotates around the year so that each month—including Ramadan—comes at a different time each year. It takes 33 years for any particular Islamic month to make the complete cycle); (4) pay alms to the community to help the poor; and (5) pilgrimage at least once in their lifetime to Mecca where they circle the *Ka'ba* seven times and perform other sacred rites.

Islam accepts many of the teachings of Christianity and Judaism. It accepts the belief in one God and in the messages of Moses and Jesus. However, Muslims believe that there is no Trinity ("the Father, the Son, and the Holy Ghost") and that Muhammad was the last and final messenger of God. They believe that some of God's messages were falsified and that Muhammad was sent to correct the record (Spenser, 1986A). After Muhammad's death, the followers of Islam split into two groups: the Sunni Muslims (90 percent of all Muslims) and the Shia Muslims (Spenser, 1986A). Iran is the only country in which Shia Muslims (93 percent of the population) have control. The Shia Muslims in Iran are governed by religious (Islamic) rules. Religion and state are one and religious leaders are also political leaders.

Arab and Persian cultures are high context with a casual view of time. People don't worry about missing appointments if something else seems more important. Middle Easterners value courtesy and hospitality and will be friendly to strangers (Lipson and Meleis, 1983).

Muslims believe that their ultimate fate is in God's hands and is predetermined, but fatalism does not extend to the belief that everything in life is predetermined. Also, of course, many Arabs in the United States are Christians (Lipson and Meleis, 1983).

Family Structure and Interactional Styles

For Arabs and Persians the extended family is the most important social unit (Lipson and Meleis, 1983; Spenser, 1986A; Sharifzadeh, 1992). All marriages are expected to result in many children. There is a strong preference for male children (Sharifzadeh, 1992). Families are male dominated and individual interests are subordinate to family interests. Roles of men and women are separate; women are in charge of the children and housework while men are the breadwinners and conduct family affairs that occur outside the house. The person at the top, usually the oldest and most educated male, makes the decisions. This reflects the high values placed on social status (Lipson and Meleis, 1983). Loyalty to family and efforts to improve family status result in high values for hard work, thrift, and perseverance (Naff, 1980). Men are expected to bring honor to the family (Lustig, 1988).

Family members visit each other spontaneously and frequently. Children maintain close contact with parents after marriage and are expected to care for their parents in old age (Lipson and Meleis, 1983). Arab immigrants in the United States are especially fearful that their daughters will be pressed into early sexual relations by their peers. Sexual permissiveness in the United States is a concern of many immigrants (Sharifzadeh, 1992).

Religious doctrine does not allow Muslims to marry outside their religion. However, in the United States Muslim men do marry Jewish or Christian women. Muslim women are more likely to follow Islam and marry Muslim men (Elkholy, 1988). Since Muslim women are expected to follow the religion of their husbands, if they married outside the faith they and their children would be lost to Islam. Interfaith marriages increased with the second wave of immigrants (Naff, 1980). However, intermarriage of Arabs with other ethnic groups is most likely to occur among Christian Arabs (Elkholy, 1988).

In the United States, family structures may be limited in size and as a result individuals may feel isolated (Lipson and Meleis, 1983). The rapid acculturation of first wave Arabs resulted in a breakdown of the extended family, and because peddling and small businesses required him to be away from home for long hours, the father's dominant family position was weakened. When children married, they frequently started their own households. Gradually the traditions of arranged marriages, segregation of sexes at social gatherings, covering the heads of females, and drop-in social visits were abandoned (Naff, 1980). The second wave immigrants are bringing cultural traditions back into U.S. Arab communities.

Communication

When greeting each other, Arabs may spend several minutes in introductions and polite exchanges before beginning any serious discussion. Interpersonal relations and "small talk" are important (Lustig, 1988). For Arabs, conversational distance is about two feet, uncomfortably close for Americans who prefer a five foot or greater distance. This close distance is said to be due to the need to "read" the other person's nonverbal facial and eye expressions (Lipson and Meleis, 1983). Some Arabs even wear dark glasses indoors to hide their eyes from the view of others. In the U.S., many people are taught not to stare into someone's eyes, so this careful attention to the eyes may seem very strange (Hall, 1979). Hand gestures are also very important to Arabs. Americans who are not familiar with Arab cultures should learn not to use the left hand for any public gestures or interactions such as handing out or accepting papers, and especially not to use the left hand for eating. The right hand is for public matters: the left hand is for private (toilet) matters and is considered dirty. The bottoms of the feet are the lowest part of the body and should not be shown to another person. Arab men may greet each other with a kiss on the cheek and may hold hands when walking together; they use much more body contact than American men (Harris and Moran, 1987).

Language is very high context. Arabs know more about each other than Americans do (Hall,

1979). Voice qualities (pitch, inflection, etc.) convey part of the message. When speaking English, an Arab may use Arabic intonations and give the wrong perceptions to an American (Lustig, 1988). When two Arabs are conversing they are very animated and may speak in loud voices as if they are arguing. Verbal aggression is intended to reduce actual violence (Lustig, 1988). When there is a disagreement, Arabs tend to use outsiders (third persons) to intervene in the dispute. The law in the Middle East is "if there's a fight and somebody is injured, the crowd is guilty because the crowd didn't stop it" (Hall, 1979, p.53). This means that you can tell anyone almost anything in public because others will stop you from hurting someone or from getting hurt. Communication is more volatile, but less risky, presumably because the speaker is not entirely responsible for what is said (Hall, 1979).

Some topics of conversation with Arabs should be avoided. Don't ask questions about or discuss a man's wife or his daughters who are older than 12 years of age. Other sensitive subjects include Israel, politics, and religion (Harris and Moran, 1987). It seems doubtful that such strict precautions are necessary in the United States. Arabs value privacy and many do not communicate easily with health professionals. In verbal communication, Arabs may tend to be repetitious to emphasize important points.

Health Beliefs and Practices

Arabs respect Western medicine but may retain some traditional beliefs. Evil eye is a "look" received from an envious or jealous person who has the power to inflict an illness or accident on the person being envied. Amulets may be worn to ward off the evil eye.

Some foods are considered incompatible and if eaten together in the same meal could cause illness. There is some belief in balancing hot and cold foods. Other beliefs in the cause of illness include exposure to cold and dampness, sudden fear, and emotional upset. In addition, some Arabs may believe that illness is punishment from God for sins (Lipson and Meleis, 1983). Similar health beliefs may be held by Iranians (Behjeti-Sabat, 1990).

Traditional treatments for illness include the use of herbal teas and many over-the-counter drugs. The availability of prescription drugs in Middle Eastern countries has encouraged a tradition of self-treatment (Meleis, 1981). There is a stigma against mental illness, so any trauma of relocation to the U.S. may be expressed in somatic symptoms such as "nerves" and headaches. Recent immigrants are particularly subject to stressful experiences. Arab and Persian clients will not seek psychiatric help (Lipson and Meleis, 1983; Behjati-Sabet, 1990).

Western medicine is expected to be strong and effective. Arabs prefer intrusive treatments, such as injections, to pills. At a minimum Arabs and Persians will expect to receive a prescription from a medical visit. However, they may fear hospitalization because that is where people go to die (Lipson and Meleis, 1983).

Arabs depend on others to make medical decisions for them in a crisis, but they don't ask for help; it must be offered (Meleis, 1981). One or more family members will accompany a person to a medical appointment and expect to be included in decisions with the patient. The person accompanying the patient may appear to be very pushy and demanding to the health professional, who needs to realize that this supportive behavior is a demonstration of concern and an attempt to get the best possible treatment for the patient (Lipson and Meleis, 1983).

Health Status in the United States

Middle Eastern diets are high in complex carbohydrates including grains and legumes. Traditional diets are low in fat. However, as people become more affluent they tend to consume more meat and saturated fats, increasing the risk for cardiovascular diseases, obesity, and diabetes. In countries where women use clothing and veils to completely cover themselves, there is a potential for vitamin D deficiency (Packard and McWilliams, 1993).

Food and Nutrition

The preferred meats of Middle Eastern diets are lamb, chicken, and seafood. Only small amounts of beef are consumed because the arid climate makes it expensive to raise cattle. Preferred fruits and vegetables include dates, eggplant, figs, guavas, lemons, limes, olives, oranges, onions, peaches, pears, peppers, and squash. Rice, wheat bread, cracked wheat (bulgur), and legumes are staple foods. Consistent with a high prevalence of lactose intolerance, very little milk is consumed; however, goat and sheep milk cheeses and yogurts are eaten and used in cooking. Olive oil is used in some frying and is added to foods which are eaten cold. Other fats and oils are used generously in cooking and deep fat frying.

Implications for Health Care

Because of their strong family/friend/kinship structure, many Arabs and Persians distrust outsiders. They need to know someone well in order to develop a relationship. A health professional needs to become an insider. Even though they are very courteous, Middle Easterners are not likely to discuss their innermost feelings unless the health professional has gained their trust (Lipson and Meleis, 1983). To accomplish this requires considerable time and understanding. It will help to share some personal information with the patient. Also, sharing of food or beverage (either by offering or accepting) will increase trust. Under no circumstances decline an offer of food or beverage. If an invitation is accepted, then the hospitality must be returned. When visiting an Arab, be careful about admiring a possession because your host may feel obliged to give it to you. Of course, you can decline the offer, but it is better to avoid the situation (Harris and Moran, (1987).

Arab Americans expect health professionals to provide effective treatment, but not personal care (Meleis, 1981). Family members and friends are expected to provide personal care and support in the hospital and will visit around the clock (Lipson and Meleis, 1983). Expectations also vary depending on the country of origin. Modern Arab countries with high incomes from oil have free health care. People from these countries may treat the health professional as an employee (Meleis, 1981).

Middle Easterners have difficulty understanding why a physician needs to use tests and ask questions in order to diagnose. Since physicians are experts, they should know the answers. Arabs and Persians may be very impatient if not provided with immediate answers. The patient may expect that the health professional who makes decisions will also take responsibility for the outcome. The person with the education and the experience should make the decisions, not the patient (Meleis, 1981; Packard and McWilliams, 1993). In a clinic interview it is important to watch for answers that are intended to please the interviewer. The development of a trusting relationship will help elicit direct answers (Lipson and Meleis, 1983). After a few years in the United States, Middle Eastern immigrants become acculturated and use Western medicine, but in cases of serious illness may revert to cultural patterns. Older, male physicians are perceived as having higher status than young males or women physicians (Lipson and Meleis, 1985).

Middle Easterners do not give up hope when a person is seriously ill. The illness should be discussed with the family and not the patient. In case of serious illness, information should be given in stages and not discussed again. The health professional should not convey the feeling of giving-up or of hopelessness (Lipson and Meleis, 1983). If death does occur, grieving is vocal and can be disturbing to others (Meleis, 1981).

JEWS

The State of Israel was established in 1948, and both Jews and Palestinian Arabs claim it as their homeland. Most American Jews are not immigrants from Israel (Farber, Mindel, and Lazerwitz, 1988), but have arrived in the United States from several nations in four waves. First, the Sephardic Jews were expelled from Spain and Portugal in the Middle Ages to Asia and Africa. Some of these Jews from Asia and Africa then came to the United States and settled in New York City beginning in 1654. The second wave was German Jews who entered the United States from 1840 to 1880; many became peddlers across the country or owners of small stores. Eventually some became quite wealthy as financiers and owners of major department stores. The third wave was eastern European Jews who arrived from 1881 to 1930 to escape persecution and laws that restricted their rights. The Jews of European origin are called Ashkenazim (Farber, Mindel, and Lazerwitz, 1988). The fourth wave began in the 1970s and continues today, made up mostly of Soviet/Russian Jewish refugees and immigrants entering the U.S. for religious freedom and for better economic status (Wheat, Brownstein, and Kvitash, 1983).

Today, most Jews in the United States are descendants of the third wave of immigrants (Farber, Mindel, and Lazerwitz, 1988). Jews make up less than 3 percent of the U.S. population. Generally, they are successful; only an estimated 6 percent of Jews in the U.S. live in poverty. Most are middle class and are professionals or self-employed. A high proportion have college degrees and many are university professors (Banks, 1984).

Family Structure and Interactional Styles

Unlike their European ancestors, American Jews have small nuclear families and are the most successful of American ethnic groups when it comes to family planning. The fertility rate among U.S. Jews is now below the level needed to replace the Jewish population and is about half the rate found in Israel (Farber, Mindel, and Lazerwitz, 1988). The small families have provided Jewish parents an opportunity to participate more fully in the labor force and to provide higher levels of education for their children than other ethnic groups. Children are motivated to be high achievers through parental praise and expressions of pride.

Of the American Jewish population about 11 percent is Orthodox, 40 percent Conservative, 30 percent Reform, and 19 percent have no preference. Of these, Orthodox Jews have the strongest traditional practices, such as keeping kosher dietary practices. The remaining groups adhere to traditional practices in decreasing order. For example, divorce is highest among those with no denominational preference. Jewish families are likely to have family members close by and to have frequent contact with them (Farber, Mindel, and Lazerwitz, 1988).

Jews have a heritage in which learning is almost considered an obligation; the value of education continues in the United States. Marriage is also important, and divorce rates are traditionally low (Farber, Mindel, and Lazerwitz, 1988).

Health Beliefs and Practices

Since most American Jews have resided in the United States at least one generation and because most are descendants of European ancestors, it is reasonable to assume that Western medicine is their first treatment choice. Jews do not have taboos about mental illness and are more likely to seek psychotherapy than Protestants or Catholics. In addition, Jews are less likely than Protestants and Catholics to have severe mental problems (Farber, Mindel, and Lazerwitz, 1988).

Health Status in the United States

Because of their relatively high socioeconomic status, health care should be readily available to most people of this group. Studies show that in the United States, Jewish people under 55 years old have lower mortality rates than the general population. However, for Jews over the age of 55, mortality rates are higher than for the general population. Several theories have been proposed to explain this phenomenon; Fauman and Mayer (1973) suggested that the most likely reason is a lifestyle of overabundant diet and lack of exercise.

There are very low rates of heavy alcohol consumption among Jews (Farber, Mindel, and Lazerwitz, 1988). Although most Jews drink some alcohol, it may not become a health problem because of its symbolic use in religious practices and consumption with food when used socially (Glatt, 1973).

Tay-Sachs disease is a genetic disorder that is 100 times more prevalent among Ashkenazi Jews than Sephardic Jews and the non-Jewish population in the United States. Tay-Sachs disease results in a progressive loss of cerebral function; death usually occurs by two years of age (Myrianthopoulos and Aronson, 1973; Fraikor, 1977).

The Jewish population in the United States is older than any other ethnic group. Their high median age of 35.2 years in 1980 reflects low fertility rates, marriages outside the Jewish religion (with children no longer classified as Jewish), and longevity (Schmalz, 1981). The median ages for other United States ethnic groups in 1980 included Japanese 33.6 years; Whites 31.3 years; Chinese 29.6 years; Asian Indians 29.2 years; Pilipinos 28.6 years; Koreans 26.1 years; Blacks 24.9 years; Latinos 23.2 years; and American Indians, 22.9 years (Momeni, 1984).

Food and Nutrition

Jewish food practices are heterogeneous in the United States because there are many countries of origin. However, because of Jewish dietary laws (see chapter 5), there are also similarities. Traditional Ashkenazic Jewish foods adapted into American diets include bagels with cream cheese, rye bread, corned beef, and pastrami. In the United States, many foods are processed using acceptable kosher practices. Consumers are able to identify authentic kosher foods by the ⓤ or K symbols on the label. Most Jewish foods in the U.S. originate from Ashkenazic (European) Jewish tradition, while Israeli foods are traditionally Sephardic (Middle Eastern) (Higgins and Warshaw, 1989).

Implications for Health Care

Recent Russian Jewish immigrants might pose problems for the health professional, but this is the result of the Soviet medical system and not the Jewish affiliation. When Soviet Jews applied for emigration they had an immediate decrease in status with restricted job and educational opportunities. Permission to leave the Soviet Union took years for some and the waiting period was difficult. Emigrants were often required to move their elderly parents with them in order to obtain permission to leave. These elderly people have caused the greatest problems in the U.S. health care system (Wheat, Brownstein, and Kvitash, 1983).

In Soviet/Russian health clinics, appointments had little meaning and if clients couldn't be seen the day of the appointment they would have to return. So, some clients would arrive very early for their appointments and complain frequently about their symptoms in hopes of being seen; others would arrive late, knowing that the appointment schedule would be behind. Either behavior could cause problems for the U.S. practitioner.

Other recommendations for health professionals who have Russian clients were described by Wheat, Brownstein, and Kvitash (1983). Russian patients should be told what to do. To involve the patient in decisions means to the patient that health professionals don't know what they are doing. The use of laboratory tests and x-rays means that the patient is seriously ill because these procedures are not common in Russia. The ready availability of medicines in the United States suggests to the client that these medications are not very effective, because drugs are not easy to obtain in the Soviet Union. The client may associate the length of hospital stays with the quality of care; the longer the stay, the better the care. In order to obtain the best care it may be believed that bribes of money and gifts are necessary. Without bribes in the United States, care must not be of the best quality. Russian Jews may be demanding and complaining, but with a little understanding of their expectations health professionals are able to improve relationships (Wheat, Brownstein, and Kvitash, 1983).

References Cited

Banks, James. 1984. *Teaching strategies for ethnic studies*, 3rd edition. Boston: Allyn and Bacon, Inc.

Behjati-Sabet, A. 1990. The Iranians, Chapter 5 in *Cross cultural caring*, edited by N. Waxler-Morrison, J. Anderson, and E. Richardson. Vancouver, B.C.: University of British Columbia Press.

Elkholy, A. 1988. The Arab American family, in *Ethnic families in America*, 3rd edition, edited by C. Mindel, R. Habenstein, and R. Wright, Jr. New York: Elsevier.

Farber, B., C. Mindel, and B. Lazerwitz. 1988. The Jewish American family, in *Ethnic families in America*, 3rd edition, edited by C. Mindel, R. Habenstein, and R. Wright, Jr. New York: Elsevier.

Fauman, S. and A. Mayer. 1973. Jewish mortality in the United States, Chapter 3 in *Ethnic groups of America: their morbidity, mortality, and behavior disorders, Volume 1, The Jews*, edited by A. Shiloh and I. Selavan. Springfield, IL: Charles C. Thomas Publisher.

Fraikor, A. 1977. Tay-Sachs disease: genetic defect among the Ashkenazi Jews. *Social Biology* 24(2):117-134.

Glatt, M. 1973. Alcoholism and drug addiction amongst Jews, Chapter 28 in *Ethnic groups of America: their morbidity, mortality, and behavior disorders, Volume 1, The Jews*, edited by A. Shiloh and I. Selavan. Springfield, IL: Charles C. Thomas Publisher.

Hall, E. T. 1979. Learning the Arabs' silent language. *Psychology Today* August, p. 45-54.

Harris, P. and R. Moran. 1987. *Managing cultural differences*, 2nd edition. Houston: Gulf Publishing Co.

Higgins, C. and H. Warshaw. 1989. *Ethnic and regional food practices: Jewish food practices, customs, and holidays*, edited by A. Bertorelli, K. Sucher, and M. Wheeler. Chicago, IL: The American Dietetic Association and Alexandria, VA: the American Diabetes Association.

Lipson, J. and A. Meleis. 1985. Culturally appropriate care: the case of immigrants. *Topics in Clinical Nursing* 7(3):48-56.

Lipson, J. and A. Meleis. 1983. Issues in health care of Middle Eastern patients. *The Western Journal of Medicine* 139:854-861.

Lustig, M. 1988. Cultural and communication patterns of Saudi Arabians, in *International communication: a reader*, 5th edition, edited by L. Samover and R. Porter. Belmont, CA: Wadsworth Publishing Co.

Meleis, A. 1981. The Arab American in the health care system. *American Journal of Nursing* 81:1180-1183.

Momeni, J. 1984. *Demography of racial and ethnic minorities in the United States*. Westport, CT: Greenwood Press, p. 39.

Myrianthopoulos, N. and S. Aronson. 1973. Population dynamics of Tay-Sachs disease: I, reproductive fitness and selection, Chapter 11 in *Ethnic groups of America: their morbidity, mortality, and behavior disorders, Volume 1, the Jews*, edited by A. Shiloh and I. Selavan. Springfield, IL: Charles C. Thomas Publisher.

Naff, A. 1980. Arabs, in *Harvard encyclopedia of American ethnic groups*, edited by S. Thernstrom, A. Orlov, and O. Handlin. Cambridge, MA: The Harvard University Press.

Packard, D. and M. McWilliams. 1993. Cultural foods heritage of Middle Eastern immigrants. *Nutrition Today* 28(3):6-12.

Schmelz, U. 1981. Jewish survival: the demographic factors. *American Jewish Yearbook* 81:61-108.

Sharifzadeh, V. 1992. Families with Middle Eastern roots, Chapter 11 in *Developing cross-cultural competence; a guide for working with young children and their families*, edited by E. Lynch and M. Hanson. Baltimore: Paul H. Brookes, Pub. Co.

Spenser, W. 1986A. The Middle East, Islam in ferment, in *The Middle East*, An Annual Editions Publication. Global Studies; Guilford, CT: The Dushkin Publishing Group, Inc.

Spenser, W. 1986B. *Country Reports, in The Middle East*, An Annual Editions Publication, Global Studies. Guilford, CT. The Dushkin Publishing Group, Inc.

Wheat, M., H. Brownstein, and V. Kvitash. 1983. Aspects of medical care of Soviet Jewish emigres. *The Western Journal of Medicine* 1239:900-904.

DISCUSSION QUESTIONS

for

**Ethnic Americans
for the Health Professional**

INTRODUCTION

Individual study and involvement are essential parts of the learning experience. The questions in this guide are intended for individual study to assist students in contributing to classroom discussions. The questions are presented on a separate page for each chapter in the textbook to allow space for responses.

In many classrooms, students are required to complete specific writing requirements. Pages in this workbook are perforated for easy removal from the binding. They may be inserted into a typewriter or computer printer to be completed as written homework assignments. They may also be used in any order if the instructor prefers a different format.

In addition to the specific questions provided on these pages, students should be familiar with any new words presented in the text chapters. Instructors may ask students to add one discussion question of their own to those provided here. Student questions may be used for classroom discussion and for examinations.

Well-written answers to these questions will synthesize personal experiences, text information from previous chapters, and topics from current news. It is particularly important to include discussions of personal experiences to expand on the content of the text. This is because content related to culture and interactions among people change over time and differ in various geographical regions of the United States. Also, class discussions which include personal experiences and knowledge add a reality to the content that may otherwise be absent.

Name _____

Discussion Questions: *Chapter 1, Culture*

1. What aspects of U.S. culture apply to you?

2. Do any of these aspects of U.S. culture seem to be incorrect from your viewpoint? Would you like to add any more American cultural traits?

3. Be sure you understand and can discuss the definitions. (No written response needed.)

4. Describe your impressions of what it is like to live in poverty?

5. Based on your own knowledge and experiences, identify a way in which the phrase "all men are created equal and have equal opportunities" does NOT apply to women in the U.S.

Answer below and on the back.

Name _____

Discussion Questions: *Chapter 2, Demographics*

1. As you read through this chapter and study the tables, note some advantages and disadvantages of being female in the United States.

2. Why is it necessary to be cautious about racial/ethnic data collected by the U.S. Bureau of the Census?

3. From Table 2-2, note the two or three U.S. cities with especially high proportions of each ethnic group. From your knowledge of U.S. history, can you explain why these cities have attracted these ethnic groups?

4. (Answer this problem immediately after each statement.) Identify the racial/ethnic group in the U.S. with the:

    a. highest median family income:

    b. lowest median family income:

    c. fewest households headed by women:

    d. most households headed by women:

    e. overall, lowest health status as measured by mortality rates:

    f. highest rate of deaths from homicide; male and female:

    g. highest rate of deaths from lung cancer; male and female:

    h. population with the highest percentage of smokers:

    What impact does the female smoking rate have on this total?

    i. highest rates of deaths from cirrhosis, male and female:

    j. lowest per capita income among Whites/Blacks/Hispanics/Native Americans:

    k. lowest number of deaths from heart disease:

    l. population with the highest percentage of college degrees:

Answer 1 through 3 below and on the back.

Name _____

Discussion Questions: *Chapter 3, Multicultural Communication*

1. Explain ways in which communication may be disrupted.

2. Demonstrate the three kinds of gestures and act out the emblem gestures.

3. How does the communication style of women differ from that of men? In what way does the non-verbal communication style convey the stereotype of male superiority?

4. Try out a body position typical of males; now try a "feminine" body position.

5. What nonverbal behaviors do you notice when conversing with another person?

Answer below and on the back.

Name _____

Discussion Questions: *Chapter 4, Health Beliefs and Practices*

1. Explain the difference between disease and illness.

2. What evidence is provided that suggests that Western medicine (allopathic) isn't always the best? For what conditions could another medical system be safely used?

3. Describe a treatment that you or a family member has used that would be called traditional or folk medicine.

4. If you are the health care provider and your client is not following your treatment recommendations, what can you do to improve compliance?

Answer below and on the back.

Name _____

Discussion Questions: *Chapter 5, Food, Culture and Religion*

1. What food changes have occurred in the U.S. in the last 50 years?

2. Describe the unequal distribution of food in the world.

3. What are the food restrictions for Jews? for Muslims? for Christians?

Answer below and on the back.

Name _____

Discussion Questions: *Chapter 6, United States Immigration Policy*

1. What immigration law (date) completely changed immigration patterns in the U.S.? What are three important aspects of this law?

2. Subsequent to the passage of the law changed immigration patterns (Item 1), most immigrants have been from these geographical areas:

3. Explain why early (1850-1920) Asian immigrants were predominantly male?

Answer below and on the back.

Name _____

Discussion Questions: *Chapter 7, Gender*

1. What changes are occurring that make distinctions in family gender-roles less important? (Think of some yourself.)

2. Describe gender differences in nonverbal behaviors.

3. What evidence is provided of sexual discrimination? Are you aware of other forms of sexual discrimination? Give an example.

4. Compared to Blacks, does being White increase the income of females significantly? Describe the income of White males compared to Black males.

Answer below and on the back.

Name _____

Discussion Questions: *Chapter 8, Native Americans*

1. Many American Indian tribes became extinct after Europeans settled in America. What are the reasons?

2. What are some advantages of living on a reservation for American Indians? Disadvantages?

3. Discuss cultural factors (values and beliefs) characteristic of Native Americans.

4. Describe the family structure and interactional styles of Native Americans living on reservations. What does it mean for a tribe to be matrilineal?

5. Describe the health status of Native Americans. What health differences exist between males and females? (Also, refer to Table 2-5).

Answer below and on the back.

Name _____

Discussion Questions: *Chapter 9, Latinos*

1. Describe the value orientations of Latinos for social harmony, religion, time, family ties, children, and extended family. What is the traditional role of women in the Mexican American family?

2. What are some traditional Latino beliefs regarding the causes of illness?

3. Describe the health of Latinos compared to other ethnic groups. Which group (Mexican, Cuban, or Puerto Rican) has the poorest health? Refer to Tables 2-5 and 9-3.

4. Despite an apparent risk for mental illness, the actual rate appears to be low in this group. What factors contribute to this paradox?

Answer below and on the back.

Name _____

Discussion Questions: *Chapter 10, African Americans*

1. Explain the reasons for emphasis on self-treatment and traditional medical care among some Blacks.

2. What are some characteristics of Black family life? Explain the social forces that contribute to the high number of single mothers among Black women.

3. Summarize the health status of Blacks in the U.S. What are some ways that racial discrimination affects health status?

4. According to Kong, what is the cause of hypertension among minorities? Describe a second theory related to genetic selection.

Answer below and on the back.

Name _____

Discussion Questions: *Chapter 11, Chinese Americans*

1. Describe some Asian values. Indicate ways in which Asian values conflict with acculturation.

2. What are the income levels of Asians in the U.S.? (Refer to Table 11-1.)

3. List any stereotypes you may have regarding Chinese Americans. If you are Chinese, describe the effects that stereotypes have on you.

4. Describe the "philosophical principles" and their development into a medical system (Chinese medicine).

5. How do the "social rules" influence Chinese (Asian) behaviors? Give examples.

6. From the reading and your own experiences, develop a list of some advantages and disadvantages of living in a Chinatown.

Answer below and on the back.

Name _____

Discussion Questions: *Chapter 12, Japanese Americans*

1. Identify the names of Japanese "generations" in the U.S.

2. Describe the Japanese values of *gaman, enryo, haji, koko,* and time.

3. Despite their general good health, Japanese Americans are prone to high rates of some disorders. Describe some specific health problems.

4. Describe Japanese family life in Japan, and explain what life is like for a woman in Japan.

Answer below and on the back.

Name _____

Discussion Questions: *Chapter 13, Korean Americans*

1. Describe the causes of racial tension between Koreans and Blacks in Los Angeles.

2. What factors lead to a high divorce rate among Koreans?

3. Explain why an Asian might say "yes" when he/she really means "no."

Answer below and on the back.

Name _____

Discussion Questions: *Chapter 14, Southeast Asians*

1. What characteristics describe the first and second waves of Southeast Asian refugees?

2. What values are placed on family structure? How does life in the United States threaten the traditional family? What role changes occur for S.E. Asian women in the U.S.?

3. How do Vietnamese values affect their health beliefs?

4. What is the most common mental health problem affecting refugees?

Answer below and on the back.

Name _____

Discussion Questions: *Chapter 15, Pilipinos and Pacific Islanders*

1. Describe the effects of sex and race on Pilipino income in the United States.

2. Describe Pilipino values and define the terms: *bahala na, hiya, amor propio, utang na loob,* and *pakikisama*.

3. Indicate some potential communication difficulties which may occur between an immigrant Pilipino client and a U. S. health professional.

4. What are the health problems of Pacific Islanders who live in the U.S. mainland?

Answer below and on the back.

Name _____

Discussion Questions: *Chapter 16, South Asians: Asian Indians*

1. What religions are "Western" and where did they originate? What religions are "Eastern" and where did they originate?

2. What American values are disliked by Asian Indian parents?

3. Describe the lifestyles of Asian Indian families in the U.S.

Answer here and on the back.

Name _____

Discussion Questions: *Chapter 17, Middle Eastern Americans*

1. Characterize some values (family, context, time-space) of Middle Eastern Arabs in the U.S.

2. Describe some health beliefs and treatment expectations of Middle Eastern Arabs.

3. Describe the traditional communication style of Arab/Persian immigrants.

4. What are some guidelines for health professionals who work with Middle Eastern Arabs?

5. What problems might a health professional expect when the patient/client is a recent immigrant from the former Soviet Union?

6. Describe the typical family lifestyle of American Jews.

Answer below and on the back.

Index

A

Accidental deaths 2–5t, 9–3t;
  African Americans 84;
  Latinos 70;
  Native American 55;
  Pacific Islanders 131
Acculturation 2, 8;
  Arabs and Persians 143, 145;
  Asian Indians 136, dietary 137;
  Chinese 97;
  Immigrants, dietary 34–35;
  Japanese dietary 107;
  Latinos, 71, 73;
  Native American, dietary 57;
  Pacific Islanders 132;
  Pilipino, dietary 128–129;
  Southeast Asians 117,
    dietary 121, 122;
  Syrians, early 141;
  Women 111
Acupuncture 99, 112
Adobo 81
Advertising, alcohol and tobacco 72
Affirmative response in counseling 23;
  Asian Indians 138;
  Asians 112–113;
  Latinos 66;
  Southeast Asians 118, 122
Africa/African: family life 79;
  languages 81;
  P-time 10;
  slaves 79;
  slaves in Cuba 69;
  world view 78
African American 77–92;
  accidental deaths 84, 2–5t;
  AIDS/HIV 15, 17, 84, 86, 2–5t;
  alcohol use 174, 177, 178;
  cirrhosis 15, 84, 86, 2–5t;
  death rates 15, 86, 2–5t;
  diabetes 17, 84, 85, 2–5t;
  education 78, 80, 84, 2–3t;
  heart disease 84, 87, 2–5t;
  homicide 84, 2–5t;
  households headed by women 14, 78, 80, 2–3t, 2–4t;
  income 14, 43, 78, 80, 94, 2–3t;
  infectious diseases 15, 84, 2–5t;
  population 147, 2–1t, 2–2t;
  poverty 77, 82, 117, 2–3t;
  smoking (tobacco) rate 72, 85, 2–6t;
  stroke 84, 2–5t;
  suicide 84, 2–5t
Age(d) (also see elderly) 26
AIDS/HIV 2–5t, 9–3t;
  African American 15, 17, 84, 86;
  Latinos 15, 17, 70, 72;
  women 44
Alaska: health care 51, 55;
  indigenous people 49;
  suicide rates 56
Albuquerque, NM population 2–2t
Alcohol (use/abuse/alcoholism) 15;
  advertising 72;
  African Americans 72, 84, 86, 87;
  Chinese 100;
  Christians 35, 36;
  Japanese 107;
  Jews 147;
  Latinos 71–72;
  Native Americans 15, 53, 55–56, 57;
  Pilipinos 128
Allopathic medicine 27, 29
Alternative medical systems, use of 29
Am duc 116
American: culture 11;
  doctors 28;
  honesty 19;
  medical practices 27–29;
  nature 20;
  traditions 11;
  values 10–11, 105, 117, 3–1t
American Indian (see Native American)
American Samoa 129
Ancestor worship: Chinese 96, 97;
  Hawaiians 130
Androgynous 42
Anemia: Native Americans 57;
  Southeast Asians 119
Animistic religion, Southeast Asians 116, 119
Anthropologists 1
Antibiotics, use of 28, 137

Arabs and Persians 141–145;
  evil eye 26, 144;
  polychronic time 10
Arizona: Latino population 64
Arizona Indians: diabetes 17, 56–57;
  population 49;
  unemployment 51
Arranged marriages 103
Ashkenazim Jews 147
Asian Americans (also see Asian Indians, Chinese, Japanese, Korean, Pilipino, and Southeast Asian): accidental deaths 2–5t;
  AIDS/HIV 17, 2–5t;
  California 93;
  cancer 2–5t;
  cirrhosis 2–5t;
  citizenship 37;
  communication 22;
  death rates 15, 2–5t;
  diabetes 17, 107, 2–5t;
  education 2–3t, 11–1t;
  Hawaii 93;
  health status 15;
  heart disease 2–5t;
  homicide 2–5t;
  households headed by women 96, 2–3t;
  immigrants 37, 39, 93;
  income 13–14, 94, 2–3t, 11–1t;
  infections 2–5t;
  lactose intolerance 107;
  modesty 1;
  population in U.S. 2–1t, 2–2t, 11–1t;
  poverty 2–3t, 11–1t;
  smoking rate 2–6t;
  stroke 2–5t;
  suicide 2–5t;
  terminology 2;
  Western medicine, fear of 113
Asian Indians 133–140;
  demographics 93, 110;
  education 133, 134, 135, 136, 11–1t;
  income, wages 133, 135;

population in U.S. 93, 147, 2–1t, 11–1t
Assimilation 8, 37
Atlanta, GA population 2–2t
Ayurvedic medicine 29, 136

B

Baby bottle tooth decay 57
Bad air 68
Bagoong 128
Bahala na (also see fatalism) 126, 127
Balance (also see harmony) 45, 127
Baltimore, MD population 2–2t
Bangladesh 133
Baptist 79
Bathing practices, Japanese 1
Baton Rouge, LA population 2–2t
Beliefs and values (also see values) 1–2, 19
Benevolence 95
Berdache 53
Berkeley, CA population 2–2t
Bhutan 133
Bilis 68
Birmingham, AL population 2–2t
Birth weight, low 86
Black(s) (see African American)
Black civil rights movement 78
Black English 81–82
Blood imbalance beliefs of African Americans 26, 29, 82–83
Blood loss, fear of, Chinese 98, Asian 113, Southeast Asian 118
Blood pressure, treatment for low 28, (see hypertension)
Boarding schools, Native American children 50
Body language 21, 22
Bottom of foot, beliefs, Arabs/Persians 143, Southeast Asian 122
Bracero 63
Brahman (Priests) 135
Breadfruit 131
Breast feeding infants, Hmong 121–122;
Latino 73
British medicine 28
Buddhist/Buddhism, Asian Indians 134, 135;
Chinese 95;
Korean 110;
Southeast Asian 116
Bureau of Indian Affairs, U.S. 49, 50
Businesses, Chinese 93;
Korean 109, 110, 111–112;
Syrian 141

C

Calcium, African American 88;
Chinese 100;
Japanese 107;
Latinos 73;
Pacific Islanders 131;
Vietnamese 121
California, Asian Indians 133, 134;
Asians 93;
Central and South Americans 64;
Koreans 109;
land ownership 37;
Latinos 64;
medical practice 69;
Native American unemployment 51;
Native population 49, 50;
Pilipinos 125;
Puerto Ricans 64;
Southeast Asians 116, 120
Cambodian (Kampuchea) 115, 119–120;
smoking rates 17
Canada, Asian Indians 133
Cancer 2–5t, 9–3t;
African Americans 15, 84, 86, 87;
cervical 15, 70;
Cuban Americans 70;
Hawaiians 15;
Latinos 70, 72;
Mexican Americans 70;
Pacific Islanders 131;
Pilipinos 128
Carbohydrate, acculturated diets 34;
complex, in U.S. diets 33, 107;
sugar in U.S. diets 33
Caribbean health beliefs 84
Caste system in India 134–135, 137, 138
Castro, Fidel 64, 69
Catholic, African American 79;
Latino 65, 66;
Pilipino 126, 128;
Southeast Asian 115
Caucasians 3, 133 (also see Whites)
Central and South Americans 64, 66, 71, 9–1t;
breast feeding of infants 73
Central Intelligence Agency (CIA) 116
Cherokee 49
Ch'i, Chinese medicine 98, 99;
Korean medicine 112
Chicago, IL population 2–2t;
African American 78
Chicano 63
Child birth, Chinese 98;
Pilipino 127;
Southeast Asian 122
Children, Arab and Persian 142, 143;
Asian Indian 134, 136, 137;
boarding schools for Native American 50;
Chinese 96, 98;
dietary needs 34;
child care 41, 79;
Japan 105, 106;
Latino diets 72;
Native American 52–53;
Pacific Islanders 130;
Pilipino 126;
poverty 11;
single fathers 42
China 93, 109, 115;
Taoism 134
Chinatowns 37, 93, 94, 96, 97, 98
Chinese Americans 93–102;
education 96, 97, 11–1t;
Exclusion Act 37, 93;
immigrants to U.S. 37, 96, 97;
implications for health care 112–113;
income 93, 94, 97, 120, 11–1t;
male to female ratio 37, 93;
population 93–94, 147, 11–1t;
poverty 97, Western medicine, fear of 113
Chinese medicine 29;
Chinese 97–98;
Japanese 106;
Koreans 112;
Southeast Asians 118;
diagnosis 98;
treatment 99
Chiropractic medicine 27–28
Cholesterol (serum), Latinos 70
Christians, Arabs and Persians 142, 143;
Asian Indians 134, 135, 137;
dietary restrictions 35;
Korean 109, 110;
Latino 66;
Pacific Islanders 130;
Pilipino 125;
Southeast Asian 116
Churches, African American 78–79
Cirrhosis 2–5t, 9–3t;
African American 15, 84, 86;
Latino 15, 71;
Native Americans 55
Citizenship 125, 133–134;
freed slaves 37
Cleanliness, Japanese 106
Cleveland, OH population 2–2t
Clients 19, 20, 23, 25 (also see patients);
expectations 23, 29, 147;
negotiation 30
Coconut 131
Coin rubbing 99, 119
Cold air (wind) 127
Communicable diseases (see infectious diseases)

Communication, African Americans
81–82, 88;
Arabs and Persians 143–144;
Asian Indian 136;
Chinese 97;
gestures 143, 144;
Japanese 106;
Koreans 112;
Latinos 67;
multicultural 19–24;
Native American 53–54;
non-verbal 19, 21–23;
Pilipinos 126–127, 129;
rules of 20–21;
Southeast Asians 118;
verbal 19, 21, 143
Communist 115, 116
Compromises 11
Confrontation, avoidance 19;
Japanese 104, 112–113;
Pilipino 126–127
Confucianism, Chinese 95;
Korean 110;
Southeast Asian 116
Conjunctivitis 119
Context, communication 19, 21,
118, 142, 143–144, 298;
food 35;
high 21, 81, 118;
low 21
Cook, Captain James 129, 131
Corn, religious use 57–58
Corresponding (five) elements 95,
99, 112
Counseling 23
Cow, sacred 135
Creole 81
Crimes/criminal justice, African
American 80, 84;
Native American 55;
violence by males 41
Cross-gender role, Native Americans 53
Cuba/Cubans 64;
AIDS/HIV 9–3t;
accidental deaths 9–3t;
cancer 70, 9–3t;
cirrhosis 9–3t;
death rates 9–3t;
diabetes 9–3t;
education 9–1t;
females 66;
folk healers 69;
health care access 69;
heart disease 9–3t;
homicide 9–3t;
income 9–1t;
infections 9–3t;
poverty 9–1t;
smoking rate 72;
stroke 9–3t;
suicide 9–3t;
traditional medical beliefs 69

Cultural, bias 1;
healers 25;
pluralism 8, 12;
shock 8
Culture 7–12, 136;
American 9, 21, 22, 3–1t;
characteristics 7;
food and religion 33–36;
illness 25;
of poverty 11
Cupping 99, 112, 119
Curanderos 29, 67, 68, 69–70

D

Dating 117
Death, meaning of "four" in
Japanese 113
Death rates 15, 55, 56, 2–5t, 9–3t;
African American 86;
Arab and Persian 145;
Japanese 107
Decision makers 11, 25;
Arabs/Persians 143, 144, 145;
Japanese 105;
Jews 147;
Native American 52, 58;
Pilipino 126;
Southeast Asian 117
Demographics 13–18;
African Americans 77–78;
Arabs and Persians 141–142;
Asian 93;
Asian Indian 93, 133–134;
Chinese 93–95;
Japanese 93, 103–104, 110;
Jewish 146;
Korean 93, 109–110;
Latino 63–65;
Native American 49, 50, 51;
Pilipino 93, 125;
Southeast Asian 115–116
Dental health, Native American 57
Denver, CO population 2–2t
Derogatory terms 82
Detention camps, internment of
Japanese 103
Detroit, MI population 2–2t, African
American 78
Dharma 134
Diabetes, 2–5t, 9–3t;
African American 84, 85;
Arabs/Persians 144;
Asian Indians 137;
dietary changes 34;
Japanese 107;
Latinos 15;
Mexican American 70–71;
Minorities 17;
Native American 55, 56;
Pacific Islanders 131;
Pilipinos 128;
Southeast Asian treatment 119

Dietitian 19
Discriminate/discrimination;
African American 78, 84;
Asian Indians 133, 135;
Chinese 93;
definition 8;
Koreans 110;
Pilipinos 125;
Southeast Asian refugees 116;
women 43–44
Disease vs. illness 25
Diversity within groups 2, 7
Divorce, African American 78, 81;
Korean American 111
Domestic violence, Native American
57
Dominate culture, definition 11
Drug abuse, African American 84,
87

E

Eastern orthodox (Greek), food
practices 35
Education 2–3t, 9–1t, 11–1t;
African American 78, 80, 84,
87, 88;
Arab and Persian 141;
Asian Indian 133, 134, 135, 136;
Chinese 96, 97;
effect on alcohol consumption,
Latinos 72;
factor in selection of medical
system 26;
Japanese 103, 104, 105;
Koreans 110, 111;
Latinos 64;
nutrition 33;
Pacific Islander 129;
Pilipino 125;
Southeast Asian 115;
Whites 80
Egalitarian, Asian Indians 136;
definition 8;
Pilipinos 126
Eggs in diet, Pacific Islanders 131
Elderly 11;
African American 78, 79, 83,
88, 89;
Arab and Persian 143;
Asian 94;
Asian Indian 136;
Chinese 93, 95, 96, 98;
Japanese 105;
Jews 147;
Korean 111;
Latino 66;
Pilipino 126, 127, 129;
Southeast Asian 117
Elements (five) in Ayurvedic
medicine 136 (also, see corresponding elements)
El Paso, TX population 2–2t

Emancipation 79
Emotions 23;
  suppression by Asians 113;
  suppression by Southeast Asians 118
Empacho 68
Employment, African Americans 77, 78, 79, 81, 84;
  Arab immigrants 141;
  Asian Indians 138, 134, 135;
  Chinatowns 96;
  Korean Americans 133;
  Mexican immigrants 63;
  Pacific Islanders 129
English language, Asian Indians 136
Entitlement, definition 8
Environment, Native American beliefs 51–52
Eskimo diets 57
Ethnic, definition 8;
  terminology for ethnic groups 2–3
Ethnocentrism, definition 9;
  by health care providers 26
European immigrants 39, 49
Evil eye, Arabs 144;
  example of 26;
  Latinas 68
Extended family: African American 79, 80;
  Arab and Persian 142, 143;
  Asian Indian 134, 135;
  Chinese 96;
  Japanese 105;
  Latino 66;
  Native American 52–53;
  Pacific Islander 130;
  Southeast Asian 115, 116–117
Eye expressiveness 23
Eye contact, African American 88;
  Asian Indians 136;
  Asians 113;
  in communication 21, 22, 23;
  gender 42;
  Latinos 66, 73;
  Native Americans 58;
  Pilipinos 129;
  Southeast Asians 122

F

Face/shame, Asian value 19;
  Japanese 104;
  Pilipino 126, 127, 129
Fallen fontanel, folk belief among Latinos 68
Family associations, Korean 110
Family influence in health care 26
Family structure and interactional styles: African American 79–81;
  Arab and Persian 143;
  Asian Indian 135–136;
  Chinese 96–97;
  Japanese 105;
  Jewish 146;
  Korean 111–112;
  Latino 65–66;
  Native American 52–53;
  Pacific Islander 130;
  Pilipino 126;
  Southeast Asian 116–118
Fat: acculturated diets, high in 34;
  diets of Japanese 107;
  diets of Latinos 71, 73;
  diets of minorities 17;
  diets of Native Americans 57;
  diets of Samoans 131;
  diets of Southeast Asians 120;
  Middle Eastern diets 145
Fatalism/destiny, among African Americans 78;
  among Japanese 103, 104;
  among Muslims 142;
  among Southeast Asians 116, 118;
  example of 20;
  in poverty 11;
  low income 25
Father/husband, Japan 104, 105;
  Southeast Asian 117, 118
Fertility rate, Asian 116;
  Hawaiian 129;
  immigrants 39;
  Jews 147;
  Korean 111;
  Latino 66
Filial piety, Asian 95, 96;
  Japanese 104;
  Southeast Asian 116, 117
Filipino (see Pilipino), terminology 2
Fish (see Meat and fish)
Florida: Cuban immigrants 64
Flushing 128
Flushing syndrome 100
Folk medicine/healers (also see traditional medicine), African Americans 77;
  universal use of 27;
  Chinese medicine 99;
  Latino 69;
  Southeast Asians 118, 119
Fontanel, fallen 68
Food: acculturated diets 34–35;
  American 33–34;
  away from home 33;
  balance in diet 34;
  beliefs 34;
  edible 33;
  health, influence on 27, 30, 141;
  Kosher 35, 146, 147;
  patterns in United States 33;
  preparation by African Americans 87;
  preparation by Chinese 100;
  preparation by Hindus 137;
  preparation by Jews 35;
  religious practices, use of 35–36, 135, 137;
  selection and culture 33;
  selection by African Americans 87;
  world distribution of 34
Food and Nutrition: African American 87–88;
  Arab and Persian 145;
  Asian Indian 137;
  Chinese 100;
  Japanese 107;
  Jewish 147;
  Korean 112;
  Latino 72–73;
  Native American 57–58;
  Pacific Islander 131;
  Pilipino 128–129;
  Southeast Asian 120–122
Food, culture, and religion 33–36
Food preparation, African American 87–88;
  Chinese 100;
  Hindus 137;
  Jewish 35;
  Southeast Asian 121
Forced assimilation of Native Americans 50
Four humors 9–2t
France, hospital care 28
French, in Southeast Asia 115, 118, 121
Fright, loss of soul among Asians 98
Fruits and Vegetables, African American 88;
  Chinese 100;
  Japanese 107;
  Latino 72–73;
  Pilipino 128;
  Southeast Asian 119, 121

G

Gall bladder disease, Latinos 70
Garden work, Pacific Islanders 131
Gary, IN population 2–2t
Gender 41–47;
  biological differences 41;
  communication 22, 42;
  differences in child care 41;
  equality, Blacks 81;
  income differences by sex and race 43, 80;
  income of medical professionals 44;
  life expectancy in third world 44;
  masculinity 41, 42;
  medical care discrimination 44;
  posture and gestures 42–43;
  roles 41–42;
  roles, Latino 65–66;
  sexism/discrimination 43;

smoking rate 2–6t;
stereotypes, African American women 81
Generational conflicts: Arab and Persian 141, 143;
Asian Indian 135–136;
Chinese 97;
Japanese 103;
Korean 111;
Latino 66;
Southeast Asian 117
Generational groups, Japanese 103
Geography, Southeast Asia 120
German doctors 28
German Jews 146
Germany, evil eye 26
Gestures 22
God parent 126
Gout 128
Grandparents: Latino 66;
Native American 52
Group affiliation 10, 20;
African Americans 79;
Arabs and Persians 143;
Japanese 104, 105, 106;
Korean 111;
Pacific Islander 130;
Pilipino 126
Guam/Guamanian 129 130, 11–1t
Guerrilla soldiers 115

H

Harlem health care 96
Harmony/balance: African American 78;
Asian Indian 136, 138;
Chinese 95, 96;
Japanese 106;
Native American 51–52;
Pilipino 127;
Southeast Asian 116, 118
Hawaiian/Hawaii 129, 131, 11–1t, 2–2t;
Asians in 93;
cancer 15;
Japanese in 103;
Natives, terminology 2
Head of Household (also see Households headed by women), African American 78;
Latino 65, 66
Health beliefs and practices 25–30;
African American 82–84;
Arab and Persian 144;
Asian Indian 136–137;
Chinese 97–99;
choices of treatment 26;
Japanese 106;
Jewish 141;
Korean 112;
Latino 65, 67–70;
Native American 54–55;

Pacific Islander 130;
Pilipino 127–128;
Southeast Asian 118–119;
traditional 19
Health care 1, 12;
African American 77, 86;
barriers to 68, 69, 84, 117, 127;
Chinese 99, 100;
decisions 26;
expectations: Jamaican 84;
expectations: Latino 69, 73;
expectations: Native American 58, 59;
Native American 51, 55, 58;
Pacific Islander 129;
Southeast Asian 117, 120, 122
Health professionals: African American 87;
attitudes 26;
use of alternative care 30;
communication 25;
community knowledge of 27;
Native American 59;
questions for clients 29;
rapport with clients 20, 23;
sexism among 44;
values 23
Health promotion and disease prevention, for African Americans 78, 88;
low income groups 25;
unfamiliar concept 30
Health status of African Americans 84–87, Arabs and Persians 144;
Asian Indians 137;
Chinese 99–100;
Japanese 106–107;
Jews 146–147;
Latinos 70–72;
minorities 15, 17;
Native Americans 15, 55–57;
Pacific Islanders 130–131;
Pilipinos 128;
Southeast Asians 119–120
Heart disease 2–5t, 9–3t;
acculturated diets 34;
African Americans 84, 85, 87;
Arabs and Persians 144;
Cuban Americans 70;
German treatment of 28;
Latinos 70, 71, 72;
Mexican Americans 70;
Mormons 36;
Native Americans 55;
Pacific Islanders 131;
Pilipino 128;
women 44
Heating 128
Hepatitis 119
High blood, low blood, bad blood beliefs among African Americans 29, 83, 89
Hindu/Hinduism 134–135

Hispanic (see Latino)
Hispanic Health and Nutrition Examination Survey (HHANES) 73
Historical Review: African American 77–78, 79, 80–81, 89;
Arab and Persian 141–142;
Asian Indian 133–134;
Chinese 93–94;
Japanese 103–104;
Jews 145–146;
Korean 109–110;
Latino 63–65;
Native American 49–51;
Pacific Islander 129–130;
Pilipino 125;
Southeast Asian 115–116
HIV (see AIDS/HIV)
Hmong 115, 116, 118, 119, 120, 122
Hoe cake 87
Holidays/vacations in Japan 105
Homeopathic medicine 27, 28
Homicide 2–5t, 9–3t;
African American 15, 84;
Asian/Pacific Islander 15;
Latino 15, 71;
Native American 55;
Southeast Asian 115
Homosexuals, minority group 11;
Native American 53
Hong Kong 94
Honor/face, Asian values 96, 97
Hot/Cold balance, Arabs 144;
Chinese foods 98;
foods 68;
Latinos and Asians 26;
Mexican American 67;
nutritional quality 34;
Pilipino 128;
Southeast Asian 118, 119
Households headed by women 2–3t, 2–4t;
African American 14, 78, 80;
Chinese 96;
Southeast Asian 117
Humors, Ayurvedic medicine 136
Hypertension 34;
African American 83, 84, 85;
Asian Indian 137;
Japanese 107;
Latino 70;
Native American 56;
Pacific Islander 131;
Pilipino 128;
Southeast Asian 119, 121

I

Illegal immigrants (see Immigrants, illegal)
Illinois, Puerto Ricans 64
Illness beliefs: African American 26, 82–83;
  Asians 26;
  causes of 25–26;
  Latino causes of 26, 67–68;
  Native American causes of 54, 67–68;
  Southeast Asian 118
Imbalance: blood 26;
  cause of illness 20, 25–26, 130;
  hot/cold 67–68;
  lack of harmony 26;
  treatment for 29
Immigrants: Arab and Persian 141, 142, 143;
  Asian 39;
  Asian Indian 133, 134, 135, 136;
  Chinese 37, 93, 96, 97, 99;
  Cuban 69;
  European 37, 39;
  illegal 39, 63, 64, 65, 74, 77, 79;
  Japanese 37;
  Jewish 145–146;
  Korean 109, 110, 111;
  Latin American 39;
  Pacific Islander 131;
  Pilipino 125;
  professional 39;
  recent 39, 94–95, 113;
  Southeast Asian 115–116, 120
Immigration (policy): preference categories 39;
  quota system dropped 39;
  time-line 6–1f;
  United States 37–40, 128
Implications for health care:
  African American 88–89;
  Arab and Persian 145;
  Asian Indian 138;
  Chinese, Japanese, Koreans 112–113;
  communication 23;
  food, culture, and religion 44;
  health beliefs and practices 30;
  Jewish 147;
  Latino 73–74;
  Native American 58–59;
  Pacific Islander 132;
  Pilipino 129;
  Southeast Asian 122
Incarceration, African American 84
Income, 2–3t, 9–1t, 11–1t;
  African American 77, 78, 86, 87, 94, 104, 128;
  Asian Indian 133, 135;
  Asian refugees 120;
  Chinese 93, 97, 120;
  effect of on health care selection 26;
  effect of sex and race on 43–44;
  Guamanians 130;
  India 133, 134;
  Japanese 104;
  Korean 111–112;
  Latino 64, 72;
  low (see poverty);
  Native American 51;
  per capita 14
Individual success/independence 10, 20
Infant mortality, African American 84, Native American 50
Infections/infectious diseases 2–5t, 9–3t (also see Communicable diseases);
  African American 15, 84;
  Asian Indian 137;
  Chinese 100;
  Native American 55;
  Pacific Islander 129;
  Southeast Asian 119
Inferiority 11
Injections: African Americans 84;
  Arabs 144;
  Asian Indian 137, 138
Injuries, African American 15
Interactional styles 10
Interpreters, guidelines 21;
  Japanese 106;
  Latino 66;
  Pilipino 127;
  use of children as 21
Intestinal parasites 100
Islam (Muslim) 134, Arabs and Persians 141–142;
  in India 135, 137;
  marriage 143;
  Western religion 142;
  Vietnam 116
Israel, creation of 141, 145;
  foods in 147
Issei 103, 104

J

Jail (see incarceration)
Jains 134
Jamaican, traditional medicine 84
Japan, children and women in 105;
  education 105;
  Korean influence 109;
  Shintoism 134
Japanese Americans 103–108;
  bathing practices 1;
  California land ownership 37;
  confrontation avoidance 113;
  demographics 93–94, 103–104;
  education 104, 105, 11–1t;
  emotions, suppression 113;
  eye contact 113;
  immigration 37;
  implications for health care 112–113;
  income 94, 104, 11–1t;
  monochronic time 10;
  number four 113;
  population in U.S. 93, 147, 11–1t;
  poverty 11–1t;
  sexually open 1;
  social harmony 112–113;
  values 104–105, 106, 107, 112–113;
  Western medicine, barriers to 113, fear of blood loss 113
Jews/Jewish 145–147;
  food customs 35;
  Israel: creation 141;
  kitchen organization 35;
  kosher 35, 146, 147;
  population: age of 10;
  religious practices 142, 143, 146

K

Kava 131
Kim ch'i 112
Kite flying 10
Koran 142
Korea 109
Korean Americans 109–113;
  demographics 93, 109, 110;
  education 110, 111, 11–1t;
  income 111, 11–1t;
  population in U.S. 93, 109, 147, 11–1t;
  poverty 11–1t
Kosher foods 35, 146, 147

L

Lactose intolerance: African American 87, 88;
  Arab and Persian 145;
  Asian 107;
  Chinese 100;
  Japanese 107;
  Latino 73;
  Native American 58;
  Pilipino 128;
  Southeast Asian 121
Land ownership, Asian Indians 133;
  in California 37;
  Japanese 103
Language, barriers 21;
  communication 21;
  Korea 112;
  Pilipino 127
Laos 115, 116, 121
Laotians, smoking rate 17
Latino(s) 63–76;
  accidental deaths 2–5t;
  AIDS/HIV 15, 17, 70, 72, 2–5t;
  cancer 70, 71, 72, 2–5t;
  cirrhosis 2–5t;
  death rates 15, 2–5t;

diabetes 17, 70, 2–5t;
education 64, 2–3t, 9–1t;
four humors 9–2t;
heart disease 70, 71, 72, 2–5t;
homicide 2–5t;
households headed by women 2–3t, 2–4t;
income 14, 64, 2–3t, 9–1t;
infectious diseases 2–5t;
pica 1;
polychronic time 10;
population 64, 147, 2–1t, 2–2t;
poverty 72, 117, 2–3t, 9–1t;
racial categories 13;
smoking (tobacco) 72, 2–6t;
stroke 70, 2–5t;
suicide 2–5t;
terminology 2
Left hand, use of by Arabs 143, by Southeast Asians 122
Leprosy, Pacific Islanders 129, Southeast Asians 122
Life expectancy, African American 84;
European 28;
in third world 44;
Jews 147
Liquor stores 72
Literacy test, immigrants 37
Laredo, TX population 2–2t
Los Angeles, CA population 2–2t, Korean 110, Pilipino 127
Lumpia 128

M

Machismo 66
Magic, beliefs among African Americans 82, 84;
beliefs among Chinese 98;
beliefs among Latinos 65, 68;
beliefs among Pacific Islanders 130;
beliefs among Pilipinos 128;
in cause and treatment of illness 26
Majority rule 11
Mal aire 68
Mal ojo (see evil eye)
Male to female ratio, Chinese 37, 93
Malnutrition: African American 88;
Latino 88;
Native American 57;
Pacific Islander 131;
Southeast Asian 119
Marriage: African American 79, 80, 81;
Arab and Persian 142, 143;
Asian Indian 133, 135;
Chinese 93, 96;
Japanese 103;
Jewish 146, 147;

Korean 109, 111;
Southeast Asian 117
Marquesses islands 129
Matriarchy 9;
African American 81
Matrilineal 9
Meat and fish: African American 87, 88;
Arab and Persian 145;
Asian Indian 137;
Japanese 107;
Jewish selection and preparation 35;
Korean 112;
Latino 73;
Muslims 35;
Native American 57;
Pacific Islander 131;
Pilipino 128;
Southeast Asian 120, 121;
traditional American diet 33–34
Mecca 142
Mediators (go-betweens) 126–127
Medicaid, Latinos 69
Medical pluralism, among Asians 99;
among Southeast Asians 119;
among Pilipinos 127;
among Koreans 112;
traditional medicine 29, 30
Medical system, factors in selection 26–27
Medicine man (also see Shaman), Hawaii 130;
Native American 54–55
Mediterranean: evil eye 26;
polychronic time 10
Mein 115, 118, 119
Melting pot 8
Memphis, TN population 2–2t
Mental health/illness: Arab and Persian 144;
Asian Indian 136–137;
Chinese 98, 99–100;
Japanese 107;
Jews 146;
Latino 68, 71, 73;
Native American 55, 57;
Pilipino 128;
Southeast Asian 119–120
Meridians 98
Methodist 79
Mexican American (also, see Latino) 29, 63–74, 9–1t, 9–3t;
cancer 70;
extended family 66;
health beliefs 67;
income 63;
smoking (tobacco) rates 72;
women 22
Mexico/Mexican: alcohol consumption 71–72;
evil eye 26;
territory 63, 70

Miami, FL population 2–2t
Middle Eastern Americans (see Arabs and Persians; Jews) 141–147;
Arab and non-Arab countries 141;
education 141;
evil eye 26;
infant mortality 141;
languages 141;
literacy rate 141;
polychronic time 10;
socioeconomic status 141;
space, personal 22
Milk, use of by African Americans 88;
Arabs and Persians 145;
Asian Indians 135;
Chinese 100;
Japanese 107;
Jews 35;
Latinos 73;
Southeast Asians 121
Minorities 1, 11;
advertising of alcohol and tobacco 72;
diabetes 17;
population changes 14;
tuberculosis 15;
values, confrontation avoidance 19
Miscegenation laws 37, 93
Mixed heritages in census 13
Mnemonic: LEARN 30
Modesty: Asians 1, Asian Indians 138;
Chinese 97, 99;
factor in health decisions 26;
Latinos 66;
Pilipinos 126, 129;
Southeast Asians 118
Monochronic time (M-time) 10, 19, 22;
Japanese 104
Montana, native population 49
Mormon 36
Mortality rates: 2–5t, 9–3t;
African American 15, 84–85, 86;
Jews 146;
Latinos 70
Mothers, working 42
Moxibustion 99, 112
Multicultural communication (see communication)
Muhammad 142
Murder (see homicide)
Muslims: African American 87;
Arabs and Persians 141, 142, 143;
dietary traditions 35;
Ramadan 35

N

Nail that sticks up is hit 105
Name order: Korean 111;
  Southeast Asian 118
Nationals 39
Native Americans 49–62;
  accidental deaths 2–5t, 55;
  AIDS/HIV 2–5t;
  alcohol abuse 15, 53, 55, 56, 57;
  cancer 2–5t, 56;
  cirrhosis 55, 56, 2–5t;
  death rates 15, 55, 56, 2–5t;
  diabetes 17, 55, 56–57, 2–5t;
  education 51, 53, 2–3t;
  heart disease 55, 56, 2–5t;
  homicide 55, 56, 2–5t;
  households headed by women 2–3t;
  income 14, 51, 2–3t;
  infectious diseases 55, 2–5t;
  population 2–2t, 147;
  poverty 50, 53, 2–3t;
  smoking rates 17, 2–6t;
  stroke 56, 2–5t;
  suicide 55, 56, 2–5t;
  values 20, 51, 52, 54, 59
Natural causes of illness 26, 82–83, 127;
  treatments for 29
Nature 52
Navajos (Dine) 51, 54, 58
Nepal 133
Newark, NJ population 2–2t
New Jersey, Puerto Ricans 64
New Mexico, Native population 49, Latino population 65
New York (city), Puerto Ricans 64, Blacks 77–78
Nirvana 134
Nisei 103–104, 106
Nuoc-mam 121
Nutrition(al): deficiencies 34, 121–122;
  diet quality 34;
  education 33;
  status 121

O

Obesity, acculturated diets 34–35;
  Arabs and Persians 144;
  Asian Indians 137, diabetes 17;
  Hawaiians 131;
  Latinos 70–71;
  Native Americans 56, 57;
  Samoans 131
Objectives of book 3
Occupational therapy 20
Oklahoma, Native population 49
Oregon, Asian Indians 133
Osteopathic medicine 27
Osteoporosis: African Americans 88;
  Latinas 70, 73

P

Pacific Islanders 129–132
Pakistan 133
Palestinians 141, 145
Pancit 128
Patis 128
Patient (also see client): attitudes of Blacks 78;
  education 30;
  expectations 58, 144, 145;
  perspective 29;
  use of alternative methods 29
Patriarchal, Arabs 143;
  Chinese 96;
  Japanese 105;
  Korean 111;
  Vietnamese 117, 143
Philadelphia, PA population 2–2t;
  African American 78
Pica, African American 88;
  Latinos 73
Picture-book brides, Japanese 103;
  Korean 109
Pidgin 81
Philosophical principles, Chinese 95
Pilipino/Philippines 125–129;
  demographics 93;
  education 125, 11–1t;
  evil eye 26;
  immigration 39;
  Nationals, designation 39;
  Population 93, 147, 11–1t;
  terminology 2
Pima Indians, diabetes 17, lactose intolerance 58
Placebo effect 29
Poison, beliefs 98
Polychronic time (P-time) 10, 19, 22;
  Japanese 104
Polynesians 2, 129
Population, in U.S. Asian 93–94;
  Jewish 147;
  Korean 110;
  2–1t, 2–2t, 2–3t, 11–1t
Pork, African Americans 87;
  Jews 35;
  Muslims 35;
  Pacific Islanders 131;
  Southeast Asians 120–121
Postpartum beliefs 34, 57, 68, 127
Poverty 11, 25, 2–3t, 9–1t, 11–1t;
  African American 77, 82, 117;
  Asians 94;
  Chinese 97;
  culture of 11;
  food distribution in 34;
  Jews 146;
  Latino 72, 117;
  Native American 50, 51;
  Pacific Islander 130;
  Southeast Asian 117

Pregnancy 19–20;
  beliefs 34, 57, 88, 112, 128, 136
Prejudice 9
Preventative health care 25
Professional goals vs. client values 20
Professionals, Asian Indian 133, 135;
  Arab-Persian 141, 142
Prostitution 93
Protection (from illness) 128
Protein: classified as "hot" food 34;
  Eskimo diets 57;
  food sources 33, 107;
  Japanese diets 107;
  Latino diets 72–73;
  Native American diets 57;
  Pacific Island diets 131
Proxemics (space) 22, 143
P-time (see polychronic time)
Puerto Rico/Puerto Ricans (also see Latinos) 9–1t, 9–3t;
  convulsions 73;
  demographics 63–64;
  family 166;
  generational conflicts 66;
  health care access 69;
  health status 1;
  smoking rate 72
Purification rites, Japan 106

Q

Questions to identify alternative care 29

R

Race 9, 125;
  census, 1990, 13;
  conflicts 93, 110, 133;
  geographical groups 13;
  primary groups 13
Racism 9, 26, 37;
  African American 77, 78, 80, 82, 88;
  Japanese 103
Ramadan 35, 142
Rape 81, 115, 120
Rapport/trust 20, 21, 23, 127;
  African American 88;
  Arab and Persian 145;
  Latino 66, 73;
  Native American 58;
  Southeast Asian 122
Reciprocity 95, 126
Refugees, Asian 94–95;
  Central American 71;
  Chinese 93, 99–100;
  immigration 39;
  Russian Jews 146;
  Southeast Asian 115, 116, 119–120

Reincarnation, Hinduism 134;
　　Native American 52;
　　Southeast Asian 116, 120
Religion: African American 79;
　　animism 134;
　　as cause of illness 26;
　　Buddhism 95, 110, 116, 134;
　　Christianity/Christian 35, 52, 95,
　　　　116, 130, 134, 142;
　　Confucianism 95, 110, 116, 134;
　　dietary customs 35–36;
　　Eastern 134;
　　Hinduism 134;
　　influence on health care 26;
　　Islam (Muslims) 35, 116, 134;
　　Jainism 134;
　　Judaism 35, 134, 142, 143, 146;
　　Pilipino 128;
　　Shintoism 106, 134;
　　Sikhism 134;
　　Taoism 95, 110, 116, 134
Religious groups 11
Relocation camps, Southeast Asian 115–116, 117
Reservation life, Native American 50
Reserved behavior, Japanese 104
Righteousness 95–96
Roman Catholic (also see Catholic) 65
Roosevelt, Franklin D. 104

S

Sacramento, CA population 2–2t
Saigon (Ho Chi Minh City) 115
Saint Louis, MO population 2–2t
San Antonio Heart Study 71
San Francisco, CA population 2–2t
Sansei 104, 105, 106
Savings, Asian Indians 135;
　　Japanese 104
Sedentary lifestyles, Samoans 131
Self-control, Japanese 104
Self-esteem: African American 77, 78, 80;
　　Native American children 53;
　　Pilipinos 126, 129;
　　poverty 25;
　　Southeast Asians 120, 122
Self-reliance 10
Self-treatment 77, 83, 88, 119, 127, 144
Sephardic Jews 146
Seventh Day Adventists 35
Sexual relations, Latinos 66
Sexual values 1, 129, 143
Shaman (medicine man) Korean 110, 112;
　　Latino 67;
　　Native American 54, 55;
　　Southeast Asian 119, 120
Shin-Issei 104, 106

Shinto religion 106
Sickle-cell anemia 85–86
Sikhs 134, 135
Silence in communication 23, 54
Single fathers 42
Sino-Japanese war 109
Slaves/slavery, African American 77, 78, 79, 81, 85
Smoking (tobacco) 2–6t;
　　African American 84, 2–6t;
　　gender differences 17;
　　Latinos 72;
　　Pacific Islander 131, rates of 17
Social harmony: Korean 112–113;
　　Latino 65;
　　Southeast Asian 118, 122
Social Organization 19
Social reciprocity 95, 118
Social rules, Chinese 95–96
Social Security 11
Social support, African American 79, 89
Socioeconomic status: African American 78;
　　Arab and Persian 141;
　　health beliefs 29;
　　Jews 146;
　　Latino and alcohol use 71–72;
　　Koreans 111;
　　Minorities 25;
　　Pacific Islanders 129, 131;
　　Pilipino 129;
　　Southeast Asian 119;
　　Western medicine 26
Sodium in diet, Chinese 100;
　　Japanese 107;
　　Pilipino 128;
　　Southeast Asian 121
Somatization 29;
　　Arabs and Persians 144;
　　Asian Indian 136;
　　Japanese 107;
　　Latino 73;
　　Southeast Asian 119
Soul (or spirit) 9;
　　African American 78, 83–84;
　　loss of 54, 55, 65, 67, 98, 120, 130
South Asians (see Asian Indians) 133–140
South Dakota, Native unemployment 51;
　　population 49
Southeast Asians 114–124;
　　income 94, 120;
　　smoking rates 17
Soviet/Russia 115, 146, 147
Space, personal 22, 42–43;
　　in offices 10
Spanish 125
Spirits (bad and good) 26;
　　African American 78;
　　Asian Indian 137;

　　Chinese 96, 98;
　　Japanese 106;
　　Korean 110;
　　Latino 65, 67, 68;
　　Laotian 118;
　　Native American 52, 54, 58;
　　Pacific Islander 130;
　　Pilipino 127;
　　Southeast Asian 116, 118, 119;
　　Vietnamese 116
Spiritualist, Latino 68
Spirituality of Native Americans 51, 58
Spokane, WA population 2–2t
Sri Lanka 133
Starvation 34
Stereotyping 1, 9, 19, 29, 66, 94
Stroke 2–5t, 9–3t;
　　African Americans 15, 83, 84;
　　Cuban Americans 70;
　　Latinos 70;
　　Mexican Americans 70;
　　Mormons 36;
　　Native Americans 56
Student(s), in classrooms 23;
　　visas 133–134
Suicide 2–5t, 9–3t;
　　African American 84;
　　Chinese 100;
　　Japanese 105;
　　Latino 73;
　　Native American 55, 56;
　　Southeast Asian 119
Supernatural beliefs about illness,
　　African American 78, 84;
　　ethnic clients 30;
　　Korean 112;
　　Latino 65;
　　Pilipino 127;
　　Southeast Asian 120;
　　traditional medicine 25–26;
　　world view 20
Supreme Court of U.S. 133
Surgery, fear of, Chinese 98;
　　Southeast Asian 120, 122
Sweat baths, Native American 55
Syphilis experiment (Tuskegee) 89
Syrian peddlers 142

T

Tagalog 2
Tahiti 129
Taoism, China 95;
　　Korea 110;
　　Southeast Asia 116
Taxes 93
Tay-Sachs Disease 147
Tea 107
Terminology 2–3, 49
Texas, Latino population 64
Thalassemia 128

Time and space orientation 10, 19, 22;
  African American 78;
  Arab and Persian 142;
  Hinduism 134;
  Japanese 104;
  Latinos 65, 73;
  monochronic time 10, 22;
  Native American 52, 59;
  Pilipino 126;
  Polychronic time 10, 22;
  Southeast Asian 118, 122
Tobacco, use of 35, 36
Toddy 131
Touch 22, 23, 43, 66, 118, 122
Traditional medicine 25, 26, 27, 29;
  African Americans 26, 29, 77, 78, 83, 84, 88;
  Arab and Persian 144;
  Asian Indian 136–137;
  body and mind 29;
  care 9, 69–70;
  conflicts with Western medicine 29, 30;
  Latinos 69–70;
  Native American 50, 54–55;
  Pilipino 127, 128;
  referring patients 29;
  social support 29;
  Southeast Asian 118–119;
  supernatural events 26;
  systems 26–27
Trail of tears 49
Translator 21
Treatment of illness 26–27, 29
Treaty of Hidalgo 63
Trichinosis, among Southeast Asians 119, 120
Trinity 142
Trust (see rapport)
Trust territories 129
Tuberculosis 15–17;
  Chinese 94–95, 100;
  Native American 15–17, 57;
  Pilipino 128, 129;
  recent immigrants 15, 100;
  Southeast Asian 119
Tulsa, OK population 2–2t
Tuskegee syphilis experiment 89

U

Unemployment/under-employment 125;
  Native Americans 51;
  Southeast Asians 117
United Nations 115
United States government, Bureau of Indian Affairs (BIA), mismanagement 50;
  food distribution program 57;
  food stamps 57;
  immigration policy 37–40;
  Native American, care of 50
Unnatural illness 26, 82–83
Untouchables 135

V

Value(s) 7, 10, 3–1t;
  African American 79, 80, 89;
  American 10–11, 19, 20;
  Arabs and Persians 142;
  Asian Indians 134–135, 135–136;
  Chinese 95–96, 97, 112–113;
  differences 19–20;
  harmony with nature 51–52;
  Japanese 104–105, 106, 112–113;
  Korean 111, 112–113;
  Latino 65, 67, 72;
  male 43;
  Native American 20, 51–52, 59;
  Pacific Islander 130;
  Pilipino 126;
  silence 54, 59;
  Southeast Asian 116, 117, 118, 120;
  traditional 19–29
Vegetables (see fruits and vegetables)
Vegetarian 35, 137
Venereal diseases 129
Vietnamese (also see Southeast Asian) 115, 122, 11–1t;
  income 94
Vietnam War 115
Violence, African American 87;
  Chinese 93
Voice characteristics 23

W

Washington (state), Asian Indians 133
Welfare 78, 117
Western medicine (also see health care) 25, 26;
  African American 77;
  Arabs and Persians 145;
  Chinese 99;
  Jews 146;
  Asian Indians 136, 138;
  Asians 113;
  fear of 26;
  Japanese 106;
  Korean 112;
  Native American 58–59;
  Pacific Islanders 130–131;
  Southeast Asians 118, 119, 120
Wetback 63
Western Samoa 129, 130
White(s) 2–1t, 2–3t, 2–4t, 2–5t, 2–6t, 9–3t, 11–1t;
  AIDS/HIV 17;
  a minority group 13–14;
  education 80;
  health status 15, 17;
  income 14, 51, 64, 82, 94;
  population 14, 147;
  poverty rate 117;
  smoking rate 72;
  terminology 3
Wind 98
Witchcraft 26, 54, 65, 67, 68, 82
Women 11;
  African American 81, 83;
  AIDS/HIV 66;
  Arab and Persian 143;
  Asian Indian 134–135;
  Chinese 37, 98;
  diets 34;
  employment increases 33, 42;
  equality/discrimination 41–42, 44;
  income 42, 44, 117;
  Japan 105;
  Korean 111–112;
  Pilipino 126;
  Southeast Asian 117
Women, Infants, and Children program (WIC) 19
World view, African American 78–79;
  Chinese 95–96;
  definition 9;
  communication 20;
  Japanese 104–105;
  Korean 110;
  Latinos 65;
  Middle Eastern 142;
  Native American 51–52;
  Pacific Islanders 130;
  Pilipino 126;
  Southeast Asian 116, 118
World War II 103–104, 109, 115, 125
Wounded Knee massacre 49–50
Wright brothers 10

X

Xenophobia 9

Y

Yin/yang 26, 34, 95, 98, 99, 112, 116, 119
Yonsei 104, 106